ALL RISE

Ministry with Justice-Involved Women

Lynn O. Cooper
and
Karen K. Swanson

All Rise: Ministry with Justice-Involved Women

Institute for Prison Ministries
Wheaton College Billy Graham Center
501 College Avenue
Wheaton, IL 60187

For ordering information, please contact: Institute for Prison Ministries at 630-752-5727 or visit www.prisoninstitute.com

ISBN: 978-1-7351829-0-2

To the women and men
who participated in the research.

KKS

. . .

For my mother, whose faith and
determination enabled
our family to rise.

LOC

Contents

Introduction

The mass incarceration of women is a disturbing trend in American society. A 2018 report estimates 99,000 women are living in state prisons, with another 89,000 women in local jails. More than one million women are on probation or parole. A history of abuse and trauma, health problems, parenthood, and poverty add to the "collateral consequences" of incarceration when these women look for work, housing, and financial support after release.

Despite an on-going body of scholarship examining male offenders, less is known about females under correctional control. In the past, social scientists, practitioners, and theologians were largely inattentive to women's experiences, but there is progress in terms of understanding women's pathways out of crime and gender differences that lead to recidivism.

However, there are few recent and relevant books for Christians working in faith-based programs with women who are under control of the criminal justice system ("justice-involved women"). The purpose of this text is to give voice to the experiences of these women and improve important ministry outcomes for those faithfully working on their behalf.

It is also a call to action for God's people to demonstrate mercy and justice for justice-involved women. As individuals, churches, and communities become informed and engage in this important social issue, Kingdom work is elevated.

Under the auspices of the Institute for Prison Ministries, the authors merged interviews, surveys, and site visits with over 550 individuals to gain this perspective. A total of 38 states were represented in this study. Our informants were justice-involved women, chaplains, volunteers, ministry leaders, psychologists, and prison administrators who together enabled us to create this comprehensive, data-driven text.

Whether you are interested in social activism, spiritual formation, or practical help, this book will provide the background to do this work well. Amid the harsh realities of these lives, we hope you will also see the grace, intelligence, and beauty of these women as they encounter the real possibility of change.

Organization of the Book

This book introduces a user-friendly overview of the important themes and practical realities of female correctional ministry. It creates a realistic look at the challenges inherent in change. Primary readers are Christians who wish to serve justice-involved women—the ministry volunteers, chaplains, and organizational leaders engaged with this population. Additionally, this text opens the door to congregations, community members, and other nonprofit agencies interested in female justice initiatives. A glossary of terms is included in Appendix A.

The text also assumes an audience among those who have already faithfully served these women, and who desire to move toward greater understanding of their work. For these individuals, the book provides "best practices" for justice-involved women living within jails, prisons, and reentry programs.

There are four sections to the text. The first three chapters provide an overview of justice-involved women in order to clarify their personal experience, community issues, and economic impact. This first section (chapters 1-3) summarizes the problems, and the process of incarceration from arrest, to jail and imprisonment, to parole and probation. It gives us a common language for understanding what justice-involved women undergo before their arrival in prison, and profiles the characteristics and unique problems faced by female offenders. Section One is especially valuable for those new to work in correctional ministries, or for community activists seeking this engagement.

The second section of the book (chapters 4-6) focuses on the socialization of incarcerated women, and the creation of their new "normal". Aspects of correctional control structured by jail and prison culture are illustrated.

Chapters 7-9 comprise the third section of the text, raising issues of reentry and recidivism. This section sets up ministry initiatives to promote lasting change once women are released from prison, as well as what will help these women stay out once they leave jails and prisons. It raises the challenges psychologists face with individuals having a history of abuse and posttraumatic stress. Sections Two and Three are especially helpful for volunteers' understanding of how justice-involved women "do time" in and out of their incarceration experience.

The final chapters (10-14) constitute the fourth section of the book that underscores the role of correctional ministries in creating lasting change by incorporating the perspective of chaplains, volunteers, ministry leaders, and prison administrators. The section ends by highlighting "best practices" in correctional programs and aftercare ministries. Section four will be especially beneficial to experienced volunteers, chaplains, ministry directors, and correctional officers.

Overview

Chapter 1 focuses on the problems created by a wave of mass incarceration in our society. It sets the stage for understanding the problems chaplains, staff, and volunteers will face in their ministry work. We learn that justice-involved women are more likely to be incarcerated for non-violent drug and property offenses. More than incarcerated men, women are less likely to receive opportunities to earn time off sentences by following the rules or have access to programming resources. Justice-involved women will face more disciplinary actions (as well as more severe sanctions) as compared to male inmates with similar behavior. After release, women may become victims of mandatory arrests, and remain longer on probation and parole.

Chapter 2 paints a portrait of justice-involved women by looking at the unique challenges they face. Apart from the larger issues of mass incarceration, women face different problems than their male counterparts, and their tenure in correctional facilities make these problems worse. Most of these women have a history of abuse, trauma, and mental health issues before incarceration. Many are mothers who were primary caregivers before incarceration, so the welfare of her children is a high concern and motivating factor. They have different health needs, involving reproductive healthcare and treatment for substance use that facilities designed for men frequently fail to offer. Influential to their future is the number and quality of programs accessed, mental and physical health care received, amount of family support, length of time spent in custody, and spiritual care.

Chapter 3 introduces a basic understanding of how the criminal justice system works, with relevant legal terminology. It gives a comprehensive, but easy-to-read overview from initial arrest to sentencing to release. It explains the incarceration process in order to understand what jail residents are facing as well as what women within prison systems have already endured. It is important to point out that this chapter is solely informational. It reminds us that jail and prison ministry workers stand outside the legal system. Lacking confidentiality privileges, they must not ask justice-involved women about their case and they do not give legal advice.

Chapter 4 looks at different issues involved in the correctional control of female prisoners by introducing five approaches currently used in jails and prisons. We learn that correctional control of women affects their vulnerabilities regardless of age, crime, or treatment services needed. Few correctional settings have programmatic resources or specially trained staff to address these issues, and necessary rules and regulations at correctional facilities place these women at greater risk. Safety, operating costs, administrative leadership, and employee training will always be important guideposts, but this chapter raises hopeful signs of change in a new era of gender-responsive correctional control.

Chapter 5 introduces correctional institutions as distinctive cultures, and sets up the process of social interaction that teaches newcomers the values and standards of their new environment. Justice-involved women focus on how to become members of a new group. It enables newly incarcerated women to fit in and interact appropriately as they are accepted by other residents. The collective narrative of representative justice-involved women underscores the fact that whether correctional facilities adapt policies and practices that are more punishment-based or strive to create therapeutic communities, incarceration is both dehumanizing and difficult.

Chapter 6 conveys the experience of female incarceration through the words of justice-involved women who discuss the prison code. These are the norms of the group and rules for behavior in the personal and public spaces of the correctional facility. The development of relationships, reference groups, "families" and cliques are noted. The phenomenon of same-sex engagement during incarceration ("gay for the stay, straight at the gate") and distinctive patterns of working through conflicts provide a helpful context for ministry workers who want to understand institutional life.

Chapter 7 examines lingering reactions to correctional culture and reverse culture shock experienced as women transition from incarceration to release. "Doing time" adds the voices of correctional leadership, volunteer staff, and recent research in order to identify three emotional themes that will impact positive change after release. We look at ways to minimize the effects of reverse culture shock before women transition to freedom. Most newly incarcerated women adapt to their new "normal" through the help of insiders who show them the ropes and will need this same help in readjustment after doing time.

Chapter 8 revisits earlier data in order to construct a new portrait of those women who are coming home. Moving from emotional responses to incarceration culture shock, the practical problems of reintegration into communities are addressed. Financial issues, including economic marginalization, and relational aspects of identity (e.g., gender norms, trauma, dysfunctional partnerships, family reunification, spiritual growth, mental health, and substance use) are used as realistic markers for success.

Chapter 9 focuses discussion on the challenges of parole and probation as women transition from jails and prisons. Constructing plans for reentry addresses the risks and needs in each stage. The transition stage (prior to release) looks at the practical needs of housing, employment, food and clothing. The community stage (following release) examines issues of accountability and support. The collateral consequences of a felony conviction are discussed. Finally, three dominant reentry perspectives drawn from our interviews and surveys express why some justice-involved women are reluctant to leave the structured world of prison, anxiety about being able to have what it takes to make it, and their desire to be 'normal'.

Chapter 10 approaches the impact of abuse and trauma experienced by many justice-involved women from the perspective of clinical psychologists and counselors. Strategies that helpers use when working with abused women are introduced, such as nonverbal acceptance and reflective listening. The relationship between stress, trauma, self-efficacy, and resilience is illustrated. Rethinking weaknesses as strengths can enhance the impact of a faith community to care and help make sense of what these women have experienced, providing a practical "ministry of presence".

Chapter 11 looks at the experiences of chaplains and program directors that use principles of spiritual formation in their work with justice-involved women during and after incarceration. The Christian idea of spiritual formation very simply is the forming, conforming, and transforming of the human personality—body, mind, and spirit—into the likeness of Jesus Christ. This chapter draws information from interviews and surveys that focus on the challenges of creating life change, as well as well-known theologians who have discussed these ideas.

Chapter 12 focuses on the experiences of over 500 people who faithfully volunteer to work with justice-involved women. The United States correctional system relies heavily on religious volunteers to meet the spiritual needs of those in custody or reentry. However, there is little research about these volunteers, and existing studies are often facility or ministry specific. We incorporate illustrations from the volunteer's point of view to highlight the nature of their work, the tensions created by their service, and strategies they find effective in working with justice-involved women. The manner in which the volunteer responds to these tensions determines whether her work experience will be a positive or negative one.

Chapter 13 revisits adaptations of the five approaches to correctional control (criminogenic risks, strengths-based, trauma-informed, evidence-based, gender-responsive care) to ministry applications with incarcerated women. The challenges each presents to administrators and leaders, as well as the ability to measure "success" within correctional ministries is raised.

Chapter 14 focuses on institutional and reentry programs for women. We talk about ways to engage life behind bars and build effective reentry programs. Best practices for maximizing volunteer time within prisons and communities, working with correctional staff, and turning the odds of reintegration in their favor are raised. However, effective programs for justice-involved women must do more than give volunteers the necessary knowledge and skills to fulfill the organizational mission. They must offer encouragement and reframe "success" in order to understand how spiritual transformation affects moral formation to create change. We highlight what one state has done by way of prison reform. Their changes bring hope for the future of incarcerated females and those who work toward their success.

About the Authors

Dr. Karen K. Swanson has been involved in correctional ministries for 21 years. She has been the Director of the Institute for Prison Ministries in the Wheaton College Billy Graham Center since 2005. In this role, Dr. Swanson has been engaged in teaching courses in correctional ministries, training volunteers and program directors, developing a certification program for chaplains, and hosting yearly professional conferences. As both leader and volunteer, she has been a strong advocate for those affected by mass incarceration.

Dr. Swanson's vision was for a data-driven book for a varied audience who shared a willingness to learn more about the problems, process, and people affected by mass incarceration. The immediate purpose is to train the next generation of workers in healing premises, providers, and programs that encourage Christian formation. This is the daily work of the Institute for Prison Ministries.

Dr. Swanson also wanted a volume that would allow justice-involved women to tell their own stories, in their own words. She wanted a comprehensive text that would speak of the large number of experienced volunteers, ministry workers, correctional officers, and prison administrators who have given generously of their time and energy over time. This validates the importance of their work and underscores their creation of a place that allows spiritual change to take place every day.

While Dr. Swanson brings the practitioner's perspective, Dr. Lynn O. Cooper applies social science research from her areas of expertise: organizational communication, group dynamics, and social influence. Dr. Cooper is Professor Emerita of Communication at Wheaton College, where she taught graduate and undergraduate courses for over four decades. For this text, she interviewed and surveyed over 550 justice-involved women, chaplains, volunteers, ministry leaders, psychologists, and prison administrators from 38 states in order to provide a data-driven foundation for this work.

Special thanks goes to Yazmin Spearman for her capable and engaging assistance with interviews. We thank early readers of this text Kristi Miller-Anderson, Deb Gore, Dail Duncan, Kate Mongeon and Elissa Cooper—for their invaluable feedback and attention to detail. Finally, we are deeply thankful to Laurie Nichols and Mary Smoot for their hours editing and proofing.

We conclude with a word of appreciation for all who serve justice-involved women and their families. Many working within the criminal system daily provide sacrificial efforts that advance mercy and justice. Those on the front lines—the chaplains, volunteers, and reentry staff—are vital in creating real change. Special thanks go to those working in small faith-based non-profits who are investing in these women and helping them transition back into society.

We know this ministry can be financially challenging and hard to measure in terms of success. It is discouraging at those times when a woman relapses or returns to illegal activity. This is a ministry that is never completed because it is a mercy ministry. However, growth occurs, and you have elevated both the individual who is served as well as the name of Christ.

Most importantly, to those of you who have been justice-involved women and been transformed, your stories give us all hope. Your courage and faith in the face of incredible odds gives us the encouragement to continue in this important work. Together, we all rise.

1

. . . . . .

Lock Her Up

***"I was shipped off that Friday** and got to the receiving area, which is very scary. I was very scared and humbled because I didn't know what to expect. I was depressed. I'd lost everything. I had three children; that was the breaking point for me. I went in receiving the third day after they did all these tests on me, because they run tests on you when you first get there and you have to follow these rules and protocols. I didn't want to leave my room. I didn't want to go out in the fenced gate and look outside. It was like I didn't know how I got myself in this situation because I have always been a good stay-at-home mother and did things in the church ... It devastated my life because I was 27 when I went in and I'm 32 now."*

– Formerly incarcerated woman

The number of women behind bars has skyrocketed since the late 1970s, increasing by more than 834 percent over nearly 40 years (Wagner & Sawyer, 2018). In fact, the United States is one of the top incarcerators of women in the world, with nearly 219,000 women imprisoned, and another million women on parole or probation (Kajstura, 2018). The disproportionate imprisonment of women in local jails can be attributed to expanded law enforcement efforts, tougher drug sentencing laws, and the unique barriers women face because of having a felony record (Sentencing Project, 2019). Whatever the cause, mass incarceration of women is a disturbing trend in modern society, and the focus of chapter one.

Changing patterns in the criminal justice system

Our country changed in the mid-1970s from a society that believed incarceration would facilitate better behavior once prisoners were returned to their communities, to one that took a tougher stance on criminals. With this change, and especially with the War on Drugs rhetoric, Americans used imprisonment to inflict pain ("just desserts"), stop criminal activities ("incapacitation"), or just keep lawbreakers far away from others ("containment") (Haney, 2001).

Abandoning the goal of rehabilitation resulted in less programming, and social and mental health services for inmates inside and outside of prison. Correctional administrators verify that *"Support services to facilitate the transition from prison to the free world environments to which prisoners were returned were undermined at precisely the moment they needed to be enhanced."* Many jails and prisons are still outgrowing these attitudes from the last century.

Jails are correctional facilities designed to hold arrested individuals who are awaiting trial. **Federal prisons** are used to house individuals convicted of breaking federal laws. Prisoners who have committed violent crimes are more likely to be in **state prisons**. State prisons are often considered to be less safe than federal ones because more violent criminals live in them.

While most states have only one or two institutions for women, some facilities are considered "unisex" and house both male and female inmates in separate areas (Davidson, 2018). When prison rates skyrocketed during the Reagan Administration, **private** (for-profit) facilities were created. These facilities added more variance in institutional practices over safety and cost-effectiveness for both male and female prisoners (Joy, 2018).

The quality of living standards between prisons varies within individual states despite standards that exist for managing these large populations of people. However, concerns about quality of living standards and programming remain unresolved.

Specific data regarding women's incarceration is difficult to track because of the larger scale of male imprisonment, but several patterns exist. First, while men make up 93 percent of the prison population and 85 percent of the jail population, *the female population has grown at a far faster rate*, increasing at twice the rate as men since 1980 (Wagner & Sawyer).

The differences in justice reform between men and women are even more dramatic at the state level. In terms of the percent of change in the numbers of women and men in state prisons since the prison population peaked in 2009, women have fared worse than men have in 35 states, where the women's prison population has:

- grown, while men's populations have declined;
- continued to outpace the growth of men's populations; or
- declined, but less dramatically than male populations.

Second, *nearly half of incarcerated women are held in jails.* This is in sharp contrast with the total incarcerated population, where state prisons hold twice as many people as those in jail. Exact numbers are challenging given the decentralized and overlapping systems of mass incarceration for women, but a 2018 report estimates 99,000 women are housed in state prisons and 89,000 women are in local jails.

Only 16,000 females are incarcerated in federal prisons. Smaller numbers of justice-involved women go to territorial prisons (500), Indian country jails (700), and military lock ups (30). There is no reliable data on the women who are in civic commitment, a legal process of involuntary commitment involving treatment in a psychiatric hospital or in the community. However, psychiatric facilities confine 22,000 justice-involved people every day. An additional 7,000 females are in immigration detention (Kajstura).

One reason given for the higher percentage of females in jails rather than prisons is attributed to space limitations. There are simply fewer dedicated facilities for women. State and federal agencies (e.g., Immigration and Customs Enforcement, U.S. Marshals) may contract with local jails to house women.

Additionally, large numbers of incarcerated women have not yet had a trial or been convicted of a crime and reside in jails. Sixty percent of women under local control are awaiting trial. Though not considered a flight risk, avoiding pre-trial incarceration is challenging for lower income women who cannot afford bail. Even after conviction (often for misdemeanors), 25 percent of women remain at the jail serving their sentence of less than one year.

*"**When they went into prison**, they often had been in dire situations prior to coming, meaning they had either used drugs [or] been on drugs prior to ever getting to a prison. They may have been in domestic violence situations, which was more often than not. They may have been involved in prostitution. They may have been involved in a string of petty crimes that ultimately led to a conviction...Women cope with prison differently than their male counterparts, too, because women typically in prison have weight, and that weight is children and/or grandchildren... "*

–Reentry Director

While there is a decline in prison population, *incarceration in jails remains relatively stable.* This has important consequences for justice-involved women and their families (Kaebel & Cowhig, 2018). Even though jails are closer to home, it is harder to stay in touch with family. In jail, communication is more restricted, and phone calls are expensive for the 80 percent of incarcerated women who are mothers. On average, justice involved women are in their early to mid-thirties and most have never been married (Zeng, 2018).

The indeterminate time in jail causes greater psychological distress, and there are few avenues for proper physical or mental health care. Additionally, the National Inmate Survey (2011-2012) study indicated *a disproportionate number of justice-involved women were sexual minorities* (33 percent), whose gender identity may lead to more discrimination in treatment and sentencing than heterosexual women (Meyer et al, 2013). They were more likely to be sexually victimized as children. Sexual minorities are more likely to be sexually victimized while incarcerated. This group also tends to receive harsher punishments, which adds to their trauma.

While a breakdown of the prison population by race and ethnicity is harder to find, most estimate that half the women in prisons are white (53 percent). A disproportionate number of female prisoners are black or African American (29 percent), despite the fact black Americans represent only 13 percent of the United States population.

Native American women are also overrepresented in prisons and jails. The breakdown of incarcerated groups by race and ethnicity include Hispanics (14 percent), American Indian and Alaskan Natives (2.5 percent), Asian Americans (0.9 percent), and women with Native Hawaiian or Pacific Islander heritage (0.4 percent). *People of color face higher rates of poverty and lack the financial resources to avoid prolonged incarceration.*

Women are [52 percent] more likely than men to be incarcerated for non-violent drug and property offenses (Wagner & Sawyer). Drug crimes include drug possession and distribution. Property offenses include burglary, fraud, car theft, theft, and other property crime. Public order crimes consist of illegal weapon possession, driving while impaired by alcohol or drugs (DUIs), prostitution, and loud disorderly conduct.

> ***"I did a total of five years of incarceration:*** *one year in jail, four years in prison. Jail and prison are totally different. That's my experience, and that was because of a drug addiction. I became seriously addicted to cocaine, so it led me to criminal activity. I went from working with lawyers and managing the law office to walking the street, just doing anything and everything to get that money for my drug addiction."*
>
> – Formerly incarcerated woman

An additional 7,300 females are in youth detention facilities, whose charges include technical violations, drug offenses, and person, property and public order crimes. Minors may also be involved in "status offenses" or conduct that is illegal for youths but legal for adults. Status offenses include underage drinking, skipping school, or running away from home.

Men are more likely to be incarcerated for violent offenses (56 percent). Violent crimes include assault, robbery, rape/sexual assault, manslaughter, murder, and other violent crimes.

Number of Female Offenders by Crime and Facility (Kajstura)

	Jail	**State Prison**	**Federal Prison**
Public Order	17,000	10,100	2,500
Drug	26,000	24,600	7,200
Property	28,000	26,600	2,400
Violent	17,000	36,600	600
Other	500	1,000	100
	88,500	98,900	12,800

Three unique variables characterize incarcerated women more than incarcerated men, and they contribute to the slow progress in releasing women from imprisonment (Sawyer, 2018). First, women receive less "good time" while incarcerated. "Good time" enables a justice-involved woman to earn time off her sentence and move toward parole by following the rules. Justice-involved females face more disciplinary actions as well as more severe sanctions for similar behavior when compared to male inmates.

Second, there are fewer diversion programs available for women. These programs represent opportunities that allow inmates to engage in rehabilitative and educational activities that can shorten their years in prison.

"You got out three times a day, *otherwise you're locked in a room. The difference between [jail] and coming to prison is [in prison] you go outside. You can walk around and do what you want, but you cannot sunbathe or any of that stuff... The last six months I was there they hardly opened [the doors], saying they're short on staff so they close [recreations] down. If they see one person with a sleeve halfway up, they close it down because 'You're sunbathing...' In wintertime, they use 'It's too cold out there.' So that's the difference between [jail and prison]—that, and at least [in prison] you have more to do."*

– Formerly incarcerated woman

A third factor differentiating justice-involved females from their male counterparts may involve a widening net of criminalizing women's survival efforts. Often stemming from abuse, this can include the over-criminalization of drug use and prostitution. It can also involve mandatory arrests when women run away or fight back against domestic violence.

Incarceration is expensive. Recently, the government spent more than $167 billion to arrest, convict, and incarcerate citizens. Although different in individual states, the fee to cover the average cost of incarceration for federal inmates in 2016 was $34,704.12 ($94.82 per day), and $36,299.25 ($99.45 per day) in 2017. The average annual cost to confine an inmate in a residential reentry center was over $29,000 ($79.69 per day) in 2016, and more than $32,000 ($88.52 per day) for 2017 (Hyle, 2018).

However, incarceration represents only a small part (17 percent) of women under correctional supervision. *Over one million women are on probation and parole.* Three out of four women under control of any U.S. correctional system are on probation (Kaebel & Cowhig, 2018).

Probation is a sentencing alternative to imprisonment. The court releases convicted defendants under supervision, as long as certain conditions are observed. Conditions may include fees and meeting with probation officers. That often presumes the woman has employment, reliable transportation, and childcare. Women end up violating their probation not because they commit crimes, but because they are unable to meet obligations stemming from probation supervision.

A small percentage of justice-involved women (9 percent) are on parole. Parole is supervised release into a community prior to the completion of a sentence. This is a result of a decision by the state Board of Pardons and Parole, and subject to conditions imposed by the Board. Like women on probation, they must comply with conditions of supervised release. These conditions include employment, safe housing, and substance abuse treatment. The conditions require reliable transportation and childcare before they can be reunited with their children.

Desistance and Justice-Involved Women

> ***"We know two things are certain:*** *that mass incarceration doesn't work, and that programming does… Recidivism rate is the end all, be all, and regardless of how you account for it, how long you go out, the truth is that the needle hasn't moved. Whether we put $100,000 or $100 million into reentry, if the recidivism rate doesn't change, then it's not the program we're delivering. It's the way in which we deliver it, and the content and value in which we have it."*
>
> – Warden

For justice-involved women, desistance or stopping criminal activities requires changes in thinking and behaving. Like any behavior change, it is often a difficult process that varies by individual. Desistance has two phases: primary and secondary. Primary desistance is a crime-free gap at some point during the course of a persistent or habitual offender's life. Secondary desistance involves both stopping the offending behavior as well as a personal identity transformation of the woman to a prosocial citizen. That is, she no longer views herself as an offender or criminal (Serin & Lloyd, 2009). The real test of rehabilitation is when women reenter society. Will they stop engaging in illegal conduct and engage in prosocial behaviors?

Institutional Programs

State and federal prisons provide correctional programs for women in custody. Institutional programs in female facilities include academic areas, substance abuse treatment, work and vocational training, development of life skills, dealing with histories of domestic violence, reentry, and religious education. A few prisons offer nursery programs for incarcerated mothers who give birth behind bars.

Jails offer few or no programs depending on their size, location, and resources committed to programs. Additional factors limiting jail programs are the high population turnover rates, jail architecture with few spaces dedicated for classes, less resident movement, limited staff availability, and fewer resources than prisons.

The programming objectives for females within correctional institutional programs are treatment and rehabilitation to provide healing and improve their behavior, both before and after release from incarceration. These positive behavior changes enhance public safety by lowering recidivism and promote safety inside the institution by reducing misconduct. However, input from female participants, information about how volunteers are managed, and how women in custody are impacted are largely ignored in studies (Huang, et al, 2014).

Some leadership styles and programs are more effective than others. Overall, measuring effectiveness is largely ignored by ministry workers, program administrators, and researchers.

Another issue is prioritizing the prison's goal. As with any organization, prisons must deal with mission drift as they receive many requests for programming from ministries and organizations. As one warden noted, *"You can't give more of your attention to another organization's mission than you give to your own."* She gave the example of a volunteer wanting to give guitar lessons to any woman who wanted them. While some women may enjoy this, playing a guitar does not not address any criminogenic risks or needs important to the prison for inmate rehabilitation.

> "***The piece that gets a little hairy*** *[for prison administrators] is that people think we're here to serve them or their organization or their thoughts or their ideas. But we have a mission here, and [need to] stay focused on that mission because when you tell [the stakeholders] it's not [our mission] then they get all offended... I think if someone would want to volunteer, call and ask the organization what volunteer opportunities there are. Then the answer is given [along with] the parameters of what we have available... Corrections is different I think because there are not well-defined volunteer job descriptions, roles, or responsibilities. What corrections in general gets is calls for requests to provide something that the caller wants to provide, and then historically [prison staff] have scrambled around trying to meet the needs of the caller."*
>
> – Warden

There is an understanding that whenever a person, ministry, or organization wants to come into a corrections facility, it requires additional work by corrections administrators and staff. Each volunteer approved to enter must have a background check and be recorded in an updated database. In many places, annual Prison Rape Elimination Act (PREA) training is required.

Names of volunteers and materials must be approved prior to the event. Volunteers must be checked, and their belongings approved prior to and the day of the event. Administrators express their frustration with organizations and ministries that want to accomplish their mission when it does not help them accomplish the mission at the prison, which is probation or parole. A better approach is to ask prison administrators or the chaplain: how can we come alongside you in meeting your mission?

A final issue is motivational. Prison life occurs in shifts, with most morning activities taking place within the rooms where incarcerated women prepare their educational or employment assignments. The pace of the dayroom picks up as activities are announced, but the inmate's room and the unit she lives in is the place where much of the social life is in a woman's prison (Owen, 1998).

Formal programming activities allow the women to move about the prison, and in some states, receive work-time credits that can reduce their prison sentences. In the process of adjustment, the women develop relationships and routine activities that both structure the day and provide growth. Not surprisingly, some women become engaged in institutional programs to get certificates to show the judge they are engaging in prosocial behavior without actual change.

"Nothing Changes if Nothing Changes"

PEW conducted an analysis of publicly accessible data from 23 states that reported reliable prison admissions and release data to the Bureau of Justice Statistics between 2005-2015. They found a 23 percent drop in recidivism or return to criminal behavior (Gelb & Velazquez, 2018). This is hopeful research, since reducing recidivism improves public safety, reduces taxpayer spending on prisons, and reintegrates formerly incarcerated people successfully into the community.

However, the PEW study has limitations. It did not have access to re-arrest information, or data on individuals released from prison in one state and subsequently incarcerated in another. Likewise, it did not include individuals in the study who have died. The good news is that the PEW data underscores the fact that meaningful improvement in recidivism does occur.

Women entering the criminal justice system and later transitioning from incarceration will face several challenges (Snodgrass, 2019). Success in navigating the system will depend upon the woman's incarceration experience, the number and quality of programs accessed, mental and physical health care received, amount of family support, length of time spent in custody, and spiritual care. The profile of women coming home tends to suggest that they will also face the challenges of a:

- **dysfunctional family**—often headed by a single parent and no loving father, movement to other homes or foster care, and a family member who is incarcerated
- **parental responsibilities**—the majority have dependent children under 18 years old
- **limited education**—almost half have no high school diploma or GED, and have learning disabilities
- **substance use**—there are high rates of drug and alcohol abuse
- **unemployment**—there are high rates of unemployment or underemployment
- **trauma**—more than 90% have experienced physical or psychological incidents
- **mental illness**—there are high rates of mental and emotional disorders
- **poverty**—high levels of poverty leads to entry into the community of the "New Urban Poor" that is marked by inadequate schools, few male role models, and lack of employment opportunities

In later chapters, we will discuss the challenges of navigating incarceration culture and reentry culture shock, meeting parole requirements, and reintegrating into society. We will examine the healing process that centers on emotional trauma and the process of spiritual formation experienced by justice-involved women. The roles played by prison administrators, psychologists, trained chaplains, and volunteers in creating this healing are highlighted. Finally, we will look at features of correctional care and effective ministry programs that foster true transformation and change.

Questions for Reflection

1. What is the profile of justice-involved women in your community?
2. What are the needs of women transitioning from jail or prison into your community?

2

. . . . . .

A Portrait of Justice-Involved Women

"I want to get a job. I want to save money. *I want to pay my bills here. I want to save money to get my own place, get furniture. I'd like to reconcile with my husband and son... I'd like to continue going to church and doing Bible studies. I like that. If I do have grandchildren, I would like to see them, even here, even though they can't come into the house. I would like to go out with them. If my son or whoever has them would take me in their car, I would pay them for gas, and we'd go do something. I would like to have pictures of them, just normal things grandparents do... We used to be so close: my husband, I, and my son. We used to be so close, and it's killing my heart that my one crime has caused all this havoc. I have done my time. I admit I'm wrong, I'm totally wrong... I took the easy way out and lost it totally... He didn't deserve what I did, but it's too late now. I can't take it back."*

– Formerly incarcerated woman

Justice-involved women differ from male counterparts regarding the types of crime they commit, personal histories, and pathways to crime. Not surprisingly, these women face different problems than incarcerated men, and their tenure in correctional facilities make these problems worse. This chapter paints a portrait of justice-involved women. A history of abuse and trauma, health problems, parenthood, and poverty add to the "collateral consequences" of incarceration when the justice-involved woman looks for work, housing, and financial support after her release. Each of these will be discussed in turn.

Collateral Consequences of Incarceration

***"Some people try to figure out people,** not really knowing their background or where they come from, because you really don't get to know them… I grew up in a very abusive home. I lost my mother when I was four. I was the only survivor of a truck wreck. I had a stepmom who didn't like me so much. It seemed like she wanted to tear me up. She put me in counseling ... They always would want me to talk about my past and let me go after I just poured out all these things. "Okay, have a nice day." I guess I started acting out… Well, how do you deal with it when you go home? What do I do? Do I just sit there and think about what happened? … I would get myself in trouble or I would hurt someone."*

– Formerly incarcerated woman

The Challenge of Early Life Experiences

Poverty is a major risk factor for delinquency. Female adolescents from lower-class backgrounds tend to live in tougher neighborhoods. They may have less satisfactory school experiences, and greater risk of dealing with premature motherhood (Van Wormer, 2010; Bloom, Owen, & Covington, 2003). They may lack supportive networks at home; nearly half of incarcerated women were homeless a month before their incarceration.

Young women of color often grow up in contexts that are markedly different than their white counterparts. Women of color are more likely to experience living in a single-parent home, with a relative, or in the foster system. They are more likely to engage in gang membership. Many women of color experience the impact of racism and classism in victimization and the prosecution of crimes along with racial trauma.

***"I got into a bad situation where I was wrongfully accused.** I was with my children's father ... He's part of the drug cartel and I was just basically his puppet because I loved him so much. Long story short is he had a lot of drugs in the car I was driving, and I ended up going to jail for it. He ended up running away because he was an illegal immigrant and so that all fell on me... I sat in County for a year. Nobody bonded me out or anything ... It's an eye opener. It's an experience you never want to go through. I'll never go through it again. I would* *rather be single and have to work two jobs than depend on a man because you never know. You could fall into the trap that, you know, you get blamed for somebody else's mistake. Or the hand of one's the hand of all, and then you're there with them. Or if you're not there, you're taking the penalty for that."*

– Formerly incarcerated woman

Justice-involved women have experienced higher rates of physical and sexual abuse in their childhoods and adult background than women in the general population. Estimates claim that almost one in four women may be a victim of sexual assault during her lifetime. Women in prison are three times more likely to have a history of abuse than males in prison.

"I spent six months in [hospital] because I had to have my jaw wired shut... *The scars all over my face you see are from my ex who broke my jaw and my ribs. I lost a baby because I told him I was tired of this life and I was leaving with our kids, because the life that he was living wasn't the life I wanted. And even though there was money, it wasn't good money. It wasn't clean money. It wasn't right money. Right way: work 9 to 5 and come home and be with your family. It was drug money… he got it the illegal way and it caused our [troubles]. I was telling him, 'This has got to change. I'm leaving you.' Plain and simple ... I found drugs in our house, and I flushed them down the toilet. Then one day he beat me up and this all led to going to prison. I mean it was just a rough situation before I went there. I went straight from the hospital to prison; [that's] how it works."*

– Formerly incarcerated woma

More than their male counterparts, incarcerated women are more likely to have at least one currently or formerly incarcerated family member. About 50 percent of women and 37 percent of men had an immediate family member who had been incarcerated (Snodgrass, 2019). Studies show that relationships in the formative years of most women in the correctional system are characterized by disconnection and violation rather than behaviors that foster growth.

The Challenge of Psychological Health Conditions

The disturbing gender disparity in recent prison populations consistently shows how prisons make the unique problems of women worse (Frost, Greene, & Pranis, 2006). For example, women are more likely to enter prison with a history of abuse, trauma, and mental health problems. Even in a "secure" prison environment, females are more likely to face sexual abuse by correctional staff or other incarcerated women (Kajstura, 2018).

> ***"I have anxiety issues.*** *Like I get really, really stressed easily because I've seen so much happen in prison. I've seen somebody get cut with razor blades. I've seen a lot of things that are really graphic, and I was scared to say anything because I didn't want it to happen to me... Besides that, I've lost my children; [the state] removed them from me. There's just so much darkness in prison... The only light you see is from volunteers coming in to minister the Word."*
>
> – Formerly incarcerated woman

Incarcerated females are more likely to experience serious psychological distress, for which treatment in prison is often inadequate or unavailable (Frost, Greene, & Pranis, 2006). Since prison health systems are usually designed for men, healthcare treatment may fail to help incarcerated women. There are always exceptions, and there is movement toward prisons becoming more gender responsive. However, even if the prison is attuned to the unique needs of women and provides gender-responsive services, the experience of being imprisoned has a powerful impact.

> ***"I was so depressed because I had never been to prison before.*** *First time offender, and [I] got really, really depressed one night and tried to kill myself. I slit my wrists. I lost a lot of blood [and] had to be hospitalized. That experience was rough because here I am in the hospital and they've got me chained to this bed... Because I lost so much blood, I could feel myself going out, and I wanted to go out. It's crazy, because you want to die. You don't want to experience all of this pain..."*
>
> – Formerly incarcerated woman

Mental health is important and influences how we handle stress, relate to others, and make choices. Mental disorders relate to a person's psychological, emotional, and social well-being. Incarcerated females were more likely than incarcerated males to meet the threshold for serious psychological distress (20 percent of female prisoners compared to 14 percent of males). Incarcerated females were also more likely to be told by a mental health professional that they had a mental health disorder (66 percent and 35 percent respectively) (Bronson, et al, 2017).

"I did take mental health classes. *I did take [classes for anxiety] that calmed me down. I took any class they could offer. They'd say sign up for this. I'd sign up for it just to see how it was. I stayed busy ... When I got back to the dorm, it was time for lights to go out every day. I didn't want to be around all the people that were so negative... I'd seen so much whenever they were fighting—like I had blood all over the floor in my hallway. I had just stood there getting ready for work in the morning [but there was a fight] because some girl took her girlfriend's stuff, or some girlfriend slept with her other girlfriend."*

– Formerly incarcerated woman

Some women do not welcome receiving a mental health diagnosis when they are evaluated in prison. Even though this insight may help them put some pieces together privately, there is a stigma with this diagnosis. Mental health needs that require medical attention are difficult, but when prisoners get care, it can create more problems.

"They go to a psychiatrist. *Then what they ask for, they usually just hand it to them. They don't really get the counseling they need. See that's what happened to me when I came out. I fell back into the drugs because I didn't know I [really] needed mental health counseling."*

– Formerly incarcerated woman

The Challenge of Physical Health Conditions

Psychological health and physical health can be intertwined. When mental health dips it also negatively impacts eating and sleeping.Incarcerated females are more likely than incarcerated males and the general population to report ever having a chronic physical condition such as cancer, high blood pressure, stroke-related problems, diabetes, heart- or kidney-related problems, arthritis, asthma, and cirrhosis of the liver.

They are also more likely to have an infectious disease such as tuberculosis, hepatitis, and HIV (Maruschak & Berzofsky, 2016). While incarcerated females were less likely than males to be overweight, they are more likely to be obese or morbidly obese.

In prison, there are medical attention teams to deal with health issues, but they have limited availability. One justice-involved woman noted: *"They didn't have medical attention all that much... They give it to them, but it was sorry the way they were treated medically down there."* This was echoed by a justice-involved woman who suffered from migraine headaches. *"If you didn't purchase [medicine] off the canteen, you had to suffer yourself."* Overall, a skeptical attitude toward medical help was expressed.

> ***"There's medical help, but the thing [is]...*** *the doctor there is a quack. I mean our doctor was a veterinarian, so I just don't think she really took her job seriously. There were people who were over-medicated and died in our prison system. They didn't wake up, so I was scared to take any medicine from anybody in there."*
>
> – Formerly incarcerated woman

Women who have experienced homelessness or substance abuse may already be at risk for malnutrition. Nutrition status can affect pathways to the brain that are important for decision making, and may impact the ability to counter thinking errors.

During their stay in jail and later in prison, fresh fruits and vegetables are rarely on the menu. Popular items purchased in the canteens tend to be chips. Vending machines in visitation rooms might have a few choices for more variety, but tend to feature high sugar and high caffeine items that contribute to anxiety.

Incarcerated females may fare worse in overcrowded jail systems because of the increasingly longer length of time spent there before sentencing. One young woman spoke of first coming off drugs, and then spending an additional 10 months in jail before sentencing.

> ***"I had gotten head lice in the jail,*** *and a staph infection in my eye. They were giving me shots of antibiotics and everything. The staph was spreading because they ignored it for so long in jail. I ended up very, very sick. All these things were going on with me when they tried me. When my lawyer came into the jail to talk to me, I wasn't in a good mental state, I wasn't in a good physical state. I just remember him stating, 'Your family members signed these statements on you'… That was very hurtful in itself, just knowing that they actually signed these voluntary statements [against me]."*
>
> – Formerly incarcerated woman

The Covid-19 crisis demonstrates the difficulty of maintaining social distance and reducing the spread of disease. But even with significant precautions, prison is not good for your health in other ways.

> ***"[Prison] opened my eyes up*** *and taught me 'don't take life for granted' because I got sick when I got out. I have Hepatitis C and have to go for liver [tests] ... I got it from prison… It's so easy to get things from… being around. They don't segregate women that have AIDS and people that don't anymore; they leave them all together. You're going to live around people that are just really disgusting. They don't clean the back of themselves. They don't have [any] respect for other people. They've got blood everywhere. You live in the situation that if you don't shower, then basically you'll just be dirty … You're in a controlled environment that is locked down…that is really old, that is not cleaned properly. You're state property."*
>
> – Formerly incarcerated woman

There is no current data on how many incarcerated women are pregnant. Past surveys (2004, 2002) by the Bureau of Justice statistics found 3 percent federal, 4 percent state, and 5 percent of women in jail reported being pregnant (Maruschak, 2006, 2008).

There are more than 200,000 women in U.S. prisons or jails each year, and roughly 6 percent or 12,000 of those women are pregnant at the time they are incarcerated. Based on 2016 statistics when there were more than 110,000 women in federal and state prisons in the United States showed that although 75 percent of these women were between 18-44 years old, there was no mandatory standard for prenatal and pregnancy care (Sufrin, 2019). Until this new study, the 2004 Bureau of Justice Statistics survey (which only accounted for self-reported pregnancies) was the only data on pregnancy prevalence in prisons.

Expectant inmates struggle with hormonal changes, unsympathetic correctional staff, hunger, a lack of proper medical care, and—in some states—knowing labor and delivery will be experienced while shackled. *The First Step Act* (2018) prohibits the shackling of pregnant prisoners in federal custody except in certain cases, but 27 states currently allow shackling during labor and delivery.

Another physical condition is the reality of drug use among justice-involved women. Although data is sporadically collected, research supports a strong link between drug use and female criminal conduct. A national study of five major American cities by the Center for Prisoner Health and Human Rights (2016) showed that between 63-83% of incarcerated women had drugs in their system at the time of arrest.

> ***"This was my first time ever in trouble,*** *and for a small amount of marijuana… I went to prison, which was unusual… I had grown up in a Christian home … I was a drug addict and so I went in. I had a son at the time... He was six months old when I went to prison and my parents took him while I went in. Then I came back out, and within six months I was right back in my addiction, so it didn't even make a difference."*
>
> — Formerly incarcerated woman

The power of addiction and incarceration on a woman's mental and physical health is notable.

> ***"One of the problems that I had coming in,*** *one time in particular, was just being separated from my drug life.[It] was very hard for me because I did not want*

to be done using and you know I was mourning the loss of my kids. There was lots of grief and loss... I was very depressed and then there was a fear inside."

–Formerly incarcerated woman

Substance use is linked to issues of trauma and mental health. Approximately half of prison and jail inmates meet diagnostic criteria defined by the American Psychiatric Association for substance abuse, which may be compounded by co-occurring mental illness.

Because of this link, treatment for substance use must also include trauma healing and mental health treatment. However, the National Center on Addiction and Substance Abuse at Columbia University estimates that only 11 percent of incarcerated individuals in need of substance abuse treatment receive it in jail or prison, so most people with substance use issues relapse in the community after release. Those who do receive "help" for substance use may be worse for it.

"They shouldn't be giving them those psychotropic *and anti-psychotic drugs [in aftercare], but they give them to you now. If they don't take them all, and they come and do a search, and if they have one pill missing, they put them in jail. It's horrible. It takes us even more effort to build trust in them again, and to let them know that they don't have to sneak because that behavior comes out with them with fear. The fear tactic is compounded with the dark side of their life, that behavior that they went through prior to going to jail. That has not been addressed, so there's no rehabilitation there. That's my point."*

– Ministry Leader

The treatment for substance abuse, trauma healing, and mental health is difficult to accomplish successfully in prison because the women have to deal with other issues as well. Even if the resources were available a significant amount of human repair must take place.

"These are life skills to help them *to regain back the faculties that they lost as a result of the lifestyle and the mind-altering substances, helping them to put their lives back together, but in a more meaningful and purposeful way for them.*

Because time and time again women lose their hope prior to picking up substances of abuse. Broken relationships, domestic violence, dating, partner violence, the loss of their children, separation from their moms and their fathers, and folks that don't understand that they do suffer with a chronic illness. When one gets themselves involved with self-medicating, they have a tendency to have a time lapse because what the chemicals do is shut down the neural transmitter."

– Chaplain

The Challenge of Motherhood

Approximately 80 percent of all women under correctional supervision are mothers, and most have at least one child younger than 18 (Swavola et al, 2016). Additionally, women in prison are more likely than incarcerated fathers to be the primary caretakers of their children and were more likely to be the primary caretakers prior to arrest. Therefore, an increase in female incarceration means an increase in health issues, family disruption and insecurity (Beitsch, 2017).

"They'll say, 'I was always a good mom, *and I didn't ever do drugs in front of them. I never left my male friends around them' or whatever. But the truth is that while they were on a binge or on a weekend trip... the kids were left somewhere with an aunt, a sister or a neighbor, and they had not returned to retrieve them at the appointed time."*

– Reentry Volunteer

Five million children, roughly 7 percent of all children living in America, have a parent who is currently or was previously incarcerated (Martin, 2017). Children are the hidden victims, with little personal support or voice to be heard (Glaze & Maruschak, 2008).

Although it is difficult to predict how a child will react, they face a host of physical, social, economic and emotional challenges. Research findings on these children's risk factors are mixed, but the absence of a mother who provides primary support for the child creates multiple challenges for the family (Foster & Hagen, 2009). Communities of color seem to be especially vulnerable, as African American children and Hispanic children were more likely than white children to have an incarcerated parent (Kopak & Smith-Ruiz, 2016). Children of incarcerated mothers had much higher rates of incarceration—including earlier and more frequent arrests—than children of incarcerated fathers (Miller, 2016).

> ***"The whole experience was just so traumatic*** *and it's detrimental to your family as well. It's like you're going to prison, but you've got children at home and they're in prison too. Because you can talk to them on the phone about how you're doing and your homework and school, but it's just not the same as being there. Visits were really bad too, because you'd have so much fun. You'd hug your children. You'd color with them. You'd do all kinds of fun activities. And then when it was time to go, that was the worst because you didn't want to leave them. It's like, 'Can I go with you? Please don't go.' It was disheartening just to even have a visit, because instead of looking forward to the visit, you're knowing that they're here now, but they're going to be leaving."*
>
> – Formerly incarcerated woman

Jails and prisons restrict communication and make it hard to stay in touch with family members (Beitsch, 2017). Further, communication with loved ones is expensive. Federal prisons are more likely to be far from home, making face-to-face contact more difficult and costly.

> ***"The fact that I didn't see my kids*** *for the whole three years I was in there, or the time that I was in the jail was very hurtful. That hurt me just being a mother, being separated from my children like that. Then it hurt me that the family members that have custody of them at the time would not bring them to come visit because then I started feeling like, 'Well I guess these family members are against me too."*
>
> – Formerly incarcerated woman

If children are placed in foster care after sentencing, a prison sentence can sever family ties forever (Hager & Flagg, 2018). Female prisoners are five times more likely than male inmates to have their children end up in foster care, and they are more likely to have their parental rights taken away (Childress, 2013).

The Marshall Project analysis estimates that from 2006-2016 at least 32,000 incarcerated parents had their children permanently taken from them. Nearly 5,000 appear to have had their parental rights taken away solely because of their imprisonment, since the things that build a case against separation (e.g., spending time with their children regularly, showing up for court hearings, taking parenting classes, being employed, having stable housing) are nearly impossible during confinement.

> ***"They separated all of my kids.*** *It's sad. It's crazy. I hope to God they don't hate me. I feel like whoever they're with, I just pray to God that they're Christians and that they love God and one day I will be reunited with my children. Cause I can't see my children, I write them letters [but] they keep coming back to me in prison, so I stopped writing after a while. It is hard because I mean I gave birth to them. I can't have any more kids."*
>
> – Formerly incarcerated woman

Female incarceration was associated with lower economic resources. This was especially true if the father did not live with the family, if the child lived with a caregiver who was already responsible for other dependents, or if the child lived with a grandparent on retirement income (Martin, 2017).

The biggest predictor of problems is the strength of the relationship between mother and child. If the mother lived with the child, provided social and financial support, and created a strong bond with the child, long-term negative effects of incarceration are lessened. With support and opportunities to interact throughout the prison sentence, the challenges are minimized.

> ***"As they are cycling in and out of prison,*** *some of what is happening is that…they think their kids are okay, that a friend has them or a neighbor has them while they were out and about. Most of the time, they never [think] that their kids may have been neglected or left longer than what they thought or what they realized. One of the things that happens in that sobriety moment is 'Where are my children? Who has them? What's going to happen next?' The reality that 'my kids are with my mother', or 'my kids are with my ex and he lives in*

> *another state', or '[my kids are with] my grandmother who is 80 years old'... All of that is a real eye-opener for the offender and how they process through that."*
>
> – Chaplain

It is a sobering reality that by federal law, parental rights are terminated after children have lived in foster care for 15 out of the most recent 22 months (Hager & Flagg, 2018).

Challenges of Economic and Employment Issues

There are several barriers as formerly incarcerated women complete their sentences. Being a single parent, being the primary caregiver of minor children, and having a history of substance abuse and mental health disorders create walls. In addition, lack of education, employment history and skills, and the stigma of incarceration make it difficult to secure employment, especially employment that offers a livable wage for justice-involved women.

To cope with these barriers, many women choose illegal options for income and welfare rather than struggling to live off low-paying jobs (Duwe & Clark, 2014). Even when prisons have appropriate training or educational opportunities, incarcerated women may have other issues that are barriers to their success.

> ***"I got up at 6 o'clock in the morning.*** *I had to get to work—I worked yard crew, which is horticulture. I did that for a while. I worked in the cafeteria too, but because I had Hep C they didn't let me work around food, so I had to go to horticulture. I did the yards ... pruned and stuff like that... and about 1 o'clock, I'd go to my studies. After that, I would go ... to school. But my teacher was kind of discouraging me about things because I'm a slow learner. I'm dyslexic, so I'm going for my GED now since I'm out of prison. But I couldn't get it in there. The teacher wasn't patient with me. He didn't want to help me, and he was always rushing me. I couldn't understand things, especially algebra and stuff. I didn't get that."*
>
> – Formerly incarcerated woman

Forty-two percent of incarcerated women have not completed high school. While women in state prisons were more likely than men to have a high school diploma, or attended an institution of higher learning, they have limited vocational training (Harlow, 2003; The Sentencing Project, 2007).

Most jobs held by justice-involved women are low-skilled, entry-level jobs with low pay. Prior to arrest, 60 percent were not employed full-time, 37 percent had an income under $600 a month, and 30 percent received welfare benefits. One justice-involved woman who had been in and out of jail four times in the past year explained the lost opportunities. *"Where I was incarcerated there weren't any programs or anything like that offered to us. All we did was sit in the pod all day and watch TV."*

Given economic and employment issues, reentry and recidivism are challenging. At least 95% of all state prisoners will return to their communities. This means that over 10,000 individuals are released from state and federal prisons each week and approximately 9 million individuals are released from jail each year.

The Bureau of Justice tracked a representative sample of prisoners released in 2005 in 30 states and their arrests through 2014. Overall, 30 percent were rearrested within the first six months, 44 percent within the first year, 68 percent within three years, 79 percent within six years, and 83 percent within nine years.

The 401,288 released state prisoners were arrested an estimated two million times during the nine years after their release, an average of five arrests per released persons. Arrests were for violating terms of their parole or for committing a new crime (Alpher, et al, 2018).

> ***"Women were coming in and out [of prison]*** *and I didn't understand why. I felt like on the inside I was beating the walls, teaching and praying and helping and supporting, and some of those ladies who had the greatest responses were cycling back in. When I would talk to them, they would often drop their head and say, 'Well you know, I really had nowhere to go. I didn't have anywhere to go. I went back into the same environment, among the same people.'"*
>
> – Chaplain

One formerly incarcerated woman echoed this sentiment, and the difficulty of getting away from her past. *"Where was I going to go when I got out? Because my one sister that takes care of my mother now said, 'I wouldn't trust you around our mother. You might kill her... You got a hot temper. You don't need to be around our mother, so we don't want you here.'"* Reentry is especially challenging for women going back to rural or more remote communities with fewer jobs and less resources.

> ***"What good is it going to do for me*** *and my staff to go in there, give them information, make them feel good about themselves? No sooner than we walk out of the institution they're right back stuck with this attitude of judgment and ridicule; the attitude of punishment. It makes me sick to my stomach to even go down there because you can just see the level of care that they are being provided. I just can't wrap my mind around it. I can't accept it. So I just wait for them to come out, those that are coming to us."*
>
> – Reentry Leader

Questions for Reflection

1. Brainstorm resources available in your community that address each challenge faced by justice-involved women.
2. How do the challenges faced by justice-involved women create opportunities for ministry?

3

Entering the System

***"I ended up staying [in jail] about 10 months.** When I got to prison, they didn't even want to give me the jail credit, and that upset me because then I find out this is a mandatory three-year sentence... They originally assigned me a lawyer in the Public Defender's Office. He did not really do his job representing me [so] the case got passed on to another public defender... He was trying to convince me into this guilty plea. With him being a lawyer, and everything going on, I thought, 'Okay, well I'm going to go with what this man is saying.'... I later on found out through other inmates he was a guilty plea lawyer only. I feel he coerced me into it because he used threats and scare tactics by saying things such as, 'If you don't take this guilty plea, you can get 15 years.' I felt that I didn't have a choice. Now I have this felony on my record."*

– Formerly incarcerated woman

Knowing how the criminal justice system operates helps ministry workers understand the legal process justice-involved women experience. Chapter three introduces a basic understanding of the criminal justice system, with relevant legal terminology. The incarceration *process* is explained in order to understand the criminal justice system jail residents are facing. This sets us up to later focus on the incarceration *experience* (as opposed to the incarceration process) through the collective narrative of representative women who have been imprisoned in correctional facilities.

The Legal Process

We acknowledge at the outset that knowing how the criminal justice system operates helps ministry workers understand the legal process jail residents are experiencing. However, volunteers and ministry staff stand outside the legal process.

Ministry workers must ***not*** *ask residents about their case.*

If residents begin to share case information, stop this conversation because anything they say can be used in the court. Ministry workers do not have confidentiality privileges, and they must not give legal advice. If asked a procedural question (e.g., should the individual take a plea deal or go to trial), ministry workers can listen as she processes her options and ask questions. However, the best response is to offer to pray for wisdom, rather than give advice about what to do. These matters must be the decision of the justice-involved woman.

Classification of Crime

The following terms, definitions, and process provide a basic understanding of the criminal justice system. Knowing these terms helps ministry workers have a better appreciation for what defendants are facing. Definitions come from the American Correctional Association (2019) or are derived from the United States Department of Justice.

Crime: Conduct in violation of the criminal laws at the federal, state, or local level. The type of punishment for a crime depends on whether it is a felony or misdemeanor.

Misdemeanor: This is usually a petty offense, a less serious crime than a felony, and punishable by less than a year of confinement. Misdemeanors are sub-classified "A" through "C", with Class A warranting the maximum penalty for misdemeanors. Every state has a system for classifying criminal offenses. Common misdemeanors include petty theft (an item stolen below a particular monetary value), simple assault (an attempt to cause serious physical harm to an individual, or causing minor harm), drunk driving without causing injury, and disturbing the peace.

Felony: This is a crime carrying a penalty of more than a year in prison. Felonies have two categories: violent crime and non-violent crime. ***Violent crime*** uses force or threat of force and includes murder, non-negligent manslaughter, rape, robbery (theft through use of force or fear), and aggravated assault. ***Non-violent crimes*** are those crimes that do not involve the use of any force or injury to another person. The seriousness of a non-violent crime is measured in terms of economic damage or loss to the victim. Examples of non-violent crimes include damage to property, possession or sale of drugs, prostitution, and tax fraud.

Court People

Once an individual has been arrested, she is held in jail or released on bond until sentencing. The process of being judged guilty or innocent involves going to court to face legal charges for the alleged crime. The principal players appearing in court for the "hearing" of the case include the:

Defendant, who is the person accused of the crime.

Defense attorneys, who are the lawyers hired by the defendant or assigned by the court to defend the accused against the government's case.

Public defenders, who are lawyers assigned by the court to represent defendants in criminal matters; these are situations in which the defendant cannot afford an attorney.

Prosecutors, who are the lawyers who represent the state or federal government (not the victim) throughout the court process, from the first appearance of the accused in court until the accused is acquitted or sentenced.

The Criminal Justice Process

The process from initial encounter with an arresting officer of the law to pretrial is described in the following steps.

Step One: Arrest

The police determine there is probable cause that a crime was committed by the individual, or there is a court warrant to arrest the individual. The individual goes into custody.

Step Two: Charged and Booked

The prosecutor considers the evidence assembled by the police and decides whether to file written charges (or a complaint) or release the accused without prosecution. If charged, the accused is booked. This is where personal information is gathered (name, address, etc.), the individual is fingerprinted, and her picture is taken.

Step Three: First Court Appearance

The accused appears in court to be informed of the charges and of her rights. The judge decides whether there is enough evidence to hold the accused or release her. If the defendant does not have an attorney, the court may appoint one or begin the process of assigning a public defender to represent the defendant.

Step Four: Bail or Bond Set

The judge may decide to hold the accused in jail (detain) or release her on bail, bond, or her "own Recognizance." The latter term means the defendant promises to return to court for any required proceedings, and the judge does not impose bail because the defendant appears not to be a flight risk. To be released on bail, defendants have to hand over cash or other valuables (such as property deeds) to the court as security to guarantee that the defendant will appear at the trial.

Defendants may pay bail with cash or bond, which is an amount put up by a bail bondsman who collects a non-refundable fee from the defendant to pay the bail. The judge also considers such factors as drug use, residence, employment, and family ties in deciding whether to hold or release the defendant. Some women are incarcerated because they are too poor to pay the bond, even when set at a couple of hundreds of dollars.

Step Five: Grand Jury or Preliminary Hearing

In about one-half of the states, defendants have the right to have their cases heard by a grand jury. This means that a jury of citizens must hear the evidence presented by the prosecutor and decide whether there is enough evidence to indict the accused of the crime.

If the grand jury decides there is enough evidence, the grand jury submits to the court an indictment, or written statement of the facts of the offense charged against the accused. In other cases, the accused may have to appear at a preliminary hearing in court. In this case, the judge hears evidence and the defendant is formally indicted or released.

Arraignment. At this point in the process, the accused is brought into court, told of the charges, and asked, "How do you plea?"

Plea. If the defendant admits to committing the crime(s) charged to her, the plea is *guilty*. The plea of a person who claims not to have committed the crime of which she is accused is *not guilty*. A not guilty plea may also be used to continue with legal due process, not necessarily that she is innocent of the crime. A plea of no contest has the same effect as a plea of guilty as far as the criminal sentence is concerned, but the plea may not be considered an admission of guilt for any other purpose.

Sometimes, a guilty plea could later be used to show fault in a lawsuit, but the plea of "no contest" forces the plaintiff in the lawsuit to prove that the defendant committed the crime. Scholars estimate that 90 to 95 percent of federal and state cases are resolved through plea bargain.

Step Six: Pre-trial hearings

Pre-trial hearings are usually the first opportunity for the defendant or her attorney to meet with the prosecutor to discuss the case. There are three common pre-trial motions. The first is a ***motion to dismiss,*** such as in a misdemeanor case where the defendant believes there is not sufficient evidence to charge her with the crime. The second is a ***motion to suppress*** certain evidence, which would be appropriate in a case where the defendant believes that the evidence was collected in violation of some of her constitutional rights. The third is a ***motion to postpone*** the trial (a "continuance"), in order for the attorney to have more time to obtain evaluations or other documents needed for the case.

Step Seven: Adjudication

Adjudication is the name for the trial process. The majority of cases are resolved by plea agreements rather than trials held before a judge or jury. Several things can occur during adjudication.

Plea agreements ("plea deal") mean that the defendant has agreed to plead guilty to one or more of the charges in exchange for one of the following: dismissal of one or more changes, a lesser degree of the charged offense, a recommendation for a lenient sentence, a recommendation that avoids the maximum sentence, or making no recommendation. The law does not require prosecutors to inform victims about plea agreements or seek their approval.

Trial can be held before a judge (***bench trial***), or judge and jury (***jury trial***), depending upon the seriousness of the crime and other factors. The prosecutor and defense attorney present evidence and question witnesses. The judge or jury finds the defendant guilty or not guilty on the original charges or lesser charges. Defendants found not guilty are usually released. If the verdict is guilty, the judge will set a date for sentencing.

Verdict is entered once the judge or jury pronounces guilt or innocence. An **acquittal** involves the judgment that a criminal defendant has not been proven guilty beyond a reasonable doubt, and therefore is free. A **conviction** involves a judgment of guilt against a criminal defendant, who is sent to jail until her **sentencing** trial. With a guilty verdict and conviction, the justice-involved woman faces sentencing.

Step Eight: Sentencing hearing

The sentencing hearing is the time at which the prosecutor and defense attorney provide arguments for the type and length of sentence. There is often a range of sentencing options within the sentencing guidelines required by the state or federal government. The judge determines the sentence within those guidelines. In cases of the death penalty, the jury is given an opportunity to make a recommendation to the judge who has the final decision.

Punishment Options

Diversion refers to a voluntary program for defendants charged with a crime to complete a program (e.g., drug treatment, boot camp).

Fine is a monetary charge imposed on an individual convicted of a crime. If the fine is not paid, the individual is imprisoned.

Restitution is money paid to the victim (either a person or society as a whole).

Probation is a sentencing alternative to imprisonment in which the court releases convicted defendants under supervision, as long as certain conditions are observed. Conditions may include community service, drug testing, substance abuse treatment, or fees.

Imprisonment involves being sentenced to a length of time. In most states, if the woman is sentenced for more than a year, she is sent to a prison; for less than a year, time is served in the jail. In most cases, time served is counted toward the sentence.

Death penalty or capital punishment is used by the federal government and in 33 states.

Experiencing the Criminal Justice Process

"Going through the arrest process is very scary. *It's a horrible feeling to get your freedom taken away. Addiction already takes your freedom away. It's a choice that we make, of course, when we're sober to pick up drugs. But once we're in our addiction, we don't know. We don't have a choice anymore. Obviously getting arrested becomes a rescue, more than an arrest. But sometimes these police officers are very brutal and very dishonest. I really want to stress that there are some good police officers and there are some bad. But going through the jail process so many times, I've seen some of the worst and some of the best. Whoever is out there listening to this, just don't judge."*

– Formerly incarcerated woman

Understanding the experiences of incarceration will improve ministry effectiveness and outcomes. Individual experiences with the justice system for better or for worse vary by the arresting officer(s), size and geographical location of the jail, the corrections staff, and jail environment.

After sentencing that sends the woman to prison, the individual's experiences depend upon the location, programs available, and corrections staff. Overall, it is fair to characterize the criminal justice process as dehumanizing as well as a time of deprivation. Justice-involved women experience shame, humiliation, judgment, and loss—of identity, relationships, privacy, job, housing, car, custody of children, and control over her life. While the order and process may vary, there are common elements. The following is a compilation of several individuals' experiences.

THE ARREST

The arrest may come from a traffic stop, a warrant or the response of police to a call. After demonstrating probable cause—such as drug possession, being high or drunk and driving, possession of stolen goods, soliciting an officer, or getting into a fight—the individual is arrested. The woman is given a general pat down. One woman says it this way:

> ***"I was handcuffed with metal handcuffs** behind my back. I remember getting in the seat in the back of the cop car. It's really uncomfortable because your hands are behind your back and you have to sit on this hard, plastic seat behind the cage. After I got out of the car, they checked underneath the seats to make sure I didn't stash anything in the car."*

At some point in the process, the woman is "Mirandized" as the **Miranda Warning*** is given to the arrested individual.

The arrested individual is driven to the police station for booking. She gets out of the police car and is taken into the station to a waiting area to get processed. There, staff take all her belongings, including jewelry, and check her pockets and socks.

They inventory the woman's possessions and put them in a bag. They take her shoelaces and shoes (if staff think they can be used as a weapon) and give her rubber sandals. She is asked questions to confirm her identity. She gets fingerprinted and has her picture taken. If it is busy,

---

* *"You have the right to remain silent. Anything you say can and will be used against you in a court of law. You have the right to an attorney. If you cannot afford an attorney, one will be provided for you. Do you understand the rights I have just read to you? With these rights in mind, do you wish to speak to me?"*

staff put her in a holding cell with others until they can process her. She is thinking, *"What's going to happen?"*

The arrested woman is told her **bond** amount and she must have family, friends or a bail bondsman pay 10 percent of that amount in order to be released. This is the time when she is given phone calls to a maximum of two individuals to get the bond. If she is unable to have someone pay 10 percent of the bond, then she is transported to the jail to be processed to stay at the jail until her first court date. She is put in a holding cell with other women who smell. It can be anywhere from a few to 30 women.

> ***"Some are dope sick because they're coming down off of the heroin,*** *or crack cocaine, or methamphetamines, whatever they're doing. They are sweating, puking; sometimes they defecate on themselves. It gets pretty bad. Then you got the gang bangers who are just bad attitude—want to start fights—or you got the other girls. The prostitutes that are standing around, and they've got attitude problems too. It's just a very unpleasant place to be. You got people just strewn all over the floor, passed out. Me, usually I would be there. I would be passed out too, because we'd be in there for so many hours. Some places would give you a mat to sleep on. Some places wouldn't, so you'd just be on straight cement."*
>
> – Formerly incarcerated woman

Typically, the court date is the next day unless it is a Friday and the arrested woman has to wait until Monday. In larger jails, it may be a week to a month before she is brought before the judge. At that court date she is read her charges, asked if she can afford an attorney or needs one appointed, and is scheduled for the next court date. Bond may be changed depending upon mitigating circumstances. She is then taken back to the holding area, and "dressed out." After being strip-searched, she is given a jump suit, and goes into a reception unit.

In the reception unit, the woman sees medical and psychological personnel to determine medications or indicate if suicide watch is needed. There are multiple tests, including a vaginal exam, urine sample, and blood work. They test for pregnancy, HIV, and venereal diseases. She is given a bedroll.

"That's where they roll up this itchy, gray blanket, *and they give you a comb, little hotel size bar soap and shampoo, a plastic cup with a little tooth brush that's about two inches long and clear tooth paste that does not clean your teeth at all. You still feel like you have a sweater on your teeth when you're done brushing your teeth."*

– Formerly incarcerated woman

The process can take two to twelve hours, depending upon what else is happening at the jail.

The food given to individuals in jail is simple, such as a baloney sandwich or syrup on a peanut butter sandwich. Women do not want to show fear because this is communicating weakness. Those who are weak become the target of being bullied and victimized; for example, having food taken or getting beat up.

"It is very intimidating to be arrested and go to jail. *You never know what people are going to say, how you have to walk in. You have to keep your head strong and you cannot look weak. You can't cry... No matter how bad you may feel, you cannot show that weakness."*

– Formerly incarcerated woman

"You can tell who is in there for the first time *because they are looking scared and crying. Everyone tries to act tough. You might be scared to death inside, but you put on a tough face." You stay straight forward and just be very about yourself, and within yourself, and just stay to yourself. I always stay to myself. I never was in the gossiping or talking sh-- to other women or anything like that. I just did my own thing, kept my head up and did what I had to do to get out of there."*

– Formerly incarcerated woman

The arrested woman finds her case may take weeks, months, or years to adjudicate depending upon her attorney, the charges, the prosecutor, the judge's schedule, and the number of court cases in the county.

__"At the next court date, you take your chances__ on a public defender who doesn't know your case or your file and is obviously overworked. In the crowded local municipal courthouse, you hope the plaintiff does not show up so the case gets dropped. It's a bright, stuffy, old room with large benches for seats. The judge, the court assistant, and the stenographer are on a large bench facing towards you, elevated. Visually you know that's a seat of authority. You then realize that your freedom is dependent on being competently defended, so you take whatever money you have left and hire a lawyer."

– Formerly incarcerated woman

Waiting for a trial is another ordeal, with different concerns and issues involved. Regardless of how many times it is experienced, justice-involved women often talk in similar ways about how the dehumanization process continues.

__"I have seizures, and I had a few seizures [in jail].__ Getting a nurse to come see if I was okay, or you know, just getting medical attention is pretty much nonexistent. Mental health issues as well. A lady come in and she was put on lock down for about two months straight because she had mental health issues, so she was probably hurt more than anything."

– Formerly incarcerated woman

The Transition to Correctional Care

Institutionalization or **"prisonization"** is the process of shaping and transforming an inmate to the correctional environment. It also connotes the negative psychological effects of imprisonment (Haney, 2001). Some of the symptoms of institutionalization include:

- dependence on institutional structures and contingencies—i.e., a relinquishment of freedom and autonomy;
- hypervigilance, interpersonal distrust, and suspicion—i.e., the incarcerated woman is alert for signs of threat or personal risk;
- emotional over-control, alienation, and psychological distancing—i.e., the woman puts on a figurative prison mask that hides

emotions and lacks spontaneity;
- social withdrawal and isolation—i.e., a retreat into oneself, trusting no one;
- incorporation of exploitive norms of prison culture—i.e., taking advantage of the weak, showing sexual dominance or submission;
- a diminished sense of self-worth and personal value—i.e., loss of confidence;
- post-traumatic stress reactions to the pains of imprisonment—i.e., the harsh, punitive, uncaring nature of prison life may re-traumatize from childhood trauma, violence, physical or sexual assault, and internal chaos that leads to stress and fear.

***"It was scary because going to jail** and losing everything ... I lost so much going to jail. I would lose my apartment, or my car, or not have contact with anybody in the world, because I'm cut off from everything. It's emotionally damaging to go to jail, it really is. It lowers your self-esteem. They strip you down to nothing. You have no make-up and none of your clothes. I know that sounds really materialistic, but they strip you down to nothing. You're dressed like a boy, you have no hair ties, no nothing. The food's terrible, and you feel like a nothing. You're pretty much bottom of the barrel. It's like you're not even in the world, anymore. It's like you're exiled out. Like you're basically just in a whole other dimension of the world. It's like your life is just at a standstill until they decide they want to unlock that door and let you out, and let you be part of society again. Yeah, and your life is just, as you know it, done. It's like you're the living dead. You know what I mean? I think that's why I'm done being the person that I used to be, because I lived that way for so long. I lived in and out of jail, like a revolving door, for so long."*

– Formerly incarcerated woman

The imbalance of power between inmates and corrections staff involves the use of direct physical force. It also involves indirect force based on the prisoners' total dependency on officers for basic necessities, and the officer's ability to withhold privileges.

Additionally, searches, restraints, and isolation can have profound effects on women with histories of abuse, trauma, and mental illness. Standard correctional procedures often act as "triggers" to re-traumatize women who have posttraumatic stress disorder (PTSD). In these cases, women are vulnerable to sexual misconduct of staff and some need services that are outside the scope and practice of the facility.

Impunity means that the prisoner will not be punished for making complaints while in custody. However, corrections staff have access to inmates' personal files, which includes a record of any complaint she has made. Officers have been known to threaten the prisoner's children and visitation rights as a means of silencing the woman.

Correctional officers also issue "rules-infraction tickets", which extend the women's stay in prison if she speaks out. Prisoners who complain may be placed in administration segregation. Reported officers may be transferred rather than disciplined or prosecuted—and in some cases, the inmate may also be transferred. Ineffective procedures and reporting can increase abuse. However, sometimes the women are encouraged to tell their stories.

Release from incarceration, often called reentry, will be discussed in later chapters. By law, when the inmate has completed her sentence she is put outside the walls. The woman is given an order of release legally known as a **certificate of disposition**. This is the equivalent of jail release papers or a discharge certificate from prison. There may be a reentry plan and identification papers, but little more.

"A lot of times the women are arrested in the summertime *in very compromising outfits, and then they get released in the middle of winter in the same outfits. I have been able to find benefactors and I have bought probably $1000 worth of sweatpants and sweatshirts, sports bras and panties so that when the women get released, they aren't released in these awful situations and that's helping restore some of the dignity to them."*

– Reentry Volunteer

Questions for Reflection

1. Go to court and observe how cases are handled, or journey with someone through their case. What have you learned from the process?
2. How does understanding the legal system and being incarcerated impact ministry?

4

Correctional Control

*"**People off the streets will come into the prison** right before you go to prison. They give them an opportunity to tour around and then we tell our stories. A lot of them thought that we got something for it. We didn't get time off; we didn't get anything. We did these tours and we shared our life with them. It was really not about what we were in there for, it was about how we're going to reach these people today, if only one. I used to reach them all because I can look at them and when they'd start bringing that, I love them. They were open, too."*

– Formerly incarcerated woman

Although justice-involved women report higher rates of physical and sexual victimization while incarcerated than male inmates, fellow inmates more often commit violent acts than correctional officers (Bloom & Covington, 2008; Wolff et al., 2006). The reality is to lower operating costs, administrators may need to hire fewer employees who are paid and trained less. Necessary rules and regulations of correctional facilities co-exist with preexisting vulnerabilities that will always place justice-involved women at greater risk because correctional control of women affects their vulnerabilities regardless of age, crime, or treatment services needed. These facts raise questions for ministry workers concerned about safety and justice and are the focus of this chapter.

A government watchdog agency points to systemic problems in the way federal prisons treat women in their custody. A review of the Department of Justice's Office of Inspector General (IG) concluded that the bureau "has not managed female inmates strategically" and "needs to take additional steps … to ensure that female inmates' needs are met at the institutional level" (Jung, 2018). The report identified three particular areas in need of review and reform: trauma treatment, pregnancy, and feminine hygiene.

The IG study reveals a system that fails to meet certain basic needs of prisoners, prompting grassroots action such as the **Pregnant Women in Custody Act of 2018**, and the **Dignity for Incarcerated Women Act of 2017**.

While not law, these recent actions protest justice-involved women being treated as an afterthought in the criminal justice system. Without treatment for mental health or substance use, justice-involved women often experience high rates of relapse upon release. Female parolees face greater stigma than their male counterparts, and find fewer halfway programs, shelter beds, employment and housing available (Bandele, 2017).

This number does not adjust for the number of women who are incarcerated, but basically points out that there are fewer options for women. Without comprehensive supports in place while incarcerated, women and girls are likely to become victims again and return to custody. One member of the American Psychological Association notes:

> *Psychologists and other mental health professionals must join forces with community activists and policymakers to address the warehousing of poor and vulnerable persons in correctional facilities. To do otherwise is to look away from the individual and generational impact of violence and victimization. To isolate instead of treating those in need keeps the cycle going in the lives of countless families, at an exorbitant human and societal cost. We must return to our credo to do no harm* (Cowen, 2019).

Recognizing the need to view women as a special population under its care as well as provide appropriate treatment, the National Commission on Correctional Health Care (NCCHC, 2014) created its position on appropriate treatment. **Standards for Health Services** are the basis of NCCHC accreditation program for jails, prisons, and juvenile detention and confinement facilities.

Several impact the health care of younger women. The NCCHC recommends: 1) screening for current gynecological problems and pregnancy, 2) an initial health assessment following clinical practice guidelines for pelvic examinations and Pap smears, 3) intoxication and withdrawal management for pregnant inmates with opioid use, 4) provision of nondirective contraception counseling, access to emergency contraception and continuation of current contraceptive method while incarcerated, and 5) comprehensive counseling and assistance for pregnant inmates in keeping with their desires for their unborn children. The Position Statement found in Appendix B provides the broader aspiration of care to meet the needs of justice-involved women.

Approaches to Correctional Control

While some facilities lean toward more correctional control, and others err on the side of correctional care, five approaches are seen in work with incarcerated women. You will note some overlap among principles of each approach, which are: 1) criminogenic risk, 2) strengths-based, 3) trauma-informed, 4) evidence-based practices, and 5) gender-responsive corrections care. Since these approaches omit the spiritual component that for religious ministries is the key to healing, and many religious ministries are unsystematic in their approach, we will revisit these approaches in a later chapter in order to provide more information about implementation strategies and specific ministry questions to evaluate each approach's effectiveness.

Criminogenic Risk Factors

Researchers have identified major risk factors associated with criminal conduct that predicts recidivism (Andrews & Bonta, 2010). In addition to these risk factors, subsequent research has focused on women and identified their gender-specific risks and needs (Bloom, Owen, & Covington, 2003).

The claim is made that interventions that do not target criminogenic factors specific to women are not effective in reducing recidivism. "Gender-neutral" factors are risks and needs identified for both male and female offenders.

Criminal history. A longer history of antisocial behavior creates more settings in which crime is committed. The number and variety of illegal conduct escalates into behavior increasing the risk to reoffend. While the past cannot be changed, there are needs that can be addressed to reduce risk and change future additions to the list of offenses. One intervention is to help women identify risky situations, ways to avoid these situations, and alternative prosocial responses. Effective programs help participants develop a moral compass and problem-solving skills.

Antisocial attitudes. Thinking errors that contribute to illegal conduct are irrational or inaccurate thoughts that lead to problems, negative moods, or illegal behavior. Early research identified more than 30 thinking errors found in those who engage in criminal behavior. These thinking errors include denying responsibility, blaming others, instant gratification, an *"I'm Okay"* self-image, and closed mindedness. Programs that replace thinking errors with responsible thinking are effective in reducing criminal conduct. In Christian programs, biblical values that overlap with responsible thinking is taught.

Family conflict. Many women were raised in dysfunctional families and likely have experienced physical and sexual abuse, and neglect. They may have observed family members engaged in criminal activity. They may be experiencing family conflict with the family members who are the current caregivers for their children. Effective programs help women parent from behind bars and connect them with their families to develop and maintain healthy relationships, a benefit to both them and their children.

Lack of employment stability, achievement/educational achievement. Justice-involved women often have low levels of education and poor job skills, keeping them in low-paying jobs. The added responsibility of child-care may interfere with her ability to keep full-time employment and create an unstable employment history. Programs that help women obtain educational achievement and job skills increase the chances for successful reentry.

Antisocial associates. Justice-involved women, like most women, are relational. The difference is that many justice-involved women, because of their high rates of abuse and trauma, have difficulty establishing healthy relationships. Their relationships tend to be characterized by high levels of conflict, dysfunction and abuse. At times, the relationship with their significant other includes engaging in criminal behavior. Programs can help women develop relational skills for safe, prosocial relationships. This helps them replace antisocial peers with prosocial peers.

Substance abuse. Most justice-involved women are in need of substance abuse treatment. While Celebrate Recovery, Alcoholics Anonymous (AA) and Narcotics Anonymous (NA) provide support groups, women may be in need of treatment to deal with their addictions. Addictions treated concurrently with trauma and mental health are most effective. Ministries can partner with treatment agencies to provide this specialized care.

Strengths-Based

A strengths-based approach recognizes all women have strengths that can be utilized to increase positive behavior changes and reentry success. The following are specific strengths for women.

Family support. Even if the family is dysfunctional, having family support increases the justice-involved woman's chances for success, unless her family is engaged in criminal activity. Building family support or helping to develop a faith family who can encourage and support her efforts is necessary for a prosocial life.

Educational assets. Gaining a GED, vocational training, and college degree are considered educational assets. They increase self-esteem and the ability to be self-supporting. Building women's soft skills, such as conflict resolution, collaboration, and relational skills, increase confidence and working relationships.

Self-efficacy. The justice-involved woman must believe that her life is under her own power and control, and that she can take positive steps to improve her circumstances. This belief empowers and motivates her to be proactive rather than fatalistic. Providing positive reinforcements as she makes progress in her reentry or life plan will build confidence.

Parental involvement. One of the strongest motivators for women is her children (Cobbina, 2009). By increasing the connection with her children, motivation for prosocial change is enhanced.

Trauma-Informed Correctional Care (TICC)

TICC is a strengths-based approach that is grounded in an understanding of and responsiveness to the impact of trauma (SAMHSA, 2014). It emphasizes physical, psychological and emotional safety for both providers and survivors, and that creates opportunities for survivors to rebuild a sense of control and empowerment. TICC recognizes the higher rates of trauma histories among justice-involved women. It also sees increased potential for both new and renewed trauma within correctional facilities. Trauma is included when providing programs and services. This approach is especially sensitive to triggering trauma reactions. TICC also adjusts organizations and ministry so that trauma survivors can access and benefit from services.

Trauma Informed Care has six core values:

1. **Safety.** Physical and emotional safety is a high priority. This includes not just a safe environment but also interpersonal interactions that promote a sense of safety. Women should not be subject to spiritual abuse or judgment. Interactions should be warm and empathetic. This includes facial expressions.
2. **Trustworthiness and transparency.** Staff build and maintain trust through warmth, openness, confidentiality and care. Trust is built through a structured program that starts on time, is consistent with expectations and discipline, is clear about expectations and maintains healthy boundaries. Being honest and vulnerable without depending on female participants to meet the facilitator's emotional needs demonstrate that TICC techniques are there to serve them.
3. **Peer support and mutual self-help.** Peers or trauma survivors are those with lived experiences of trauma. Peers contribute to establishing safety and hope. Together, women build trust, enhance collaboration, and share their stories because lived experiences promote recovery and healing. In addition to sharing their stories, peers contribute to mentoring and curriculum development.
4. **Collaboration and mutuality.** The goal is to ensure equality in participation by sharing power and decision-making. Recognize

everyone has a role to play and create a sense of belonging so that healing can happen through relationships. When possible, justice-involved women are included in setting group, class or house rules.

5. **Empowerment, voice and choice.** Building on her strengths and addressing areas of need, women are empowered to identify their goals and plans for healing. Leaders may offer options, but each woman is trusted to know what she needs and what will work for her.
6. **Cultural, historical and gender issues.** There is no stereotyping or biases. Gender responsive services are offered, cultural connections leveraged, and historical traumas are recognized and addressed.

EVIDENCE-BASED PRACTICES (EBP)

Evidence-based practices (EBP) are the application of eight principles derived from empirical research and expertise on risk reduction (Bogue, 2004). The eight practices are:

1. **Assess risks/needs using actuarial instruments.** Gender-specific, credible assessment instruments are used to identify risks, needs and strengths of justice-involved women. The measurements are used to inform programming and case management. A recommended tool developed by the National Institute of Corrections and the University of Cincinnati is the Women's Risk/Need Assessment (WRNA, 2008).
2. **Enhance motivation to change.** Motivational interviewing techniques, rather than persuasion tactics, are used in coaching, substance use treatment, and case management. These techniques enhance internal motivation for initiating and maintaining positive behavior changes.
3. **Target intervention.** This practice first implements the *risk principle* to prioritize supervision and treatment resources for higher risk women. Next, the *needs principle* targets interventions to criminogenic needs. Third, the *responsivity principle* responds to temperament, learning style, motivation, culture and gender. It matches women with programs, dosage (by requiring more structure for higher risk women) and

integrates treatment into sentence or sanction requirements.

4. **Staff skill trained with directed practice.** Workers understand social learning theory, cognitive behavioral strategies, and trauma informed care. They have strong communication skills. Their work with justice-involved women promotes skill development through modeling, reinforcement, role-playing, graduated practice, and extinction.
5. **Increase positive reinforcement.** Research indicates that a ratio of four positive reinforcements to every negative response is optimal for promoting behavior changes. Workers look for opportunities and a variety of ways to provide verbal encouragement and material rewards that assist women in their progress toward positive behavior changes.
6. **Engage ongoing support in natural communities.** Research indicates that positive outcomes are more likely to be achieved when significant others are engaged in the woman's case plans. Positive outcomes are also associated with meaningful connections to the prosocial community. Staff encourage and support the development of healthy relationships with prosocial individuals both inside the facility and in the free world. When possible, this involves fostering the women's relationship with their children.
7. **Measure ongoing processes and practices.** Staff must evaluate and measure the program processes and practices. They also need to evaluate workers in their programs' effectiveness. Formal evaluation is often omitted as part of programs, with workers relying on anecdotal evidence.
8. **Provide measurement feedback.** Providing feedback to women as they work through their reentry or life plan helps them stay focused and motivated. In addition, measuring programs ensures program integrity. Is it accomplishing what it is designed to accomplish?

Gender Responsive

When working with justice-involved women, corrections experts recommend rehabilitative rather than punishment-focused efforts.

Gender-responsive practices must be implemented. Gender-responsive means creating an environment through site selection, staff selection, program development, content, and material that reflects an understanding of the realities of women's lives and addresses the issues of the participants (Bloom, Owen & Covington). This reality takes into account her unique pathway to criminal conduct, relational issues, and social/cultural factors. Elements of gender-responsive practice are:

1. **Relational.** Work with women in a relational way to promote mutual respect and empathy.
2. **Strengths-based.** Recognize all women have spiritual, educational and experience strengths that can be mobilized.
3. **Trauma-informed.** Understand her history, and that the context of abuse plays an important role in how she responds to programs, services and relationship to God.
4. **Holistic.** Provide a comprehensive case management model that addresses the complex and multiple needs of justice-involved women including the spiritual component.
5. **Culturally competent.** Provide services that value and acknowledge the diverse cultural backgrounds of women (Modley & Giguere, 2010).

The new practice of "gender-responsive corrections" allows work assignments and training specific to working with incarcerated females, and programs addressing female risks and needs. This approach better serves women. Giving women some control over their immediate living environment, including the ability to find privacy, provide for material needs, and develop personal, educational or vocational skills are essential steps toward healthy readjustment.

Given the focus of our research and "best practices" for training, we want to elaborate on gender-responsive correctional practices. Facilities that are sensitive to this concern use programming and mentoring that illustrate gender-responsive strategies, as these two examples demonstrate.

> ***"Gender specific programming in evidence-based practices is huge*** *across the nation when it comes to rehabilitation… Parenting is huge. Mentoring is huge. Parenting can include aspects of programming that allows you to take your voice and tell a story to your children like, 'Hello son. This is Mom and tonight I want to read you a bedtime story.' That whole story can be mailed to the child—or emailed to the child—and actually be read at night. The "play day" program works on reunification and bonding… It keeps a bonding and the reunification with mom that whoever your caregiver is makes room for mother to still be a part of your life. They all are goal-centered around being productive and making positive changes in the right direction."*
>
> – Chaplain

The process of rehabilitation should begin while institutionalized, but this can be challenging. A recent series on National Public Radio talked about the fact that women going to prison are entering an institution built to control men (Shapiro, 2018). As a result, women in prison (who tend to be less aggressive and confrontational) are disciplined more than men. Additionally, policies may be implemented that don't acknowledge their unique challenges.

> ***"The only negative experiences I've had*** *has come from the political environment and administrative decision, because I haven't really had negative experiences, per se, working with the women. I mean, I'm not going to say that sometimes one of them and I may have had a conflict or something like that. I'm not going to tell you that they all love me, because I'm sure that there's some that don't. But my only difficulties come from the political climate and the environment, especially when they make policies that are not going to help these ladies change. It comes from the legislators who don't have any concept of what prisons are really like. Or they may interview some disgruntled inmates who tell lies… They'll make a policy based on things that aren't even true. Then it just weakens your work when you don't really have authority to do certain things."*
>
> – Correctional staff member

In most correctional facilities, unless significant changes are made in the way women are prepared for release their progress toward a successful transition to life outside prison is limited. Several transitional services exist, such as decompression programs that socialize justice-involved women to freedom (Haney, 2001). In terms of mentoring while still incarcerated, some prisons offer reentry coordinators or other staff to provide this education.

> ***"Reentry coordinators are people who take everything*** *that the offender has done, compiles all that, makes sure all of that is there, kind of puts it in a jacket for that offender, and then they work and beat the streets outside to connect with outside resources (housing mostly) that that person can go to. They pass on all the information that the offender has done that includes her goals, what she hopes to do and all of that to that housing agency. This abridges in a few pages what has been accomplished maybe over five or 10 years in a prison. Those people hopefully can take that and extend that into community programs that now include outside job training, all the educational pieces that you did not get, continued educational programs within there. You would no longer do sobriety classes per se ... You might not be doing parenting in the same way now. You might be doing a parenting offered by the state through the Department of Human Services that would meet some criteria for getting your kids back. Those become stepping-stones to the next stage or the next level of being productive citizens in society."*
>
> – Prison reentry coordinator

Another example of gender-responsive strategies involves living units that are character programs. The character program might provide a character track as well as a spiritual life track where positive relationships are developed. Explains one participant: *"They all teach the values and morals of being upstanding citizens—one by faith and one by just good deeds. But they are one. They use the same material, just one uses the word 'God' and the other does not."*

> ***"Programming for women becomes meaningful,*** *essential and necessary for change. Sometimes when women are trying to change their past, that change becomes difficult because the environment is different. They don't get it*

> *outside of a contained environment. You can have jailhouse religion in prison and it's good. You can have programming inside a prison and it's good. But when you expand that, the reason it's good is because it's a controlled environment. You know who people are. Nobody else is coming in that environment. When they actually leave, the chaplain, the reentry coordinator, everybody is contributing so that when they… walk out the door, everything that they need, they have with them."*
>
> – Program administrator

Other benefits of correctional facilities adapting gender-responsive strategies involve the self-motivation and time available to act on that motivation. Programs and mentors can facilitate change and stable housing inside the corrections facility helps the women focus on change. *"For the majority of the re-entering women, long-term commitment is not a pattern in their life. They might be able to keep a commitment for a shorter time, but to keep going in the long term you almost need something like a material [goal] to keep them connected."* Intentional relationships can provide this motivation.

> ***"Personally, I needed that when I was in there.*** *I know a lot of other women need that. They need that connection with somebody who can help them, too. They got all these feelings going on. You got all these things going on, because they're sober. They don't have the things going on in their life that they had had for so long. They need that connection with the positive, the godly women, the recovering woman—anything that they could have. They need connection of positiveness, not so much as: 'Oh, we're just going to put you all together and be negative together.' I think they need that connection of positiveness."*
>
> – Former incarcerated woman

Justice-involved women have safety needs, but also problems with trust. Even in institutions where correctional officers treat the women well and do not tolerate bullying, the security of these programs and designated living units reinforces healing.

> ***"Because of that mob mentality,*** *a lot of the women won't let their guard down enough to let some healing begin. That is a challenge, trying to*

convince women that… You're never going to see these people again, but they have to live in that environment. [The guards] don't tolerate that kind of treatment within the unit, but then [the women] have their own private cells that they go into and that's where the bullying takes place."

– Prison administrator

A final incentive for justice-involved women to view gender-responsive strategies taking place while they are inside prison walls is economic. Faith-based programs understand this well.

"Some chaplains are good about knowing people *really well, knowing their spirit… but you want to get all that done inside because that's where it's free. The minute you walk out, there's cost associated with those services. Waiting lists associated with those services. Offenders sometimes lose [those services] outside of the perimeter of the gates… Upon going out, if there's nobody to catch their hand, bridge them over and walk with them until… they know where they're going, sometimes it's a slippery slope."*

– Ministry leader

As pointed out in Chapter 2, women in prison have some needs that are quite different than men. Managing incarcerated women requires gender-responsive strategies that reflect the unique needs of women in several areas of the corrections environment. These include offender management and supervision; classification, assessment and case management; treatment, intervention and services; community reentry; and program evaluation.

The warden or facility administrator's philosophy of punishment or rehabilitation and the level of gender-responsive strategies implemented are key to addressing the unique needs, circumstances and risk profiles of women in custody. Some prisons and jails do a better job than others of implementing gender-responsive strategies. Becki Ney (2018), Director of the National Resource Center for Justice Involved Women, states:

"Gender responsive assessment tools, *case planning and management models, and programming are growing in number and have shown* *through research to have much better outcomes with women than gender neutral tools and programming. Most criminal justice professionals who work with women will tell you how different it is than working with men; yet, they do not have the education, training, and skills to engage effectively with them. In jurisdictions where corrections staff have been trained in gender responsive and trauma informed approaches, we have seen reductions in institutional violence and misconducts, self-harming behaviors and mental health referrals."*

Questions for Reflection

1. How is your organization integrating corrections principles into your approach to ministry?
2. What are one to two changes your ministry should make to apply the principles described in this chapter?

5

PRISONIZATION

*"**I was born into the type of home** that most of the women who are incarcerated were born into, which is a home of dysfunctional parents and abuse. Because of that, I took to the streets at a young age and ended up in and out of juvenile homes. I eventually became my own adult at 16 and dropped out of high school. I was just going to take care of myself and run life my way. And I did pretty good, except I was confused inside. I made a lot of destructive choices and continued to just get worse and worse off. I didn't do a good job taking care of myself. I got involved in drugs … and eventually got to a point where I had just spiraled down to the bottom of my pit. I realized one night that I was hopeless. I had become a statistic, a throwaway by society. I was now uneducated, strung out on drugs, and living with a drug dealer. And everybody who had ever known me or known of me probably figured I was either dead or in prison by now."*

– Formerly incarcerated woman

Incarceration is a place of dehumanization and deprivation. While we recognize experiences vary from institution to institution—and correctional facilities adapt policies and practices ranging from punishment-based to therapeutic communities—"doing time" is difficult. In this chapter, we examine the experience of female prisonization. This is the process of socializing inmates into adapting behavior for survival.

Barbara Owen (1998) writes about surviving "the mix" in prisonization. The mix is characterized by a continuation of the behavior that led to imprisonment, a life revolving around drugs, intense, volatile, and often destructive relationships, and non-rule abiding behavior.

To avoid the mix, women establish their own "life-round" program. This involves interaction with other inmates, school and work, and developing their own approach to doing time. This includes negotiating the prison world and gaining respect. For some women, imprisonment offers a rare opportunity to reflect on those early life experiences and beliefs that may incline them to positive change.

> ***"It was then that I remembered Jesus,*** *whom I've always believed in, even though our home was dysfunctional. My mom would sneak us off to church on Sundays, and I always believed ... I always believed in Jesus. I always believed what I learned at church, but in my mind, He never came home with me, so He wasn't real for me. And so that night, at the bottom of my pit, I cried out to Him to save me, and meant it, and knew instantly that something had changed, but I didn't know what. Four days later, a warrant came out for my arrest. I was going to go to adult prison."*
>
> – Formerly incarcerated woman

How women do time is influenced by the length of their incarceration, age, life prior to incarceration, and ethnicity. However, studies show qualitative differences from their male "peer associates" that include developing mutual relationships fundamental to women's identity and sense of worth. It involves countering the more frequent problem of isolation and alienation female offenders suffer by discrimination, victimization, mental illness, and substance abuse. Finally, doing time is impacted by partners strongly connected with drug use, abuse and relapse.

> ***"All the people in that building were*** *... A lot of them were very mean ... [They're] not people you want to share life experiences with and things like that because they're not safe people you want to trust with information like that. Not if they're going to use the information to twist, and turn, and hurt you more. That happened to me. I learned from those bad experiences that I don't need to share anything with these people anymore because these people aren't here for me. They're not here for my spiritual growth. They're not here to help me heal. They really don't care. They're here to make a bigger mess of my life, and make me more traumatized, and then laugh about it."*
>
> – Formerly incarcerated woman

In order to transition to prison life, incarcerated women must understand what behaviors are appropriate and effective in their new context. The first thing that happens is the perception of "difference"—that is, noticing the important characteristics of their new identity in prison. Encounters with corrections staff within prison walls leads to quickly developed stereotypes.

> ***"I think they're so used to being mistreated themselves*** *by so many of the inmates, that they just assumed when they saw me, 'Okay, this girl has probably done some horrible crime' or 'She's probably like the rest of these inmates. She's going to smart mouth us. She's going to talk back to us.' That was hurtful because you stereotype me, because that's not who I am."*
>
> – Formerly incarcerated woman

Incarceration teaches women that confrontation is a risky option, even when others were getting away with breaking the rules. On the other hand, conformity to the prison norms (or a passive strategy of avoidance or evasion) ensures all members play the correct role so that the larger group does not suffer. Breaking down the experience sheds light on the formal rules and social behaviors that can stifle change and effective ministry.

The Process of Prisonization

Socialization is the process of learning acceptable ways to behave. The family is the first teacher. Rules and standards of behavior are further shaped in school, by peer groups and religious communities, and through the influence of mass media. In the same way, newly incarcerated females are socialized in a way that enables them to understand their new world and assimilate new roles within it.

Women who were incarcerated for long periods remembered the role played by older women in taking new arrivals under their protection and teaching them aspects of their new life situation. Several of the women we interviewed played this role.

> ***"Most of the time they put the young people in cells with me*** *because then I got them hooked with the character groups, got them doing things that they liked to do, get the help they need, beautify the institution, get them into a work pattern, and all this other stuff. If you don't have somebody that's going to lead them to that, well it's whack. [Otherwise] they're just sitting there not doing anything..."*
>
> – Formerly incarcerated woman

The socialization process differs by the age of the offender as well as the correctional facility. Youth facilities are usually focused on rehabilitation. According to one volunteer, *"They actually do a pretty good job of recognizing that these people are kids, and they take care of them pretty well. It's definitely not perfect, but there is a good relationship between the correctional officers and the kids in there."*

Likewise, the experience of short-term incarceration is different than a prison sentence. When a woman is arrested, she learns jails function under the formal social control of the government. Jails use laws and court officers to exercise social controls to reinforce appropriate behavior.

> ***"The first time you go into jail,*** *you are traumatized because you've never been in that environment. The first time I went into there, I didn't know they take all your undergarments if they're colored. If you have red panties or black bra, they take it. You have to adjust to all that. In jail, you really don't know what was going to happen. You're in transition, and there was not a lot of programming in jail. You're in limbo. You sleep a lot of times because you're coming off drugs, so you're getting your nourishment or your routine back on track because you're getting clean, and you eat a lot more, and then you gain weight. The needs were greater there, it's just to know what's coming. I was in and out of jail at least 10 times before I actually went to prison [but still didn't understand what to expect]."*
>
> – Formerly incarcerated woman

Learning the Ropes

When encountering prison for the first time, women have an incomplete understanding of what jail or prison will be like, and this can take many months.

> ***"You don't know what to expect when you go into jail,*** *and then you get used to it when you're in and out of jail. You become one of the people that is a 'regular'. The guards know you; the other people know you. It becomes familiar to you, and easy to go in and out unless you're facing some serious time."*
>
> – Formerly incarcerated woman

Three women compared their first impressions of the transition from jail to prison life with each other:

> **Speaker 1:** *The transition from jail to prison for me, once I was out, was amazing. It gave me the opportunity to be outside, to be around people, to go to classes, go to work and just do the things that I should've done a long time ago. You can't do that in jail.*
>
> **Speaker 2:** *In the jail that I just came from, I only got out five hours out of the day. We were locked down all the time. We had a little rec room; for an hour, we could go there. I mean, we went to the library once a day. When I was going to my prison, there was a jail that [housed us]. They don't give you socks. You have to buy your socks. You have to buy your bra. You have to buy your underwear.*
>
> **Speaker 3:** *Right, the necessities. In prison, they give that stuff to you brand new. That's another thing with jail, it's like you get used stuff that other women have used. That's not sanitary to me. I would go without any underwear, you know? Federal prison, you get brand new everything. You get brand new stuff. Once a month you turn it in, you get new stuff. They give you a razor. They give you shampoo every day, if you wanted it. I mean, it's comfortable. You could buy your own clothes, sweat outfits. You get comfortable in there after a while. Jails, they had me more tied down. That's where I feel like I was going insane.*

While jail is a prelude to incarceration, once facing "serious time" women learn prison is a unique community. In this community, inmates (not laws and court officers) impose a distinctive culture through strict enforcement of an "inmate code." This code expects loyalty to other offenders and assumes solidarity within the inmate community.

Incarcerated women deal with many surprises when they begin their new prison lives. However, many times they are still dealing with unfinished business from the people and lives left behind.

> ***"Women must cope with the shame, embarrassment,*** *and humiliation of being there... Privilege protects you from it just for so long. You can have a great lawyer and really get protected, but if drug abuse and all of that is extended, then eventually the pathway is going to be prison and jail... Some of those parents are saying their kids are at an Ivy League college or they're at a special school or whatever, when in reality they're in prison. It carries a stigma of shame, embarrassment, humiliation. Women cope by extracurricular activities. They cope through mental health and they cope through medication."*
>
> – Prison chaplain

When first socialized into this culture, the woman experiences disorientation, foreignness, and a kind of sensory overload. "Reality shock" occurs as the newcomer's senses are flooded with unfamiliar clues, made more confusing by the woman's poor physical and mental state.

> ***"I stayed in receiving for 30 days.*** *You have to be medically cleared to leave Receiving. After you leave Receiving, you get placed... When I went there, it was totally different because you're locked behind a door... I was with people that I was scared to tell that I was just a minor charge like a drug charge, and they're murderers. I've seen things that would shock you. Like I've seen a girl get dragged in the bathroom for just snitching on somebody ... I stayed to myself. I stayed in my Bible. I did classes. I did 20 hours of classes in three days."*
>
> – Formerly incarcerated woman

When transitioning to incarceration, the individual first learns formal rules from corrections officers, lawyers, chaplains, and corrections administrators. The delineation of these formal rules or "explicit norms" are conveyed most often by staff who have the responsibility of reinforcing the rules. Formal rules are meant to teach the woman how to act in this new environment, and work in tandem with prisoner roles.

> ***"Regardless of what any of the guards do****—and there's some good [Correctional Officers] in there—we understand they're trying to help us. But there's nothing that a CO can do that's going to make our lives easier if we aren't adhering to these other bylaws that we're accustomed to."*
>
> – Formerly incarcerated woman

However, formal rules can change if individual members do not play their assigned roles. When the rules change, incarcerated women may have trust issues and anger.

> ***"We stayed on lockdown a lot…*** *it was sad the way they punished everybody on that building because they say everybody is supposed to be treated the same. I didn't agree with that. They say the whole program is about teamwork, okay? They want you to work together. I'm fine with working with people, but you have to have the right team. You can't just expect people to work together if you don't have the same morals, the same beliefs… I can't work with these types of people.*
>
> *What happened was they punished the whole building. 'Everybody is on lockdown, nobody is going to go to canteen, and everybody's on canteen restrictions. We're taking your phone calls.' [In my program] You only get one 15-minute phone call a day … everybody else in the prison can use the phone multiple times a day as long as they have money to use the phone. You have to choose who you're going to talk to… Not only that, but you have to wait two months before you can use the phone at all. You can choose to call a lawyer when you get there in the building, or you can call your parents or your family."*
>
> – Formerly incarcerated woman

Beyond the formal rules, the women learn situation-specific information that helps them make sense of "how we do things" or "what matters around here". These social rules or "implicit norms" come from informal interactions with other incarcerated women. Implicit norms provide privileged information that eventually turns a new inmate into an insider. They form the basis for the prison code.

Reference Groups

Insiders generally know what to expect so little is surprising, but newcomers must learn to interpret the actions of superiors and others, and what meanings to attach to their actions. These observations and resulting judgments about the prison environment form the foundation of new beliefs, behaviors, opinions, and aspirations as effectively as family, peer groups, school, and religious communities did in the past. There are early lessons about who is in charge.

> ***"Prison is a place where you have no rights.*** *You're told when to get up, when lunch is. You don't have the privilege to say, 'I can't, I don't want it right now but maybe later I'll get it.' No. It's now or not at all. You follow the steps. You don't walk in the yard. You don't walk in the grass. You don't cut the grass. You walk up the sidewalk. You don't drop anything. You don't pick up anything. You move like you're on your way somewhere. You move with a purpose, so you get up on time. Your lights are out at a certain time. You don't choose your roommate. You lose rights while at the same time inmates have rights and privileges, but they fit within the scope of 'you are now under authority'. I'm not taking your motherhood away. You're still in authority, but here you will not exercise it. You're not in authority, you're under authority, and you'll slowly gain your privileges and rights that you came in with, if in fact you get visits."*
>
> – Formerly incarcerated woman

Assimilation into prison life is easier when newcomers have insiders' help. Specific information is given as needed. Groups of insiders create reference groups, a collection of individuals that a person compares herself to or uses as a standard to evaluate attitudes and behaviors.

Reference groups can be either a positive or negative influence, but always shape perception of reality and the value the incarcerated woman gives to her own performance and achievements.

> ***"My family, my biological family,*** *the family that God placed in my life and church people—that's who helped me. The whole time I didn't [go] without money, I didn't [go] without the things that I wanted. I didn't want*

the whole time. But most people don't have that, so what I did was gave back to those who didn't have. What we did, and honest, this is what I love so much about these women in there, for birthdays, a lot of them never had a birthday party, but we knew when their birthdays were. We had birthday parties. We had dinners at Thanksgiving and Christmas. Everybody gets presents. You walk around the rooms and put stuff on the people's bed. When the receivers come in we made sure they had everything they needed. Yeah, some of them fall to the wayside because they got from under the umbrella [but] if they were in the building with me everybody was straight... because I made sure we had a washing machine, ice machines, dryer, microwaves, everything was fixed on my building [because I made sure it happened]."

– Formerly incarcerated woman

The influence a reference group has over an individual is known as referent power, which is measured by how much the woman desires to identify with the group and how willing she is to accept group values. Incarcerated women gradually lose part of their old identity and find new roles that are in line with cultural expectations.

Past experiences may help them cope, as well as their own personal characteristics. Although most women would negatively react to this change, newcomers may be surprised by their first exposure to a prison community that seems so unlike a chaotic home life.

"In prison, it's a whole new little community; *a little city. You've got people doing your laundry, you get a job... You could work in the chapel, you could work different jobs until you get released, and you can also do more self-improvement. You can do substance abuse programs. There was actually a therapeutic community there, so you could attend that, or there was God's Pod. There are more choices to improve yourself before you get out in prison."*

– Formerly incarcerated woman

"You can get way [too comfortable] in prison, *though... That's what scares me, is how comfortable I got while I was in there. I had a schedule. I worked Monday through Friday, 7:00 to 3:00. All the stuff that I should've* *done on the outside before I ever went to jail, I was doing in prison. I got comfortable doing it. In county jail, there's really not much to do. I didn't even have people to come see me. I didn't make phone calls... [but prison was different]."*

– Formerly incarcerated woman

Another part of leaving past experiences was learning to use reference groups to cope with their new reality. Since families, friends, lawyers, and social workers were no longer available, other residents helped women learn the ropes in terms of how parts of the prison system work and how to get the help you need.

Special consideration is given to "prisonizing" members of gender-fluid communities. For example, when offenders enter jail or prison identifying themselves as "other than female" an institutional space must be created for them.

"In the first 24 hours, *we bring all the information we can get, and we determine the first placement...Within a 72-hour timeframe, we come back. The clinical psychology offender services, chief of clinical service, the chief medical officer, the chief of psychiatry, the warden, a PREA coordinator, my associate warden, a programmer, a case manager... and an intel officer all meet. Then we have mitigating factors that we assess, and we look at the best placement for the individual and for the population that they're going into. Those occur fairly frequently [and are increasing]."*

– Warden

In practice, prisonizing social behavior for new gender-fluid members often meant learning a strict PREA "zero tolerance" policy. This might mean you can shake hands, but no embracing hugs. Staff can utilize discretion in what they see, or if there is ill intent or malicious behavior. If a report is filed, inmates are reminded of their expectations, and understanding that the other person did not want this contact. Justice-involved women learn from staff *"in a correctional environment, that's setting yourself up for a bunch of things that you don't need."* In one prison, there are ethnicity, age, race, and gender trackers in every unit to create healthy interaction and the ability to influence.

Prisonization can be seen in terms of a new norm for personal health care.

> ***"The thing that was the least cared for*** *was themselves: their bodies, their teeth; just their basic general selves were not always in the best of shape. So when the drugs really dried up and they became… clean, one of the number one things was that women needed medical attention more often than their male counterparts because for the first time they were dealing with cramps. They were dealing with the aches and pains that surrounded [their menstrual period]. We hear commercials about bloating and all of this kind of stuff and as a girl we know that yucky feeling. You don't feel good. But if you're high all the time and you're buzzed all the time, some of these ladies for the first time will beat on the medical door saying, 'I need help. Something's wrong with my stomach.' They didn't know that that was … just the cycle of womanhood and the cycle of the month; the headaches that came with it and the body aches that came with it."*
>
> *One of the most positive things was that women were being cared for in very healthy terms, in ways that they could not and would not in times past… The other way that women cope in prison that is different from their male counterparts is that they may utilize mental health services more. They may feel like 'I need to talk about this. I need to figure out what's going on.' So they will see a clinician, a prison counselor or a prison psychologist or even a psychiatrist. It just depends on what type of prison, just because they are dealing with the separation issue. 'I'm sober. I really miss my kids. I don't know where they are. I promised them I'd never be apart from them.'"*
>
> – Chaplain

Unexpected negative outcomes, however, produce conflict or dissonance that can only be resolved as the woman makes sense of her situation. Prisonization recognizes the ways in which the prisoner community influences the newcomer's values and attitudes.

***"Some of them don't care,** they just don't care. They don't care if you take their phone call, they're going to get somebody else on another building to make a phone call for them, slip them a note. They're going to do something else they're not supposed to do, break another rule to get it done another way."*

–Formerly incarcerated woman

In addition, women in custody do not always get the support from those they used to count upon, those who can most help in adjusting to her new reality.

***"They don't come see you anymore.** It's a whole other process for them to be able to come and see you and fill out forms or whatever the case. Then they have to get approved, versus when you're in jail it's not necessarily the case. Then they can't be on someone else's visiting form or something, because then they can't be on yours. I think that makes a difference. Then, they take you, move you so far away, because they don't have prisons everywhere. They move you so far away. Then, they take your phone calls from you. You can call 99 times in a day from a jail. You can only call one time a day from a prison, well, 15 minutes, whatever. If you want to call that 15 minutes 15 times, one minute apiece by all means. But it doesn't work like that. You have to be on an approved list. That doesn't help."*

– Formerly incarcerated woman

***"Women don't get visits like men do,** for all the reasons you would expect. Women follow men to prison, but men do not follow women. The people that are visiting in a women's room are usually not their husbands. It's usually not their sons. It may be their granddaughters, their smaller children. It may be their mom or a best friend, but it's not their man, okay?... Men, on the other hand, their waiting rooms are packed full because their mothers are there, for sure. Their women are there. Their grandmother is there. And they wait hours upon hours to see them. Women on the other hand, the time that they do and the way that it's done, it's very different than their male counterparts in almost every way."*

– Chaplain

However, most newcomers modify their behavior and change their actions in this new setting. This can often result in negative effects toward outsiders who come in, including ministry volunteers, since prison walls not only keep prisoners in. They exclude others from this world.

> ***"If there's a thousand women [in prison]*** *and there's 300 on your unit, you know who they are… No one else is coming in. But extend that beyond the wall, and all of that sort of falls away because now it's boundless, limitless, and I'm lost. [It's not like] when I go to church. It's not that happy family where practitioners, religious clergy people come in and they know you by name. You lose that."*
>
> – Formerly incarcerated woman

Questions for Reflection

1, How does knowing how women "do time" influence your interactions with them?
2. In what ways does the correctional facility you minister in implement social adjustment?

6

. . . . .

Jail and Prison Culture

"I wasn't with the gangs or anything like that, *but you have to respect other people. You have to respect other people's property. Never snitch or else you get a jacket, which means that you're a snitch. You get a snitch jacket. There's a lot of girlfriends. They develop their own little families. There's a dad, there's a mom, there's lots of sisters. There are aunties; there's grandma and grandpa. The whole family thing is there, but again you have to respect each other like a criminal code. You don't take people's property, you don't snitch on them, and you don't take somebody else's girlfriend. The needs are to have that family contact. When I was incarcerated, I lost my parental rights to my only son, and so there's that need to have that family contact, and again you do develop that family atmosphere because you're a nurturer."*

– Formerly incarcerated woman

Members of a culture share a particular way of looking at the world, and these patterns endure over time. Insiders teach newcomers what prison culture is like and how to navigate safety within it. The cardinal rule of the prison code quickly became apparent in interviews.

In this chapter, we demonstrate the prison code and its influence in creating a unique institutional culture. This culture is a result of correctional norms and practices, as well as the interaction between justice-involved women and the facility staff.

"There's a stigma, *if you watch reality TV, about what incarceration looks like, and that's not who we are... There's accountability in everything that we do for everyone, and if someone doesn't accept it, then there's a consequence. But if they do, how much farther can we move forward... because our goal is to make inside of prisons look as close to outside of prisons as we can so that when* *you walk out the door, and you know what society expects of you, then you move forward into the world as such."*

– Warden

The consistency that incarcerated females display in adhering to the prison code indicates social norms at work. They are unplanned, unexpected results of individual interactions that together create a system of rules that inexplicitly describe what sorts of behavior is acceptable within the prison's context.

These social norms persist over time and throughout membership changes. One justice-involved woman warned: *"It's something that if you don't live by—helping others out, not talking about what you see—[breaking the social code] will affect your stay."* These norms tend to develop in small groups and expand beyond the original group that founded the norm and play an important role in creating your social identity.

***"They say that there's a prison code and everything,** but when it's a women's prison … there's just survival of the fittest. You sometimes tend to get into this little clique of people that weren't regulars or whatever ... Sometimes there would be the women that think they're better. There are the drug addicts or there's the violent crimes, and there's the white-collar crimes. I was a white-collar crime."*

– Formerly incarcerated woman

While prison culture is displayed through media as aggressive and violent (as one warden noted above) most inmates are focused on getting along and getting out. A major function of norms is maintaining social order. Within the prison, this is the means of finding and continuing balance, which comes from cooperation.

Interestingly, "finding God while you're here" is an accepted norm in jail and prison facilities. Consistent with Christian norms such as honesty and loyalty, new members learn that reciprocity, and promise keeping are a few rules of cooperation that provide stability to social groups, and this is true within prison walls as well. Peer influence works on a sense of trust that exists between the incarcerated females. It is based on personal commitment and choice; that is, the women will adopt behaviors judged appropriate by their peers.

> ***"Women clique up.*** *In the men's prisons, it's mostly racially motivated there. In women's prison, it's not at all. They clique up… when you get in it's that convict code. It's something that they live by. That's kind of how you notice people are getting better, when they kind of let go of all that, like the snitching thing, all that stuff. Once they start letting go of those concepts is when they start realizing 'I want to get better.'"*
>
> – Chaplain

Transgressions occur when peers consider some rule of conduct or taken-for-granted expectation about how the others should act is violated. There are both explicit behavioral social norms and implicit expectations that threaten the stability of prison culture when a transgression occurs.

Outsiders may have difficulty understanding the subtle and taken-for-granted norms at work in the prison, but even insiders can misread behavior. For example, is "love" showing respect or being there in times of need? Is "trust" keeping confidences or keeping the relationship exclusive? Communication is the way of building cooperative expectations within female populations.

> ***"Women are the nurturers of the family****, so you need to do that and so continue it. I think that's why the family environment is developed while you're incarcerated. Many of the women of course need mental health counseling. They need trauma healing… There are needs of contact with your husband or your significant other, your boyfriend. Again, depending on your culture, we're very family oriented. Having to have that contact with family, that's a great need that we have… It seems like we're always on the phone when you're inside. You just have to have that communication."*
>
> – Formerly incarcerated woman and volunteer

Within the larger prison culture unique individual relationships develop. These relationships, like all relationships, build on expectations stemming from individual backgrounds and experiences. How these expectations are communicated can vary. A few women cope by creating and participating in a prison family.

> ***"There's always a dad,*** *which is a girl that typically…has a more masculine haircut… no makeup. No anything. In prison you don't get a regular bra. You always wear a sports bra, so if they put on a couple of sports bras, it looks like a chest instead of a breast and they will practice that look. They will sag their pants as much as they can, and you may do a double take because just from a side view you get the image of, 'I know I'm in a female prison, but you look [like a male]'. There's the mom. The mom is that person that is pretending this is a real relationship. There's always a kid... and typically they're going to take on the role of it. They're going to have ponytails in their hair … but everybody is getting a little bit of what they need. The person who plays the role of the child is getting a lot of attention, a lot of protection. The person that plays the male counterpart is … providing a lot of safety and security. The mother is being just that, caring for them all. Then there's always a grandma or a pawpaw in there.*
>
> *You get this family and they don't really clique up but they kind of stick together and help each other out. You may not even notice it on the yard, because they all may have different things to do—somebody has to go to school, somebody has to go to work, somebody has to do this —but then in their pod and in their unit and in other times, you see this really pronounced… They'll kind of congregate with that family. It's not a clique. It's not a gang or anything like that. It really is a nurturing family where support is generated and given one to another during that time. While if these were men [in prison], they may actually pair up around religion. They may say, 'Well, we're Muslim. That means we got Muslim rights. We got this. We got that. We can have meetings. We can do that.' They may pair up for control. They may pair up in gangs. All of it is for control and to dominate and to get what they want, where women become families and nurture. There are female gangs, but they're not anything like a male gang. It's really very, very different. That's another huge aspect of prison and female prison stuff."*
>
> – Chaplain

However, virtually all relationships show some elements of dysfunction. People violate expectations, criticize one another, demonstrate undue possessiveness, are jealous, and commit acts of betrayal. It takes two to make a relationship, but only one to break it.

> ***"If you didn't do anything specifically to me,*** *I don't have an issue with you. When you do something to me, then I have an issue with you. Now, yes, we come from [background history] yada, yada, yada. And certain things—we all do certain things. Most the same, some different. But I'm not going to blame you for what happened back in there. I'm blaming you for what you do to me at this point. You know what I'm saying? If anything was said, I'm going to communicate. I want to talk about it. What's up? I need to know what's going on. Did I offend you somehow? Tell me. But some people are so used to that person responding that way or the other five people that's how they responded. That's not how I'm responding. So don't treat me like that because I'm not going to treat you the way these people did me. Because I've got to grow up. I got it."*
>
> – Formerly incarcerated woman

"Gay for the Stay, Straight at the Gate"

For a host of reasons, same-sex relationships are common in prison. Prisonization argues that the inmate community influences the newcomer's values and attitudes, which may account for this norm. These relationships are not sanctioned by formal rules, and in fact are forbidden through the Prison Rape Elimination Act of 2003 (PREA), which was an act of Congress to address the problem of sexual abuse for those in corrections custody.

However, both incarcerated women and corrections staff may ignore this behavior. Same-sex behavior is not always indicative of a homosexual orientation: there are women who basically identify themselves as being only attracted to the same sex all along, as well as women who go in the direction of same-sex relationships only in prison. According to psychologist Stanton Jones (personal communication, September 20, 2018):

> ***"The behavior can come out,*** *I think, for all kinds of reasons. It can be a continuation of a stable pattern, where the woman has a stable preference*

for same-sex partners. But it can also be an expression of loneliness, or desire to connect with somebody. Prison can be a dehumanizing experience, and under that context it can be more an attempt to establish that connection with a significant other. Sometimes that's linked with being attracted to qualities in the other person you aspire to have. Other times it can just be an extension of companionship. There's a dimension of sexual expression as well, kind of self-anxiety soothing. So there can be that kind of dimension where people are using sex for its instrumental value— to distract from boredom, to cope with anxiety, to feel better about themselves—all those sorts of motivations."

A woman can have a heterosexual orientation, but for any one of a host of reasons may become involved in a same-sex relationship. Many same-sex relationships point to a desire to establish a connection in their lives, and many incarcerated women no longer have a spouse or friends to fill this role.

According to studies of women who've been in long term same-sex relationships, the sexual dimension of the relationship becomes a minor part of the relationship involving emotional dependency or co-dependency. Psychologists see co-dependency as a kind of jealous protection of a relationship as the exclusive source of meeting emotional needs. Alternatively, according to Dr. Jones:

"I could easily imagine *a woman who [has] broken other cultural taboos. She's done things that are ... outside the normal boundaries of society. What's one more barrier? So, 'I'm in prison or jail. I'm lonely. Why not have a close companion during this time? Why not have somebody with whom I can share pleasure?' I think those things are options that a person would feel legitimately to explore when they're in prison, and it's only a kind of Christian moral structure that might be in place that would hold a person back from doing that."*

Generally, men are more immediately and viscerally moved by physical attraction. For women, sex seems to be more of an organic experience related to emotional intimacy. That is, physical intimacy is more an extension of emotional intimacy. Women experiencing same-sex relationships in prison reflect the fact that there is some plasticity to women's sexual attractions because it's more of a whole person experience.

Same-sex behavior may also stem from a history of abuse that pushes these women away from healthy male relationships. Given negative experiences with men, there may be suspicion or a lack of trust that makes same-sex behavior a safer and more satisfying option. Here again, the prison code of "don't ask, don't tell" as well as "don't interfere in another woman's relationship" is at work.

> ***"There are people there having sex in the prison system.*** *[They're supposed to] put a sheet up, but I mean there are some that don't do that at all. You had to just keep your eyes forward or not look at that if you don't believe in that stuff. If you voice your opinion, you're going to get beat down or you're going to get hurt. If you stand up for yourself, you're going to go to lock-up. If you fight back, you go to lock up; that's plain and simple. And you lose your good days. It's an iffy, iffy situation. If you snitch, you've all those people [for whom] you have to watch your back."*
>
> – Formerly incarcerated woman

Religious volunteers in the prison are often offended by the presence of "girlfriends" but should be prepared that such relationships exist and to not be shocked by them. Dr. Jones recommends listening in order to explore what the relationship means to them. If the person genuinely wants to know, "Why do Christians have a moral teaching about this?" there is an opportunity to present a bigger picture of a personal, relational God.

The Christian belief is that God is a Trinitarian reality—Father, Son, and Holy Spirit—a communion of love that was complete and full in and of itself. The Trinity did not need anyone else for happiness, but out of an overflow of that love, God created men and women in his image. Dr. Jones notes: *"It's much more important to introduce the person to the love of God for their life than it is to bring them to a confrontation with specific sins."*

In fact, women in custody may use negative reactions to come up with a sort of a test of whether the chaplain or volunteer really cares about them since these individuals can be perceived as being a proxy for the God that is proclaimed to be loving. In essence, the justice-involved woman is saying: *"I'm going to test you with what I know is going to offend you and see whether you can work through that.'"*

At that point in time, to throw up the barrier and say, "What you're doing is reprehensible to God" is more of a block to being able to share the Gospel with that person and bring real transformation. Dr. Jones counsels:

> ***"I think you can say it's much more important*** *that you make your decisions about that kind of behavior after you've had a chance to experience for yourself the love of God, and to explore whether you want to follow the person you've come to know through this Bible study, through this explorative process that you're going through. Then make the decisions because all of our moral decisions are costly, and we put aside things that have been of value to us in some way or another. We only make those decisions in light of something that we see of greater value. So find out whether a relationship with God is something that [the woman] wants to pursue. And let's deal with [their sexuality] down the way..."*

"Spirals of Silence" and the Fear of Isolation

The spiral of silence is a theory of human behavior that says an individual's estimate of the majority view influences her own expressed opinions and increases conformity to a preferred set of ideas or norms (Neuwirth, Frederick, & Mayo, 2007). Self-censorship (*"I've done a lot of jail time, so I've just learned not to get mixed up with other people's stuff")* and immersion in a limited "climate of opinion" misleads people about what is true. In such situations, individuals are less likely to express their own opinions or buck the majority view. They act as others do because of a fear of isolation.

Depending on her personality, the issue, and the situation, women silence themselves into this ever-growing spiral of conformity. Female prisoners adapt their behavior according to what they believe is the majority opinion so that they do not enact or express anything that is unpopular within the group. This reality is often reflected in narratives from women who have served time in different prisons.

> ***"There it was pretty much if you told,*** *you were going to be handled. So nobody told. Nobody saw anything. Yeah, mind your business. You just mind your own and stay in your own lane. In [prison A] they were a lot more physically violent than they were at [prison B]. It was messy. [At prison B], the girls would make stuff up just to get other girls in trouble. You don't even have to do anything wrong in that prison and you're going to get in trouble constantly. The girls there feed off that, because there is no code, really. It's just everyone for yourself…*
>
> *The code in [prison A] was you just mind your own business. My time there [at prison B] was a whole lot harder than it was in [prison A]. You got to stay in your own lane, you know? I was more boyish, so it was everyone thought I was trying to get their girlfriend or something like that. I think the two places that I went were pretty decent under the standard that I was behind the bars and not at a camp. Federal [prison] I know, is a lot different than state [prison]. It's easier. They say you do more of your time, but it's easier."*
>
> – Formerly incarcerated woman

This does not mean that disagreement, prejudice and discrimination do not exist between incarcerated women. However, more than male inmates, females are socialized to understand people unlike themselves and break artificial or arbitrary borders that separate them. One example is how the influence of social class impacted relationships.

> ***"The more money you had, the better you were doing.*** *The more people you had sending you money, the nicer the shoes you had. The more shoes, the more everything you had. That was pretty much what it was all about. If you had the most of everything, then everybody liked you. Everybody was there. That seemed to be the biggest concern that I saw: who had the most or who could do what for you or who knew which staff was what. It's just that it's criminals inside of a gate, really. It's just constantly the same thinking in there. It's nothing to change the thinking. It's just locking you up and letting you be sober to think that way, so you can think about how you're going to get around the things going on in there."*
>
> – Formerly incarcerated woman

While there tends to be less judgment based on the group to which they belong, there are lines drawn between prisoners and correctional staff.

> ***"I'm still having a hard time doing boundaries.*** *You can't compliment staff there. That's a big no-no, like, 'You got nice shoes.' You can't do that. It is still hard for me to be able to ...knock on their door or stuff like that. There, it's a big 'You Cannot.'"*
>
> – Formerly incarcerated woman

Prison culture has a debilitating effect on correctional personnel as well as the prisoners, and this effect is not lost on the incarcerated. Although they have legitimate authority to act, some corrections officers fail to do so or respond with behaviors that reinforce negative norms.

> ***"I began to feel like maybe*** *some of these staff members have been traumatized, and some of them I would actually take up for because I can see it can get to the point where they felt ... fearful for their life. Hey, fights break out... It's not that they didn't want to hold the people accountable...[but] it was not doing any good because when they try to hold them accountable, the punishment seemed to have no effect on these people. They didn't care. So they were probably, 'Who cares, let them just have sex because we've already tried to put them in lockup and they're still going to keep doing it.' I've heard some of the inmates talk to some of the staff members very, very horribly; just talk down, curse them out, tell them they're going to kill them, kill their family when they got out. That was traumatizing to hear somebody talk to somebody that way. So eventually it got to the point where a good bit of the staff started realizing, 'This person does not seem to be somebody that's trying [to change].'"*
>
> – Formerly incarcerated woman

Conflict results when there is perceived or real incompatibility of goals, values, expectations, processes or outcomes between two or more interdependent individuals or groups. It may stem from underlying causes; e.g., unequal or unjust relationships between individuals or groups (e.g., prisoners v. correctional officers). Conflict may arise from a history of oppression (e.g., sexism or racism). It may be due to different agendas (control v. freedom). It may result from the collision of strong values and beliefs (e.g., punish v. rehabilitate). Conflicts of interest also are fueled by economic problems (e.g., scarce resources, understaffed facility).

It is not unusual for individuals to blame marginalized groups and divert attention from those who actually wield power. "Scapegoating" or hate mongering stem from perceived economic threats and competition. However, besides creating conflict it can also lead to empathy.

> ***"I think for me what prison helped me do*** *was to root for the underdog, the people that were getting bullied or picked on and stuff. I didn't think it was cool. I stood up for a lot of people, at the same time minding my own business, not getting into the real stuff. The not-needed picking on people stuff, that just wasn't cool to me. I was friends with all the underdogs… people with handicaps and stuff like that, I just don't like people doing mean things to them for no reason. It's just sad, really. It gave me a lot of empathy. It made me sit back and realize that we are all somebody's mom. We're all somebody's daughter. We're all somebody's sister. It leveled out the whole playing field for me and help bring me to God. Yeah, it's kind of rough in there."*
>
> – Formerly incarcerated woman

Conflict is managed differently if it focuses on the actual situation rather than the larger societal context. In normal situations, conflict can be productive and be used to strengthen relationships. However, given power imbalances in prison, conflict is often resistant or destructive. Whether prisoners use silence and avoidance, the use of intermediaries to act on their behalf, intense displays of emotion during disagreement, or discussions that are emotionally calm, the concern is with protection.

Correctional personnel tend to deal with conflict through controlled mediation or isolation. Said one warden: *"We eliminated [potential violence] almost in its entirety because females are very, very, very focused on socialization, and isolation is the worst thing that you can do to them."* Women in prison tend to combine expressive/restraint and indirect/direct behaviors to create different conflict styles (i.e., avoiding, competing, accommodating, compromising, and collaborating) because of a common belief that conflict is destructive. But within a prison context, conflict may serve other purposes.

> ***"My two roommates hate each other*** *and actually want the fight, but I got between them and stopped them. Nobody liked them, but I was like, 'No, we're in the room. Y'all is peace. You don't have to like each other.' After a few days of this, all of a sudden they were whispering and talking to each other. I mean, they hate each other… I find out one of the girls didn't like me because her friend (and when I say 'friend' you know, it's her girlfriend) was using me … to get to her girlfriend at the time in another building. It was a plant. She said that I sexually harassed her, and I was like, 'What's going on?' They said that they'd seen her go up to an officer and put on her fake cry. It was a plant…*
>
> *So all the officers are talking -- you hear a little bit here and there. I called my family… The protocol [for investigating sexual harassment] was supposed to have a lot of people. You go to lock up and then they do an investigation… I went to lockup for 15 days. It was just an investigation! It was Christmas time. I didn't get stuff from my grandchildren, so I was highly upset because it's Christmas, you know... The warden, he said, 'We know this is not you.' These people know me; there's no way, that wasn't my thing. Okay? I'm not even into this, and it just blew my mind, oh my God, because I never seen it coming. But they got the investigator, and the investigator said, 'You know what? They're jealous of you. They want your job... This is a bunch of crap, you know.' And he looked all the way back in my files and their files, and he said … there was a stack of requests from inmates and staff on my behalf."*
>
> – Formerly incarcerated woman

Within prison walls, the end of relationships threatens identity and personal well-being. Disengagement can create guilt or relief, sadness or anger, anxiety or aggression. "Harassing" behaviors (e.g., verbal or physical threats or assaults, being watched, sending notes or gifts) indicate direct actions of control. Indirect tactics to break up (e.g., reducing contact, self-disclosure, being unresponsive) terminate relationships with minimal effort—unless the other fails to take the hint.

Justice-involved women must learn there is accountability for what they do. Purposeful and thoughtful communication that addresses conflict is warranted. All members have input, even if that input isn't heard or acted upon. One warden whose career included mostly male inmates noted that women under his correctional control were especially responsible in this regard.

> ***"Females, no matter what,*** *if you are doing something right, they will acknowledge it… Females, if they understand and they know that staff care, you're shifting culture. You're shifting paradigm in reference to what we do, or even shifting conversation. They're aware of it, and they acknowledge it. They are much more openly, emotionally invested in incarceration… Our staff have to be acclimated and trained to allow that to occur… redirect that thought process, provide expectations, have a conversation, and then come to consensus in reference to expectations and how you move forward. It is a big shift, and we're doing it department-wide, but I think it's had very, very impactful results… Change is hard for anyone, but as we get there [the women] are getting more accustomed to it."*
>
> – Warden

Questions for Reflection

1. As an outsider, how can you build trust within your jail or prison ministry?
2. How do you and others in your ministry respond to incarcerated women's sexual choices?

7

Doing Time

***"Unfortunately for me, I have been in and out** of the correctional system for a very long time. I've done time from South Dakota to Colorado to Nebraska. I haven't been in the penitentiary since 2001; however, I have been in lots of jails. My experience was always not a good one. While I was there, there weren't a lot of tools that I learned to be different when I got out. I learned [to do] the wrong thing. Even worse, I was doing the wrong thing … when I got out. I can honestly say there was one time that I went through a jail sentence and that program was a lot different for me. It gave me a lot of tools. It helped me to do time differently, not so much in a negative sense… but [in terms of] how to work on myself and how to continue to be different... Not only there, but as for when I had gotten out also."*

– Formerly incarcerated woman

In this chapter, we examine these themes and issues in order to understand how prison culture affects programs and reentry ministries as well as individual lives. We focus as well on some of the negative aspects that prevent positive change and look at ways to minimize the effects of reverse culture shock as women transition from incarceration to freedom.

A woman's institutionalization does not end with her release from jail or prison. Ironically, during the process of reentry women are again plunged into disorientation and anxiety. Reentry or return to her home culture sets up a period of adjustment sometimes known as "reverse culture shock." It suggests that the internal stress and anxiety leading to readjustment on the outside is significant.

Unprecedented increases in female incarceration rates, along with the shortage of facilities to deal with widespread overcrowding can adversely affect living conditions. This includes issues of prisoner safety, and access to meaningful programming.

Many of the women who participated in the interviews for this book were incarcerated in the early years of the 21st century. They experienced longer sentences under conditions of greater duress and dysfunction. However, women confined more recently and at younger ages often demonstrated transformative aspects of prisonization. That is, they gradually became accustomed to the restrictions of institutional life and dependent upon them to control their behavior.

For these women, meaningful programming was significant in teaching positive behaviors while incarcerated, as well as helping them relinquish the negative parts of prisonization upon release. In short, program-rich institutions gave these prisoners genuine alternatives, engagement in meaningful activities, and the ability to develop meaningful life skills.

> ***"When I first got to [prison],*** *I went through a mandatory, six-month inpatient residential treatment center in the prison. I would have to say it did help me to accept the things I've done and realize that I was sorry for those things and that I didn't want to be that person anymore. The only way I can make amends to a lot of the people or a lot of the things I've done wrong is to just do better myself. It was a lot of tearing you down, and very little building you up. I guess, really, in prison, that's kind of what you need.*
>
> *I did a voluntary drug analysis program. If you're qualified, you can get 18 months off your sentence: a year off and then six months in a halfway house. It's pretty intense. You're in your own little community. There's a lot of girls there. You go in front of the podium, pull people up or pull yourself up and make a remedy for yourself… I learned a lot from there; a lot of tools that I was trying to use outside. Then I got complacent...*
>
> *When you go to the halfway house, you have to do the Transitional Drug Analysis Program. That's a second part of it. You get two certifications from it when you complete it... One thing that I don't like is the certificates that we receive for the classes, we're required to take them ... Now the law is changed, no matter if you've done jail time or prison time, you have to do supervised release. And on supervised release or probation, you have to complete the same classes again."*
>
> – Formerly incarcerated woman

Reversing the Effects of Culture Shock

As seen in the last chapter, incarcerated women experience culture shock when their basic identities and assumptions about life and ways of behaving are no longer appropriate or functional. The loss of familiar signs and signals, breakdown of normal interpersonal interactions, and identity crisis enhances culture shock. Not having time to prepare for change, the involuntary nature of incarceration, the degree to which the new inmate "stands out", and her compatibility with the values and norms of prison culture can impact the degree of culture shock she experiences.

On the other hand, personality characteristics such as the woman's positivity, flexibility, and tolerance for ambiguity can mark a person who is most able to absorb shocks and bounce back from the challenges of prison and reentry. Situational and personality characteristics may impact an individual's ability to adapt to long years of imprisonment.

"I did 27 years. *I was called 24/7. Sometimes I might not even get two hours of sleep because they were always calling me to fix something, from the fence system down to the air conditioning -- everything. But with all that said, I did all of that and then when I walked out the door, they didn't even give me a shirt on my back. Not one shirt. They said they weren't prepared for me to be released... So I'm telling the head warden, 'Y'all still set me up' [but] nobody set me up so I went myself to a pre-release class… I asked the lady there to do my resume, and she did my resume. They didn't offer me any of those classes, you see. They say they got all this and that, but that's a lie. It's not the truth. They don't prepare people. They didn't prepare me to come out because everything's by computer. I didn't know anything about computers. I'm learning it now. I'm learning it. Thank God I got that intelligence …"*

— Formerly incarcerated woman

"There is room for improvement in every way, *shape and form [but] for me the most frustrating part is that I live at the end of the waterfall… The end of the waterfall is where everything ends up. There's a lot of pressure on* *myself, my management team, and my staff to do good business and put a good outcome out, when that's not necessarily always the case seven levels in front of us."*

– Warden

Based on more than 50 interviews and 550 surveys involving formerly incarcerated women, volunteers who serve in both prisons and jails, reentry program administrators, and chaplains, we looked at how a woman's "sentence" influences the way she does time. The results suggest several themes that affected her life after release, and together with situation and personality factors, each theme suggests what successful adaptation to institutional culture and reverse culture shock look like.

Theme #1: Powerlessness and Humiliation

Correctional institutions exert a powerful influence on inmates' identities and are a significant factor in marking reasons for treating people differently. A common theme expressed by justice-involved women was the negative identities given to them from the beginning process of being arrested, sentenced, and incarcerated.

"I feel like people need second chances. *I feel like your black and white piece of paper goes along with you through your whole life. Something that I did when I was 19 and may not even be who I am now, but it affects me. If I were to go to jail today, they're going to bring that up from when I was 19… I think that makes a big difference… I think that some of it's unfair and unjust."*

– Formerly incarcerated woman

The powerlessness and humiliation experienced within this process set up the expectations and behaviors that would mark their prison experience.

"The judge raked me over the coals *saying I'm a horrible person. The prosecutor was laughing at me because I had to do 15 years. He said, 'You won't get any work credits or anything like that.' If it wasn't for my work credits,*

I wouldn't have got out when I got out. I worked seven days a week in a cafeteria in a prison. But after being through that with the courts and all the prosecutors saying I'll have to do the full fifteen years I was amazed what work credits could do for you because I was considered 'violent'..."

– Formerly incarcerated woman

Control and regulation are goals of many organizations besides prisons. However, prisonization begins with the exercise of powerlessness and humiliation when markers of identity and social amenities are removed. A person is defined by defining others, which increases their feelings of powerlessness and humiliation. This process was eloquently described by a recently released individual:

"The worst thing is being dehumanized. *You're stripped of your name and are called either by your [Department of Corrections] number or your cell number. Everyone is given the same outfit... You're browbeat daily to keep you in check; yelled at for no reason but intimidation. You are treated like a bad child or pet and after years of this you believe it deep in your heart. It affects you more than you realize. Like a bear poked for eleven years I want to lash out, but I know who I am. It all starts with your name. My name is who I am, and it is taken first. 'Offender' they call us. Eleven years you might as well have been calling me 'Stupid'. I got it the first year. My offense was a long time ago."*

During the prison experience, the woman unconsciously or deliberately is made aware of her status. A specific dehumanizing vocabulary may be provided, and the hierarchical structure is reinforced.

"I experienced the guards talking to the inmates *like they were dogs and trash. One of the guards actually made a comment [when] she was on the phone with somebody and said that she 'had to go let the dogs out and feed them'. How we were treated was not a good thing. It wasn't very correctional at all."*

– Formerly incarcerated woman

The lack of privacy experienced while under surveillance defines the prison environment and sometimes reentry housing. Combined with the sense of being treated like a naughty child who must be given constant verbal direction or correction, the justice-involved woman remembers again that sense of powerlessness and humiliation, which were reinforced by camera surveillance while she was in a reentry program.

> ***"Nobody should have to be told what to do,*** *when to do it and how to do it. Nobody should have to be degraded by (which now it doesn't matter) who walks in. If I'm naked, I'm naked. Okay, but that came from prison. Nobody should have to go through that."*
>
> – Formerly incarcerated woman

Theme #2: Retaliation and Fear

Uncertainty and insecurity can lead the individual to doubt herself, and inadvertently lead to retaliation and fear. Incarcerated women may conform to expectations to avoid standing out or being punished. She may change her behavior to become closer to what the code expects. She may struggle to create a self-image that does not reflect the victimization she experiences.

A justice-involved woman may project greater confidence, loyalty, or bravado than she has or feels. If there are added institutional differences in status and material insecurity, the woman may survive by becoming dependent on existing and shifting alliances. On the other hand, she may react in kind.

> ***"I didn't trust anybody in that prison*** *because I heard if you got to be not close friends [but] a friend with a guard, if they're a 'messy guard'—which I couldn't tell if they're messy—they'll go around telling everybody what you told them. In other words, they like to cause trouble, and you don't realize it. Like they'll tell something you said, but they'll twist it around to cause you problems… You've got to watch it because they'll put you in 'crisis' if they think you're suicidal, even if you aren't. [In crisis] you get locked up in a room and they watch you. They watch you use the bathroom. There'll be toilet paper, and*

you're in there in a jumpsuit; that's all you wear. And you only get food with no utensils; you got to eat finger food. And I was afraid they were going twist my story around to make me look like I'm suicidal and I wouldn't [get out]. I didn't trust anybody there."

– Formerly incarcerated woman

Many talked fearfully about the number of women in the prison who were dealing with mental health issues. Often peers are identified as helpers and given the job of working with more violent offenders.

"I'm put in situations where you had females *in there that had seizures like I haven't ever seen. I said, 'Lord have mercy! All these people have seizures. What's going on with these people having seizures?' They call them fighting seizures. [I came] to find out that's what they came to prison for, because they jump on the police and they didn't know that they were having seizures. But I was able to subdue them without hurting them and talk them out of it. God gave me that extra super-human strength to do that. I was able to identify with what the demon [was doing] because that's what it is: they were experiencing a demon."*

– Formerly incarcerated woman

If you're always looking over your shoulder, that fear can lead to suspicion and stereotyping. Justice-involved women may lack confidence in the staff's ability to keep prison culture just, as well as safe. Some come from cultural backgrounds that are anxious about medical personnel and drugs given to inmates to control their behavior.

"Sometimes you know, the punishment can be so severe *for [a minor offense. The medical staff] gives them their pills in a pack. The majority is for headaches, but what's the other medicine?"*

– Formerly incarcerated woman

There may be personality differences or situational forces early in the relationship between the correctional officer and inmate that creates a memorable narrative. These stories get reinforced and passed along to others, often establishing a lasting negative impression early in her sentence.

> ***"[The guards] were trying to be so hard*** *on someone, like making them 'Drop and give me 25 pushups; drop and do this and do that' because you didn't follow a command, or people were abusing their authority ... There was a very, very bad Lieutenant there, and I'm just going to say it flat out: I felt like this [person] was an enemy to me. She seemed to soften up some, but... it took me praying for two years before I felt we were able to make some peace with one another. She eventually got moved off the whole building because I stayed in prayer for so long. I was literally crying to God. I mean I was in tears crying because [of] this woman. I felt she was very abusive to people. The tone, the voice she used with women was traumatizing. But if you were a bad inmate and you bullied people, she was all for them people. She was covering up their messes. It seemed like a patting on the back."*
>
> – Formerly incarcerated woman

Even once released, a sense of fear and retaliation linger.

> ***"I'm on probation for six months****. In other words, I go to [my probation officer] when he schedules me. I just went. I did a drug test and passed it. So now I don't go back [for six weeks] for another drug test. But he can come see me at any time and he can come to my work at any time he wants."*
>
> – Formerly incarcerated woman

Theme #3: Anger and Blame

Inside and outside of prison, women are encouraged to keep from going beyond organizationally drawn lines. But socialized to not complain and serve others well can be depersonalizing and stressful. Perceptions of "in-groups" may develop, and since roles are non-negotiable, incarcerated women may spend considerable time and effort working to establish their trustworthiness to both leaders and peers.

As a result, they are encouraged to reinforce the hierarchy and minimize their own individuality. This can lead to anger, resentment, and blame. In addition, women may already be carrying anger from abuse, marginalization, and cultural gender role expectations. Even women who follow the rules can be punished for it.

> ***"All these people were in here having sex in this building.*** *They're doing things they're not supposed to do, and now we're all going through this punishment…I felt it was so unfair because I was like, 'I'm not participating in any of this.' I didn't understand why staff members weren't doing their job. Why are you not writing them up, and giving them an infraction? Or putting them in punishment or isolation or lockup, rather than punishing the whole building? The whole goal was to get everybody to work together, but you can't make people do that if they're rebellious people. If they're unwilling to do that, you can't force them."*
>
> – Formerly incarcerated woman

Many angry narratives dealt with health concerns. Medical services can be limited and difficult to access within prison walls. The availability of competent and motivated staff affects health visits. Additionally, inmates who have abused these services in the past can set up current residents for inaction and misdiagnosis. A series of practical and emotional issues can develop along with physical problems.

> ***"I began to think some really horrible thoughts*** *in my head because in the prison nobody was attending to [my medical problem]. It took me nine months to get a pelvic ultrasound in prison. When I finally got the pelvic ultrasound, they said they weren't finding anything, which was great but there's still obviously something because I did not have a period. I didn't believe that stress [caused it] … Typically the doctor said, 'Maybe in six months we might get that off the stress, but after six months we do want to try and test you for other things because that is a very long time.' Men, you know, [are] very crafty in having these products that we use and depend on in normal society. They've had access prior to the women ever thinking about having that type of access. When I say that it has dehumanized them, it's because they just don't care.*

I mean you've taken everything away from me, including my family, because it's quite costly to make a phone call out. If you want to eat anything like normal foods you have to purchase it off of the canteen, which is very pricey. Families just can't afford to support a member who is incarcerated, as well as support themselves and the family and most definitely the children who have been left behind due to the mothers being incarcerated. It really puts them at a disadvantage. It's definitely not a place for human rehabilitation."

—Formerly incarcerated woman

One of the needs in correctional institutions is for more medical attention. Without proper treatment, interactive levels of anger and blame are heightened for both justice-involved women and correctional staff.

"I spent 14 and a half years in prison, *and it was like I wasn't there. They were very bad on [providing] medical attention, and they need more mental health counseling. The women go to a psychiatrist, and then what they ask for, they usually just hand to them. They don't really get the counseling they need. That's what happened to me when I came out. I fell back into the drugs because I didn't know I needed mental health counseling. [Correctional facilities] need more. When I was down there, they were getting a good prison ministry program coming in and that was good. I hear they lock down a lot now because they don't have the correctional officers, because of the way that they treat each other. The ones higher up treat them like they treat the inmates. They don't like the way they treat the inmates, so they get other jobs... It was basically the medical attention team… I know they didn't have enough mental health [care]."*

—Former incarcerated woman

The mental health issues corresponding with drug abuse were a recurring theme.

"Some of the issues that I have heard and seen *down at the Department of Corrections has me where I don't even want to engage there with the women when they're behind the walls. Because what good is it going to do for me and my staff go in there and give them the information, and make them feel* *good about themselves? No sooner than we walk out of the institution and they're back stuck with this [medical] personnel, with this attitude of judgment and the attitude of ridicule; the attitude of punishment. It makes me sick to my stomach to even go down there because you can just see the level of care that they are being provided. I can't accept it.*

"So I just wait for them to come out, those that are coming to us. Sometimes you know, the punishment can be so severe they give them their pills in a pack. The majority of them are headache medicines, but they give them psychotropic drugs, and they keep them on anti-psychotic drugs. They give them to you [while incarcerated] and if they don't take them all, and the guards come and do a search, and if they have one pill… they're done. They put them in jail."

– Reentry director

An example of how anger and blame work in tandem is illustrated in the experiences of one courageous woman who continued to face off with medical personnel in order to solve a long-lasting health issue.

"My last three years [in prison] *I walked around with part of my cervix and my uterus hanging out. That's the medical issue. Medical assistance was awful—they'll let you die in there. The doctor himself saw it and started [treatment, but] he said I kept missing appointments. He didn't tell me [about the appointments] nor did he probably even bother with them. Make a long story short: I did. I'm a grown woman. It's my health. I'm talking to you. I'm signing up for it. I'm coming. I don't care about the $5.00 [appointment fee]; don't have it any way. You see me, and you'd know you need to send me out [for treatment]. The surgeons were getting upset because I made the appointment… He could tell I overheard him tell the other doctor sitting there [say], 'Are we going to switch the system?' You all were trying not to do it, like some other people you've thrown away when they went to the hospital. I'm a lifer; you have to take care of me.*

It took family, friends and some lawyers to call him to get appointments. So three years I walked around like that. No pain medicine because I refused that. 'I don't need pain medicine. I need you to fix this. I'm not covering that thing. You see it.

I'm bleeding,' and all this stuff. I went to the urologist and he... wound up doing my surgery instead of [the other doctor]. He said, 'I'm going to get this done' so he took out my cervix immediately... But mind you now, [he] took [my cervix] from me for no reason.

I went to court, won my case, and had [the correct] surgery. It's not happening fast for a lifer [but] it's all about God... That's my miracle ... But even saying that, I had my appointment for my post-op [and] they did not tell me. I've seen the doctor here [who said], 'You got to call them out. I already paid for it'. I call two weeks later. 'Ma'am, the earliest I can get you in is four months.' I still have to go for a post-op.

The penal system! You knew I had this appointment. You didn't tell me before I left. It was already paid for. I don't have it. I'm good though. considering I have a little pain, but as far as you know ... I don't know what's going on ..."

—Formerly incarcerated woman

A final example focuses on correctional staff and drug regulation within the facility, and the difficulty of changing culture. In this case, what appears to be a healthy rule change (i.e., removing cigarettes from the facility) becomes part of creating an even larger issue.

***"I have heard quite a few stories** from the reentry women who have come to take up residential services here. They inform me that if they wanted to use drugs that they could have used them while they were incarcerated... [When I was incarcerated] I couldn't imagine any drugs or such being allowed to get in there because it's a high security or maximum security correctional facility. To date I have learned that it is very populated with drugs. Street drugs as well as pharmaceuticals— just about any other product that you would depend on or use in mainstream society can be accessed there. I think one of the biggest drawbacks that has happened in the Department of Corrections institutions is [that you can get drugs, but not cigarettes.] When they removed cigarettes. It really dehumanized a lot of the inmates."*

—Formerly incarcerated woman and volunteer

Alleviating feelings stemming from prison culture involves important identity work that is difficult to do in reentry alone. Typically, prisoners are given no alternative culture for modeling or participation, so there are few positive activities to develop prosocial behaviors. There are few opportunities for employment, which could allow this development. Social and emotional support must be carefully considered as an activity since vulnerability can invite exploitation. Even in terms of religious programming, which is often found in correctional institutions, the prison culture is influential in discouraging such activity.

"I think there's a lot of people in there *that are worried about what the next person thinks and they're not going to step out and do the next right thing or what they feel in their heart. That's a big thing in prison. It feels like every time you take a step, someone's judging you on your next move. You just don't want to be a part of the problem. The easiest way to be a part of the solution is just do what everybody else is doing.*

I know there are a couple of good strong women in there that follow the Lord. I feel like the more that those women would step out in their faith and show that, that it would make it okay for other women to do that. It's kind of a hard thing to do in prison, because everyone's going to judge you. A lot of the times, following God is looked down upon, because, 'Oh, you came to prison to know God?' That's a big thing that's always said in there, 'You didn't know God before you came to prison. Why are you going to know him now?' For me, that was hard. I knew God before, but I just chose to take a different path and handle it myself.

When I got in there and I had no other paths to take in there, God was the only one there for me. I mean, you're going to take a little bit of slack from some people for doing that… I think a lot of people are scared. It's the unknown. Change is hard, especially change for somebody who's been doing the same wrong thing most of their whole life. For somebody to say, 'Here's a card. Call me when you get out' or 'Go to this place when you get out,' they're like, 'What?' … It's hard to believe anybody loves you in there. How could anybody love me for the things I was doing before I went in there? Then, you get in there, and you're just surrounded by people that have done the same type of stuff you've done."

—Formerly incarcerated woman

In brief, to survive in prison, incarcerated women must establish relationships that enable them to figure out what is appropriate and expected behavior. These are "involuntary" relationships, since these women did not choose to become members of this community. However, they enable the women to avoid second-guessing, miscommunication, conflict, or punishment. Prosocial relationships provide an anchor against the dehumanization, fear, and anger that inevitably arise.

Most newcomers adapt to their new "normal" through the help of insiders who show them the ropes—and need this same help in readjustment after doing time. The resulting culture shock when they leave jail or prison brings on corresponding feelings of powerlessness, retaliation, and blame that can impact the efforts of even the best organized ministry. However, the ability to see growth; to thrive, to be accountable, to be comfortable with oneself, and rekindle relationships once you get out is significant.

Questions for Reflection

1. How can you prepare women for prison or help them acclimate once they arrive?
2. How can you empower incarcerated women to mentor those who are new to the prison?

8

Coming Home

"I felt fine spiritually, *but I knew deep inside there's these emotional scars, and stuff that needed to be healed so that I can move forward. From what I understand there's some other women that have this too. Maybe they just don't talk about it as much. Sometimes I feel like sharing it can help other people, but ... I felt worse the more I held all this in and didn't talk about it. I feel better trying to get it out and share with people, being honest and open and saying, 'This is what is going on. This is how I feel. This is what happened that's cause me to act this way.' I was kind of isolated in the prison..."*

—Formerly incarcerated woman

Reentry is the process of leaving prison or jail and returning to society and is the focus of this chapter. When women are released from prison, some are released on parole and others are released with no form of supervision. Similarly, women released from jail may be on probation or no supervision. Reentry involves reintegration back into society to live a crime-free life, eliminate future victims, and improve the lives of the community through public safety.

Evidence of reintegration is participation in the workforce, family, community, school, and/or a religious organization. However, reintegration implies that these women were integrated within their communities prior to prison. It assumes they now have the skills and opportunities to have safe housing, make a livable wage and have a prosocial community support system. In reality, most justice-involved women were socially excluded before prison, and their time in prison potentially excludes them further (Carlen & Tombs, 2006).

Reentry planning should begin the first day of incarceration, since 95% of those in state prison will one day be released and the jail churn is particularly high (Hughes & Wilson, 2002). All programs in jails and prisons are voluntary so not only do reentry programs need to be offered, but the women must take advantage of them. The Transition from Prison to the Community (TPC) model begins first with an institutional phase, then a reentry phase and finally a community phase.

> ***"In the initial need assessment** through our case management component, [we] get them engagement with our healthcare provider and our health services. For the first 14 days of their stay, that's what they're doing. They also are attending 12-step fellowship meetings to hear others who have come before them share what it was like for them. That helps them decrease some of the embarrassment and the shame and guilt associated [with being incarcerated] as well as the remorse. I think we have an awesome drug and alcohol component here that's very supportive and that's hopeful because they begin to see that they can live as productive members in society."*
>
> —Case worker

Reentry and Reintegration

Recidivism is the term used to describe a person's relapse into criminal behavior, or violation of parole or probation. For those who minister with justice-involved women, it is an ever-present reality (Snodgrass, 2019). Volunteers and ministry staff may not see lasting changes; recidivism is common. Those who serve in this role understand that it is also a ministry of mercy that may or may not allow them to see the fruit.

Reentry and rehabilitative work are ministries for the long-haul. Incarcerated women are sincere and believe it when they say, *"Oh, I love you and I want to connect with you. I'm going to call you."* However, life after prison often offers challenges and barriers that make it difficult to follow through on that commitment as they face more pressing issues of survival. Volunteers and reentry staff must not take relapses personally. This work will require adjusting expectation for them to follow through.

***"When somebody goes into correctional ministry** and especially women who are so relational… you realize that maybe 1% actually follow through and [contact you]. You really have to focus on the relationship and the time that you have with them while they're locked up. Sometimes they come back [to prison] for three or four years, so you have that opportunity just to keep inputting into them. The Lord told me early on when I went into the ministry full time that it was going to be a seed planting ministry… 'You're here to plant my word, and I will accomplish what I'm going to accomplish.'"*

– Volunteer

The profile of women coming home is the same as the profile of who is incarcerated, unless they have received treatment intervention while in custody to address their risks and needs. Absent intervention, women coming home are:

- nonviolent. They pose a lower public safety risk than men, since women are usually arrested or incarcerated for property and drug crimes rather than violent crimes. Violent crimes committed by women tend to be against the spouse, ex-spouse, or partner that physically or sexually abused them.
- disproportionately women of color.
- raised by single mothers or in foster care.
- uneducated. Most do not have a high school diploma or employment skills.
- unemployed, marginalized and poor. The poverty-to-prison pipeline is especially experienced by women. Incarcerated women report earning half as much as incarcerated men.
- likely to have health issues. A higher percentage than the general population has HIV, hepatitis, tuberculosis, and chronic conditions. There is also more obesity among females than males in custody.
- exhibiting low self-image. This is possibly associated with negative images and social stigmas of them as justice-involved mothers.
- victims of a trauma experience. Most have experienced physical and sexual abuse as children and/or adults.

- demonstrating mental health concerns, such as posttraumatic stress disorder (PTSD), depression, psychosis, anxiety, and mood disorders. These women are more likely to use prescribed medication than males coming home.
- involved with substance use and have addiction issues, including the type of drug used, frequency of use, or intravenous drug use.
- likely to be homeless.
- mothers of young children. Mostly, their children lived with them prior to incarceration.
- dealing with incarceration trauma. The experience of incarceration can be traumatic, and they may have experienced staff sexual misconduct.

Transition is typically more challenging for women from prison than from jail because of their felony record and being separated from family and society for a longer time. However, women transitioning from prison tend to be more motivated to stay out of crime and substance use than women who spend less than a year in jail.

> ***"They suggest that you do not work,*** *because they believe for women the healing process takes longer. They want to work through the issues that brought you to prison, whether it was not having support, abuse, or trauma. They want to try to get these issues healed, instead of covering them up... Some people might need more counseling, more therapy, more time to pray and meditate, more time to try to heal before they just go right into the workforce. Because you're dealing with anger or bitterness or maybe you're just scared of people. Because you've been mistreated for so long in the prison. You felt like staff members were so abusive and their tone of voice was so harsh. You've become almost afraid of people when you get out, even though the people ... you're around are nicer people. They're trying to help you [but] you have fear problems and trust issues due to these trauma experiences... Really I feel like anger and bitterness can be a trauma issue too because most of the time somebody is not just going to be angry and bitter for no reason. There's usually something that caused that anger or bitterness or unforgiveness... Then maybe they were unable*

to receive the help they felt they needed for so long. You can't really deal with a lot of things in prison.

—Formerly incarcerated woman

Reentry and reintegration are more complex for women than men because of the stigma given to justice-involved women, childcare responsibilities, poverty, employment barriers, possible intimate-partner violence, trauma, substance abuse, and mental health issues. There are practical issues such as housing, food, clothing, and transportation along with identified risks and needs that contributed to her pathway to crime (Snodgrass, 2019). Successful reentry and reintegration require both individual growth and a supportive environment. If a woman addresses the risks and needs contributing to offending behavior but the environment does not provide economic opportunity and support, she is less likely to desist from offending behavior.

Financial Needs and Issues

"My calls from prison were rejected. *'No, we're not going to have to take your call. No, we're not going to do this.' You've totally devastated the family, but gradually they came back. One of my needs [was] knowing that you're going to have some help when you get out. You have to have that support especially after you've done four years in prison like I did, and one year in county. It was like, 'What is going to happen to me? Where am I going to go?'"*

– Formerly incarcerated woman

Economic resources. All federal and most state prisons pay those in custody who work regular prison jobs. The average hourly wage for low-level jobs is 14 cents per hour; high-level jobs pay 63 cents per hour, but hourly wage varies by state. The following states do not pay the incarcerated for working regular jobs: Alabama, Arkansas, Florida (low level), Georgia, Mississippi, South Carolina, and Texas.

These women may work an 8- to 10-hour day without pay (Prison Policy Initiative, 2017). Employment for those in jail custody typically goes to those sentenced to jail time. There are fewer employment opportunities in jails. In addition, a few jails charge those in custody a "pay-to-stay" fee.

When released from jail, women are given the balance of their inmate account, the clothes they came in with, and a debt for jails requiring "pay-to-stay" fees. It doesn't matter that they are given shorts and a t-shirt in the middle of winter or that they may have changed sizes while in jail. When women are released from prison, they are given gate money anywhere from $50-$200 (depending on the state), the balance of their inmate account, a bus pass, and street clothes to wear. In Texas, the women are given men's clothes because that is what the state has most to give.

Those who have secure housing or someone to pick them up from the jail or prison are more likely to have access to food, clothing and toiletries. Those released with no one to pick them up have greater challenges for food, clothing and personal hygiene needs. They are also easier prey for traffickers and drug dealers.

Transportation is important to get to the parole or probation office for mandatory meetings and to get to work. While there are many options for transportation, they cost money. Public transportation may not be available, and weather may prohibit walking or riding a bicycle. A phone is needed to gain employment, and a landline may be required for those on parole or probation.

Safe housing. Incarcerated women are more likely than the general American population of women to be victims of domestic violence. They are also at greater risk of returning to or being with a new violent partner. Women with weak family ties and lack of housing options may be tempted to reside with a violent and/or substance using partner.

Formerly incarcerated women are more likely to be homeless, live in a shelter, or be unsheltered (i.e., without a fixed residence, such as staying with different friends or family members) than formerly incarcerated men (Couloute, 2018). Securing safe housing is perhaps the most immediate and critical need facing women upon their release. Those released from prison on parole or mandatory supervision, such as those who have committed a sex offense, are required to provide an address where they will live.

Without an address, they are not released. Like men, women who must register on the sex offender database have an extremely difficult time finding safe housing within their restricted housing options. Women not on parole or probation may be released without securing housing and may be homeless.

Legal documents. Identification and other critical documents are necessary for successful reentry. Without proper identification, employment and some housing options are impossible. Women need a social security card, government photo ID such as a driver's license or state ID, birth certificate, school records, and job training certificates.

> ***"When you get out,*** *everybody said that you can use your prison I.D. That's a lie. You can't use that. Those don't mean anything. You got to go to the [Department of Motor Vehicles] and get an I.D… Man, if you don't have your birth certificate and your Social Security you can't get that I.D., so you got to get your birth certificate and Social Security cards."*
>
> – Formerly incarcerated woman

Economic marginalization. Most women employed prior to incarceration were in low wage, entry-level positions, and approximately a fourth were on public assistance. There is no recognition for the unpaid care work of being a mother. For many, poverty is a pipeline to prison as they engage in property crimes to make ends meet.

Upon release, women are often returning to low-income neighborhoods, plagued with a lack of economic development, and with few employment opportunities to earn a living wage. There are additional challenges for women coming home to impoverished and rural communities with a lack of education and skills. Most notably, these women lack social capital to find employment, and bear the stigma of a felony record.

Women of color are impacted by economic marginalization at a greater rate and intensity level than white women. Gaining employment in legal occupations at any level is challenging, which is why some women resort back to illegal behavior to survive.

Empowerment is a process that includes hope, self-efficacy and social self-efficacy. Women must have hope, not just a desire that they will gain legal employment, but a belief that they can make enough to support themselves and their children. Self-efficacy is the belief that the justice-involved woman has the ability to control her life and achieve her goals.

Social self-efficacy is confidence in her ability to engage in social interactions that initiate and maintain interpersonal relationships. For example, she is confident of her ability to interview for jobs, able to submit to her boss, and work well with co-workers. For women to gain economic empowerment, they need education, vocational training, assertiveness training, and financial literacy.

In sum, economic barriers to women in transition may include gaining education, vocational training and employment. Significantly, meeting parole requirements includes employment, which constrains free time for further education or training. Meeting with her parole officer takes time away from work or school and requires transportation, so these barriers are often interrelated. Once access is gained, then issues of finding transportation, funding, computer skills, and childcare are needed to succeed.

Relational Needs and Issues

*“**My mother had some mental issues.** I didn’t know about her life until pretty much near the end of prison… She was beautiful [but] my mom was the one that abused me... and my mother was a bully. Church folks came in and it’s like, ‘Oh I know your family. I know you. I remember you were small. Yeah. Your mom was a bully. We used to see her, and we’d get on the other side of the street...’ I paid for the sins of my mom for a long time because people didn’t like my mom.*

At 13, I got pregnant and had my son at 14. [The school counselor and teacher] marked me present at school as long as I kept my grades up. If I missed work, they’d make sure to get my work, and make sure I got it. They worked with me because they said, ‘Don’t repeat history.’ And when they said that it’s because my mom would’ve graduated [but] two weeks before she graduated, she cut a principal. I graduated high school and went to college, but I didn’t finish.

That was rough, but I thank God because of my great grandmas, their friends, and all the other great grannies. I did things for them to make a little change there, just to get me stuff because my mother didn't really feed me. I grew up in the projects where you had two big freezers, two refrigerators. They had changed the locks on them, and I couldn't eat. She didn't provide for me. No allowance, no money, barely any clothes. On the other hand, she loved music. She played games. She was smart… but I learned most from my grandparents.

[My mother] had more than two or three [different sides]. So, in saying all that, with all the abuse and neglect, I don't think I'm crazy. You never know. We always prayed before a meal, so there were good sides to it. Playing games, like I said; things like that. Dancing. But then sometimes it'd turn ugly near the end. I always tried to appease her. All I wanted was her love. I just wanted her to accept me and love me."

– Formerly incarcerated woman

The sense of self-worth for women is built upon her connections with others (Bloom, Owen & Covington, 2003). Incarceration separates her from her children, family and significant others. Keeping relational connections, especially with her children, increases self-esteem as maintaining relationships let her know she is still loved and needed.

If the justice-involved woman is in a family, with people of faith, or a community that refers to her with the labels of "offender", "ex-offender", "criminal", "ex-con", or "perpetrator", she feels unredeemed and socially excluded. This negatively influences her self-esteem and significantly affects her ability to reintegrate successfully (LeBel, 2012).

Identity. How a woman identifies herself affects her reentry and reintegration since self-identity correlates with optimism. If she identifies herself as a persistent offender (one who has committed crimes over a long period of time) or career criminal (one who has a high rate of offenses, and possibly violent crimes), she is less likely to successfully desist from crime. Successful reintegration requires a new prosocial identity.

For women of faith, their identity in Christ provides them with worth, confidence, and hope. Like any change, identity change is a process and the support of others is needed. If the justice-involved woman has made an internal cognitive change, her external social environment needs to be supportive of this new identity or she will be less likely to have a successful reintegration.

> ***"These women, their journeys into prison*** *were so different than mine. They didn't have memories of family movie nights and game nights and parents helping them with homework. That was my experience. Theirs were fatherless homes, and generations of addiction where their parents were so in their own mess that they didn't protect them from being sexually abused and physically abused... So through that trauma comes a false identity of 'I'm unworthy, I have no value'. Those things needed to be addressed and that did not get addressed [in prison]."*
>
> – Formerly incarcerated woman

Gender norms. Another relational factor influencing reintegration is persistent cultural gender norms. Some cultures operate on beliefs such as "girls don't need school", "wives deserve to be hit", "childcare isn't real work", "women are the caregivers who are loyal; they rescue and care for children and partner while ignoring self". In some subcultures, these norms can be substantial influencers of behavior.

For example, the blueprint for the Strong Black Woman (SBW) is defined by five characteristics. These include: (1) an obligation to manifest strength, (2) an obligation to suppress emotions, (3) resistance to being vulnerable or dependent, (4) a determination to succeed despite limited resources, and (5) an obligation to help others, while neglecting themselves (Woods-Giscombe, 2010).

Within the faith community, the role of patriarchy may come into play. Churches that hold a traditional or complementarian view of gender roles argue that females are to have a submissive role under the leadership and authority of men, who should be heads of churches and families. Regardless of context, the strength of gender roles was seen.

> ***"What am I going to do?*** *Where am I going to go? The wrong people are out there. I can say, it was always a man we were calling on the phone, That*

was out there, still toxic, ready for you to get out. And that can be harder... to get away from than the drugs."

— Formerly incarcerated woman

Trauma. Unresolved trauma from sexual victimization can interfere with reentry. Feelings from abuse may continue to fuel depression, PTSD, and addictions long after the abuse occurs. Ideally, women have access to counseling for trauma healing and healthy anger management classes while incarcerated, since unhealthy coping mechanisms for anger and hostility may interfere with work and social relationships and result in physical and mental health problems.

"I had a problem when I went there. *I was so angry with every male, but every male wasn't my violator; my violator was. The one male that was my violator, I finally was able to forgive him. Once you start forgiving all that is a release off of your life. Then everything else can fall in place. I was able to have mental health counseling, went through all kinds of anger management. I realized that you can't manage anger. It's a root problem, so you have to get to the root of the issue and once you get there you could start to heal."*

–Formerly incarcerated woman

Women are different from men in their anger triggers, experience, and expression. For women, anger is often triggered by perceived unfair treatment or injustice. It may be influenced by experiences of trauma and marginalization.

Their expression of anger may include turning inward, contributing to depression, self-abuse, suicidal feelings, self-mutilation (such as cutting), crying, verbal abuse, and disruptive behaviors. They are more likely than men to suppress their anger because it is not socially acceptable for a woman to openly express her anger—or if they do, they are given a negative label. Social expectation depends on her culture. It may be acceptable for her to fight physically.

Dysfunctional relationships. Not every incarcerated woman is psychologically harmed by her time in prison, but most are changed by the experience of living with extreme, unusual norms under degraded living conditions (e.g., being watched, being told when to eat or go to bed) (Haney, 2001, p. 3, 8).

Prison creates distance between people and leads to dependency so that the justice-involved woman does not always know how to do things on her own. Likewise, these women are less likely to make emotional investments in relationships that are risky or unpredictable.

> ***"The façade of normality begins to deteriorate****, and persons may behave in dysfunctional or even destructive ways because all of the external structure and support upon which they relied to keep themselves controlled, directed, and balanced have been removed."*
>
> – Case worker

In addition, unhealthy or dysfunctional relationships may have contributed to women's pathway to illegal behavior. Developing new prosocial relationships can be a significant challenge without exposure to a supportive community or mentor.

> ***"Unhealthy relationships are the thing that hinders*** *people the most, because you're always pretty blind to people that are closest to you [whether a bad boyfriend, relationships with family members on drugs]. For women, it's that emotional attachment saying, 'No, but that's my foundation.' But I'm saying, 'Don't you understand? Your foundation is cracked. Where it gets you in your life is not where you want to go. Your foundation has to reflect where you want to go, not where you've been.'"*
>
> –Reentry director

For women without prosocial relationships, loneliness can drive women back to old friends and family who have or will contribute to her pathway to crime.

> ***"Most of the women*** *that I've come in contact with, I'd probably say 90% of them, are involved in some sort of toxic relationship, codependency. So it's really a matter of getting the help that they need and vocational [opportunities]."*
>
> – Case worker

Making relational changes is a process and challenging, especially for those who have never had prosocial relationships. Developing new friends is not always easy for most people, but developing prosocial friends adds the element of learning to do life with someone different from you. We tend to gravitate toward people "like us" in race, social economic status, faith, education levels, age, life circumstances and vocation (workplace or stay at home moms). For many women it requires learning to relate to someone who is different.

Family reunification and conflict. Parental involvement while incarcerated gives women hope and is a strong motivator to stay drug and crime free. In most cases, a family member cares for her children while she is incarcerated. Parental stress is more acute for single mothers who receive little support from the father(s) or other family members, and whose children are in foster care. Regardless of the situation, women preparing for reentry feel the stress of caring for their children.

> ***"I have children out there*** *that need their mother. I feel like God has other plans and purposes and things He wants me to do. I need to get this taken care of."*
>
> — Formerly incarcerated woman

Reentry may bring an increased responsibility for the physical, emotional, and financial well-being of others. One incarcerated woman was fearful of her release from prison because she would have immediate responsibility of caring for them and she did not feel she was ready. This was overwhelming for her.

There is the temptation on both the caregiver and mother to reunite the children with their mom too soon. This can be harmful to them, and the mother risks relapsing into addiction or illegal conduct. She must first get stable housing, a job, and maintain sobriety. In the gradual transition of her children into her care, she can be involved in decision making for them.

A woman's family may be both a strength and a risk factor depending on the level of conflict or support provided. Does the family engage or encourage illegal conduct, or do they live law-abiding lives? When relationships with family are restored, it can be very positive. These relationships can also be toxic.

> ***"My family held my freedom in their hands.*** *If they were mad at me, they could call my parole officer and make a false report for violating my parole or make new accusations. Even if it was false, I would go back to prison."*
>
> — Formerly incarcerated woman

SPIRITUAL GROWTH

The faith factor is omitted in risk and need assessment instruments, as well as most case management plans. Yet women who list "faith" as a significant strength when released from prison have a strong desire to continue to grow in their faith as well as assimilate into a religious community upon reentry. Women may be leaving behind in prison a supportive faith community, multiple weekly faith development opportunities and time available to devote toward spiritual growth.

> ***"The motivation for me would be*** *a different way of living… The love that was given, you want to cling onto those things. You want to be around people who love you. There's a lot of volunteers who poured their hearts out and invested in you. That's what motivates me…one of the good things about it is having that love, that circle of love."*
>
> — Formerly incarcerated woman

Unfortunately, not every woman's experience in prison involves a supportive faith community:

> ***"A lot of the people in the building*** *were worshiping Satan, and I mean literally. They will tell you they didn't believe in Christ. They were not believers. They had a Ouija board on the unit, and they were worshiping Satan. These weren't nice people. They were mean…They're not people you want to share life experiences with. It's not safe to trust them with information like that -- not if they're going to use the information to twist, and turn, and hurt you more. That happened to me, so I learned from those bad experiences that I don't need to share*

anything with these people anymore cause these people aren't here for me. They're not here for my spiritual growth. They're not here to help me heal. They really don't care. They're here to make a bigger mess of my life, and make me more traumatized, and then laugh about it."

– Formerly incarcerated woman

Adjusting to life on the "outside" requires justice-involved women to modify their spiritual practices, find a faith community, and make new friendships all while facing pressures and temptations that come with living in the "free world." Keeping one's faith a priority can be a daunting task. Even working with male volunteers and staff can be stressful.

"I was telling the program director, *'You guys don't know how to really take care of females.' I was telling them there was a time when I wouldn't be able to sit in the presence of [males] but because of God and my wanting to be different, I can sit into a meeting with them. 'You all need some women on board because y'all don't have anything set in place to really help women—and these women have all kinds of issues.'"*

– Formerly incarcerated woman

Women who are getting ready to be released need to be proactive in order to find possible churches in their community and create a new spiritual growth plan that they think will work once back home.

"When folks see that there's hope *and help in conjunction together, they're much more likely and much better equipped to be successful beyond the parameters of simply failing to return to prison. That's not success."*

– Reentry worker

"Reentry is really a problem… *inside. I see over the years [the women are] not getting rehabilitated. If I advocate for them and I try to get them into faith-based rehab with proven success rates, it is a battle in the court system to get it approved. I think there's a few reasons for that. One is it's extra work for the probation officers. If the public defender, or the DA, or whoever doesn't have any* *significant spirituality in their own life, they don't see the significance of making the person deal with all three parts of their being (mind, body, spirit) to bring them into wholeness. We're trying to fix people with just dealing with their mind and their body, and we're forgetting that part."*

– Reentry director

Health Needs and Issues

As previously noted, women often do not receive adequate health care or regular medical help in prison, which is often related to economic and staffing issues. This can create trauma and physical problems as they try to get their lives back on track after incarceration.

"The healthcare is just horrible. *I mean lots of people just die because they ... misdiagnose them. They just don't care. But to hear somebody say, 'Wait, we're not going to do this because basically it's going to cost money' makes you feel very uncared about. Great, I'm a person, I'm alive. This is not only affecting my life. It's going to affect my kids because I'm a parent. And you're just acting like my life does not matter to you because of money. I'm young. I have a future ahead of me [but] there's really no excuse to treat anybody that way. I just felt like that would be all the more reason they would want to [help] ... especially if they do have a short sentence... Actually, it worked the opposite because they said to people with longer sentences, 'You've got a long time, we're going to send you to these specialists.' But it shouldn't be that way, I think it could be equal care whether you have a long sentence or a short sentence. Because if you have a short sentence you're going be back out. You're going to get back out into society, and you have a future. They should want you help because you have a future."*

– Formerly incarcerated woman

However, it is encouraging to see that in times of crisis these populations are not forgotten. For example, the state of Illinois quickly moved to install health precautions during the Covid-19 pandemic. As signs of infection appeared in the general public, Governor Pritzker released low-level offenders, those near the end of their sentences, pregnant women, and justice-involved women in baby care programs. He proclaimed, *"An incarcerated person is a person, and my administration will not be in the business of proclaiming one life is more than another"* (J. B. Prizker, March 30, 2020).

Mental health. The added stress of release, a woman's history of mental health issues, the type of issue, and her medication needs are all concerns for reentry. Women who received medication while incarcerated need a seamless transition for accessing medication and follow-up help upon release. Women with anxiety or depression need to develop self-awareness for stress, anxiety, and depression, coping mechanisms and when and where to get help (Hardy, 2020).

Women with more severe mental issues often do not have access to psychiatric help needed to progress in prison or upon release. Justice-involved women with undiagnosed illnesses like schizophrenia may be seen as behavioral problems and left untreated.

> ***"She was always in isolation,*** *so I was the only one allowed to go in to see her, except for officers. An officer had to go in with me and I wasn't allowed to go in the actual cell. I could put my hand through the door, but I do believe that to a certain extent mental illness can be demons, or spirits. I know what I saw that night, you know. I just saw her come in ... it was just like somebody was overtaking her, and she was just in and out, and in and out.*
>
> *When I would pray with her and I would comfort her and encourage her. I would see the good side of her, and she would come out. And she would go, 'Have you talked to my mom? Can you pray with me?' Then she'd go back to the evil side. So, we went through that for many, many weeks and she had eventually got out. You know, to this day I don't know what has happened to her, but her mother said she's been sick like that all her life. It has caused her to get in serious trouble like that. But what was heart-wrenching... [Her mother] said she never had anybody to work with her."*
>
> — Chaplain

Whether involving physical or mental health issues, institutional services are one way to prepare prisoners for release in their communities. By taking the nature of prisonization seriously and making changes to the way prisoners are prepared to reenter, justice-involved women can in effect "decompress" and acclimate to new norms. With an understanding of how prison may have changed them, these women start to collect the tools they need to adjust to freedom.

> ***"Being a medical chaplain****, I use a lot of materials from the medical field to help them, especially with trauma, grief, and abuse. I use a lot of resources to try to start the healing process for them on the inside because I don't see them getting it once they're out of in prison… It's like a neglected group of people that nobody's really concerned for. We have such high standards in the medical field, but we don't in Corrections. We deal with so much grief and trauma, death, overdoses. It's dramatic all day long. It's very heavy, heavier than it is in the medical field.*
>
> *When it comes to reentry, we are so limited in what we have available for women, and with their children, too. We have addicts that are coming back out homeless, going into homeless shelters with the people they used with. How do we break the cycle? We need faith-based reentry facilities for women, and we need faith-based rehabilitation centers for addiction because what the system is doing isn't working. Your heart breaks for them because they want help. They're crying for help, but the system isn't really set up effectively to give it to them because even when you look at trauma and you see the devastation in people diagnosed with PTSD, what are we giving them for treatment? Nothing. They're not getting treatment. They're getting medicated, but they're not getting healing programs."*
>
> – Medical chaplain

The reentry process should begin long before release. In terms of physical and mental health, reestablishing family ties and addressing criminogenic risks and needs are essential for their effective functioning in post-prison roles. When women have manifested signs of mental illness or developmental disability, pre-release outpatient treatment is helpful in reacquainting reentry women into the social norms or reinstalling medical benefits.

***"I actually had a disability claim** out from my mental issues and other things I already had diagnosed before I went [to prison]. I was unable to receive the Supplemental Security Insurance (SSI) because I got a letter back from my lawyer saying that they didn't pay benefits to someone incarcerated. He said that I would have to start the process over when I got out. But when I got my medical records back from the disability office that came to me in the prison, I had found out the medical staff had told lies about me ... Well I've applied again; I'm going back to that process. I actually don't qualify for [Social Security Disability Insurance] because I haven't paid enough in, but I can qualify for SSI."*

— Formerly incarcerated woman

Justice-involved women should be prepared for reentry and not expect quick healing. It is not unusual to have other challenges after release.

***"I began to have other physical health issues.** I don't know if it was as a result of not having my mental health medication and then physical problems in my body, or if it was a combination of everything -- not being able to get help, being traumatized so many times, not being able to get the proper mental health medicine, not being able to get healthcare, just people being so mean —the combination of all of it. My menstrual cycles actually stopped for 17 months. When I came to [the reentry program] it still took me another month and a half before I was able to get that straightened out and find out what was causing that. Due to those medical issues, I had to go and see a chiropractor and go through that process. I had to basically share with the [reentry] staff what was going on and tell them that I didn't know what to do."*

— Formerly incarcerated woman

Substance use. Since most justice-involved women have substance use addictions, they will need on-going support for sobriety in the free world. Depending on their level of addiction and programs received while incarcerated, they may need treatment and/or a support group. Groups such as Alcoholics Anonymous (AA), Narcotics Anonymous (NA) and Celebrate Recovery offer support.

"That's what we try to do, *at least to the best of our ability. We try to run programs that deal with the topics that these people are suffering from —trauma, abortion, rape, all those things—but from a faith perspective. It's Christ-centered because he's the only one that's going to heal them. When they meet him there, it's life changing. It's eternally changing. It changes the whole family. We've had women that we've been able to get them into faith-based programs, versus drug court. They've come out successful. They've gone back and gotten their degrees. They've gotten custody [of their children] back and become case managers in the community, ministering to other people in the community. It can work ..."*

— Reentry director

Women who relapse may need inpatient or outpatient treatment. Early intervention and consistent treatment during incarceration is important regardless of the program but is often difficult to deliver. In the following chapter, we examine reentry plans and the challenges of healing while on parole and probation.

Questions for Reflection

1. What are ways your ministry can prepare women for reentry?
2. What church, community, and government programs and resources are available to assist reentry transitions?

9

. . . . .

Staying Home

"So, my incarcerations, I had about seven of them. *A lot of the times that I was in there, I'd be like, 'God, just get me out of this. I won't do it again.' At some of those times, I really did mean it. And then, it never failed. As soon as I got out, as soon as I walked out that door ... sometimes even within the time from the jail to my house, I would be smoking a pipe already. Because that's what I knew. I didn't know any other people. Even family. Sometimes are bad for you, triggers you. They're an addiction too, so that's not a safe place to go. So, it was really like a revolving door for me with the jail. I'd be in there and I'd say it, and I'd come back out, and I'd be right back in that door going into jail, saying the same thing. But the last time was different for me, because God knew what I needed. He knew I needed time in there, so He put me in there for five months this time. That's where I met Chaplain [name]. After that, it was just like the Holy Spirit filled me. I met Jesus through her. Then when I got out of this place, this new community started."*

– Formerly incarcerated woman

Women released from jail have some of the same challenges, issues, and feelings as women from prison, but there are also distinct differences and perspectives. Women in prison tend to be more motivated and ready to be sober, substance free, and crime-free. They have aged, been away from the lifestyle that contributed toward criminal life, and possibly changed their thinking and gained new skills to keep them free of crime.

Reentry Planning

Jail residents know that their time is short so they may not be thinking about what they need to change in their life. Rather, they think about how to get out, and possibly where they will get "high" when released. They have not hit "rock bottom" and are not ready to make behavioral changes that will keep them out of the justice system.

Women in jail are housed in their local community. They typically have more contact with family and friends than those in prisons far from home. They don't face culture shock upon release because of their short time of incarceration, and often have stronger ties with the community, family and significant others.

However, women describe jail time as "hard time" because of the lack of programming, movement, light, and recreational opportunities. Jail reentry is more likely without access to community-based agencies such as departments of health and human services, workforce development, and family and child welfare services. These agencies are likely already working with the women who are cycling in and out of jail and their families. Women from jail will still have practical needs for reentry such as food, clothing, safe housing, and transportation. They will need employment, trauma healing, substance use treatment and family support. Jails offer fewer programs and opportunities to prepare women for successful reentry, so access to community-based agencies is important.

Women who renew their Christian commitment or experience conversion while in jail may not be grounded in their faith. They need someone to disciple them and an accepting faith community upon reentry. Sometimes, women who have experienced prison are those who work well together in this endeavor, and it is not unusual for those who have served time to become involved in jail and prison ministries.

> ***"I did time with these girls,*** *so I know what their problems are and I know where their mind really is. But everybody needs a chance. When we said that our lives have been changed because of Christ, when you give your life to Christ, then that means that either you're going to allow him to do the work in you that he needs to do in your heart [or you're not]. A lot of mindsets still be of the world... When God said that 'I am', he says that I'll do the cleaning up. When they give their life that means they become a new creature."*
>
> – Formerly incarcerated woman and volunteer

> ***"It seems that the women,*** *they're mean to each other. I think it's just because of the woundedness. As far as going off to prison, it almost seems like a relief to them because then they know what their future is and what time they are doing."*
>
> – Chaplain

There are numerous needs and barriers to successful reentry. On the other end of their sentence is the need to alleviate anxiety and to satisfy the burden of care for reentry women. This requires addressing financial, relational, and health needs.

A case plan can address risks and needs during the institutional phase through programs. The **transition phase** (six to 12 months prior to release) can address some of the practical needs such as finding safe housing, possible employment, access to food, and clothing in preparation for the transition. The **community phase** follows release. In this phase, a case manager or parole officer can provide accountability and support to follow their case plan (Hardy, 2020). Navigating the transition is not easy and takes the support of family, friends, church, social services, parole, and the community.

Most assessments used for reentry plans and programs measure the risks and needs of the women. Then an individualized treatment plan is developed to address those risks and needs identified in the assessment. The assessment should be gender-specific for women, and not one used with men.

A strengths-based approach provides more strategies to increase and build on positive qualities, enhance intrinsic motivation, and help women remain out of the justice system. Rather than focusing only on deficits, this approach recognizes that all women have strengths that can assist in reentry. Strengths-based assessments tend to ask the woman to identify her personal strengths in areas such as educational assets, self-efficacy, family support, and parental involvement. In addition, the faith factor should be included as a strength: their relationship with God and with other Christians.

In the best-case scenario, strengths are identified or built while incarcerated. For some, however, this awareness comes after release.

"Near the end of the month on Friday, *we have fellowship time and see how they're doing. We celebrate their birthdays, celebrate their goals and achievements... to give them the opportunity to realize that it's more than just a job; that they can live like that too. All they have to do is educate themselves and become socially and economically empowered to be able to market themselves for higher living wages. As long as they have acceptance, being able to identify the need, the willingness to put in the action steps that it's going to take, and focus, focus, focus on improving that quality of life. I have the resources and the elements for them right now to pay for this education, but it's up to them. I want to see this for them, but they have to want to see themselves taking this opportunity... Negative self-talk and shame may resurface or continue to haunt her. These feelings of failure contribute to a loss of hope, motivation, and depression."*

– Reentry director

The Challenges of Parole and Probation

Parole and probation are not synonymous with "freedom." Women who are released ***on parole*** to complete their sentence in the free world face a variety of conditions and tasks. Violation of parole conditions will send them back to prison to complete their sentence. Requirements commonly include:

- regular reporting to a parole officer;
- finding and maintaining full-time employment;
- submitting to alcohol and drug tests;
- abiding by strict curfews (checked through electronic monitoring);
- not changing employment or address without permission;
- attending specific programs, such as anger management;
- not leaving a designated area without permission; and
- not associating with people with criminal records, including family and friends.

The conditions imposed for those ***on probation*** are related to their type of crime. Common terms or conditions may include:

- regularly meeting with a probation officer at set times;
- appearing at any scheduled court appearances;
- paying fines or restitution (i.e., monies to victims);
- avoiding certain people and places;
- not traveling out of state without the permission of your probation officer;
- obeying all laws, including minor laws such as jaywalking;
- refraining from illegal drug use or excessive alcohol use; and
- submitting to drug or alcohol testing.

In some cases, a condition of parole or probation is to wear an ankle monitor (also known as a tether, or ankle bracelet) that monitors location. Ankle monitors require a daily fee, which adds to the financial challenges of those on parole or probation. If probation violations are severe (new criminal charge or absconding), or after multiple technical violations (not paying money owed, missing a meeting, testing positive for drugs), a probation revocation hearing could be scheduled. A judge at the hearing will consider reports from the probation officer. If probation is revoked, the probationer will often be incarcerated in jail or prison (Hardy, 2020).

Collateral Consequences of a Felony Conviction

> ***"Now I have this felony on my record,*** *which upset me. I was very angry and bitter in the prison for quite a while just having to accept this because all I could see was the pain and hurt and 'what am I going to do?' But I've always had a really strong faith in God, ... and I did turn to Him, but it's still very shocking to have to accept that now I've got this felony on my record. I feel falsely charged for something ..."*
>
> – Formerly incarcerated woman

Everyone convicted of a felony experiences collateral consequences. These are legal restrictions that limit or prohibit them from accessing employment, housing, and other rights, benefits and opportunities. These

46,000 restrictions are scattered throughout state and federal statutory and regulatory codes (Malcolm & Seibler, 2017).

Frequently, they are unknown even to those responsible for their administration and enforcement. A list of all the restrictions can be found on the National Inventory of Collateral Consequences of Criminal Conviction website. Some of the more common consequences that may include being denied parental rights, residency in public housing and some non-public housing or limited areas to live. Felons may be denied public benefits such as food stamps, a driver's license, educational opportunities including student loans, the right to vote and jury service. Certain professions may be restricted, as well as employment involving a "check the box" question on applications. In addition, some international travel may be prohibited.

Collateral consequences have a negative effect on the individual and her family. For example, employment is one of several important factors in a person's successful reentry. Employment results in more positive relationships, an income for family and prosocial activities. Employers are more likely to hire someone without a criminal background than hire a woman who has one.

> ***"The interesting result is*** *the stronger effect of incarceration for women than for men. Whereas 57.1% of male job applicants with a prison record would have been called for a job interview, only 30% of women with the same prison record would have been called for an interview. This difference could reflect an additional 'punishment' for women in that they violated employers' gendered role expectations. Put differently, women with a prison record are seen as having committed two offenses, one against the law and one against social expectations of how women are supposed to behave"* (Decker, Spohn, & Ortiz, 2010, p. 57).

To remove the stigma in hiring practices, some states and employers have "banned the box" by removing the question on the application asking if the applicant has a felony. To compensate, some employers now do a background check on all applicants, and criminal records are now available on the internet.

Reentry Feelings and Perspectives

Reentry is an emotional experience. A few common observations regarding reentry from women released from prison are noted below, along with antidotes for countering these emotions.

Perspective #1: "I was more scared to leave prison than I was to go to prison" (Roos, 2017).

Women experience many fears and anxiety before release and upon reentry. Fears of rejection by family, friends, the church, the community, fear of going back to prison and losing their freedom, fear of drug relapse, fear of not being able to find a job or housing, fear of not meeting parole requirements create anxiety. Capitalizing on her strengths, having a reentry plan and support system helps alleviate these fears. Prison is sometimes an escape from the larger fears and anxiety that was part of her daily life, and ultimately provided a window into the suffering of others.

> ***"It was kind of a little break.*** *I guess it was more of 'Okay, I don't have to go through all that anymore' but yet I'm still locked up. Do you get what I'm saying? The mind… So then when I got to prison, the people come in and talk to you and stuff. 'You're safe.' I knew a weight had been lifted off me because I had a lot of nightmares, but my nightmares were the nightmares I'd had growing up. It's always the same nightmares, and they stopped ... Sometimes in prison things are triggers, so I'll holler at you because you can't say anything. You could, but you'd go to jail. I worked hard to get where I'm at… I wanted to follow the rules. [When I became a prison ministry volunteer] they did a pilot program with some of the other inmates, especially lifers. Help them calm down… I asked them, 'Are you sane? I don't have any money. But if I can help you, I will.'"*
>
> – Formerly incarcerated woman and volunteer

It is easy for women in reentry to feel overwhelmed by reentry expectations to find housing, get a job, stay drug free, and care for themselves and their children. A second area that is overwhelming is the number of daily decisions now required of them. While incarcerated, women make few decisions.

They are told what to wear and eat, where to go and when, and what to do. In the free world, it is decision overload even for the average person (e.g., think about walking down the cereal aisle and all the choices there, or the number of options on a restaurant menu). When moving from few choices to an overload of choices, it can be overwhelming and induce panic. Patience and sensitivity is important as she adjusts to all the decisions required in reentry.

> ***"In our program we say,** 'Okay for 30 days, nothing. You just do what we ask you to do for 30 days and ... we'll take care of everything.' We tell them, 'You can't go to work until all of your appointments are completed. After all of your appointments are completed, we'll get you a job. You won't even have to look for a job. We're going to do that for you.' [But by] Week three, they're looking for a job; all by themselves. We're like, 'What are you going to do? Your appointments aren't finished. You're going to go to work tomorrow and then two days later you're going to have to call in and ask for time off. What do you think your employer is going to say?' So, they're really frustrated by the amount of time it takes just to get set up to begin work... On our end, we have to continually teach [this] because people get out every month. 'Relax. We understand. We've been there.'"*
>
> *Occasionally you run into that one or two people who happen to be particularly manipulative and they are trying to circumvent the process because they just can't wait. They're frustrated and then you want them to be successful, so you get frustrated because they're trying to go around the process ... They get out. They have to deal with the debt. It's frustrating when you get out and someone tells you, 'Oh, by the way..."*
>
> – Reentry director

Women with post-incarceration PTSD may display many symptoms such as nightmares of going back to prison or jail. There may be hyper-arousal, to the extent they have trouble sleeping. They may demonstrate persistent avoidance or panic attacks in crowded public spaces. There may be avoidance of triggers that remind them of prison, such as eating food off a tray. They may have emotional numbing, where women cannot trust others, keep an emotional distance, and don't display emotions (Reichert & Bostwick, 2010).

***"It's horrible.** It takes us even more effort to build trust in them again, and to let them know that they don't have to sneak, because that behavior comes out with them. With fear, the fear tactic, it's compounded with the dark side of their life, that behavior that they went through prior to going to jail. That has not been addressed, so there's no rehabilitation there, that's my point."*

– Reentry director

***"The purpose is rehabilitation.** I'm a firm believer that healing has to precede anything else. Because people, when they've had significant trauma ... Those in the field know that if there's a trauma people freeze—socially, emotionally—and sometimes that's what's causing their behaviors, their drug addictions, their alcoholism. I believe in healing. I believe in healing first. I believe in inner healing and then you're free to take advantage of all these other opportunities. If you're not healing on the inside, you're stuck; you're frozen [and] you can't move forward."*

– Reentry director

Perspective #2: "I don't have what it takes."

Expectations about life after release can be unrealistic. Women may think when they return home that roles and relationships will pick up where they left off, that their goals of getting an education and employment will move quickly and easily. Those incarcerated often talk about how they want to start a non-profit. They may not have the procedural self-talk to be able to identify what all is needed to reach their goal of earning a GED or gaining employment. Imposing discipline and direction can sometimes be problematic.

***"Processes frustrate the snot out of returning citizens.** Their life has been on hold for a number of years typically. So even though they intellectually understand that they are not going to be able to catch up where they left off or make up for lost time, they try anyway. They have really unrealistic expectations about what life is going to be like out here because they fantasized for so many years. 'Oh,*

I'm going to do this and everything I touch is going to turn to gold and everything is going to be wonderful.' They don't have an actual connection with life on the outside viscerally, so their connection is fantasy..."

– Reentry director

In an effort to make up for lost time, women may rush into gaining custody of their children before they are ready or be anxious to "do" for their kids. They also may feel guilty for being incarcerated, and for the time away from their children. This guilt may play into an increased tolerance of children's disrespect, verbal abuse and manipulation, especially financially. This feeling can interrupt the recovery process.

Many women face problems they had not anticipated, and that they are ill-prepared to solve. The burden of care for self and others, and the needs and barriers of reentry may be overwhelming, especially for those without support and in impoverished neighborhoods. She may think, "I don't have what it takes," and the pull from her former life of illegal conduct and addiction leads to relapse. Focusing on the long-term as well as short-term goals can help.

"Some of the other positive experiences *I've had with women that lost custody of their children; somebody was awarded guardianship. A few years ago, we had a dress banquet, and one of the women I had worked with was at the banquet with her daughter. She told me she was engaged. She has a job. And all I could think of was the many times that she sat in the room with me and just sobbed about how her life was such a mess. Then I see what God can do."*

– Volunteer

Women may feel like they don't fit in, especially when they are socializing with sober, prosocial people for the first time. They may think, "I don't belong here. These people are better than me." "I have an ex-con tattoo on my forehead–everyone knows" or "If they knew my past, they would reject me." Not surprisingly, friendships often come from those who have some understanding of what they have endured.

> ***"Now since being out, I met some people.*** *This one lady who was an officer in [prison] retired and opened her own business. She's my friend. Since I got out, her husband gave me this phone. She and my cousin take turns paying my phone bill, because I have nothing. It's a blessing. [The former correctional officer] had a shop and gave me these [tote bags] and clothes. She said, 'What do you need?' I said 'I need an umbrella' so they got me an umbrella, this umbrella. I keep tearing up over that…*
>
> *And all the people that I've met from the inside, they have gotten out and stayed in contact with me all these years. One girl I call my daughter. She's been out seven years. She just came up and we went out to a cookout together. That's the first time I went there, and we had a milkshake together. I've had people that stayed in contact because they said that I meant something to them. This one girl said, 'I only have two friends, my husband and my children.'"*
>
> – Formerly incarcerated woman

Women may feel sad, empty, lost, and dejected. They may be tempted to "hide" when feeling depressed, overwhelmed by the demands and feelings associated with reentry. They often talk without much hope about employment prospects and their future:

> ***"Sometimes it's not all about the money,*** *but what they can do ... not everybody I guess wants to do a restaurant, or a plant job. Now some people might be okay with that for the rest of their lives, and some people might not mind doing it for the time being, but it might not be what they want to do when they get out."*
>
> – Formerly incarcerated woman

Those women with a clear sense of what they want to do may be blocked from obtaining their goal.

> ***"I actually wanted to go back to school*** *for cosmetology because that's what I did before I went to prison. I did graduate cosmetology school, but I did not take the state board exams due to my arrest and incarceration. They said if it had been over two years and you had not taken your state board exams then*

you were required to get back to school. I already owe $20,000 in student loan debt from the first time I went to school. I'm not sure what God's plans are for me right now, but I still would love to do that… But I don't want to go into more debt right now and they don't have funds … I've called multiple different schools in this area. It's running $18,000; you can go full-time and do it in nine months, or you can go part-time and do it in 18 months. The Pell Grant only covers $10,000, so you will still have to take out remaining in student loans, which is debt. So unless you have other funds available..."

– Formerly incarcerated woman

Patience for "ideal" employment placement is a challenge for recently released women.

"What's a big struggle for the women is *not accepting the opportunities work wise that are available…The women we're working with, especially the ones that we have working at the center… want to go find an office job. Well, you may not be able to find an office job. You may be hanging clothes up somewhere, and that's okay. Now you have experience in an office setting and we're going to try to get you that opportunity, but we can't promise it to everybody. The fields that women go into after incarceration are very limited because those types of fields have those restrictions on your background... Just getting them to accept that 'I'm going to have to take some steps back and build back up. I'm not just going to get that job that I'd just love to work at.'"*

– Reentry director

Anger may lie under the surface at all times. The source of anger may be fears, injustices, feeling overwhelmed, rejection, unhealed trauma, not making progress fast enough, the barriers to transition, and lack of support. She may have outbursts or depression. Anger may be triggered by male authority figures after incarceration. Having formerly incarcerated female mentors available when they first come out of prison would be helpful, as well as building upon past prison experiences to create a supportive community.

*"**With my own issues, [I received] a lot of self-help**... A lot of my healing wasn't so much from staff, it was more from each other. We lift each other up in prayer. They used to put me in the middle and they were a circle around me, my friends, and prayed for me. Anytime I was off the wagon, as they say, and I'm in my sin, they loved me. 'Hate the sin' is what they prayed for me. They kept me uplifted. That says a whole bunch because a lot of people don't do that. People, they mess up. They're shunned. The churches do that. People don't do that—if that's your family, why are you shunning them? It's just like church is coming into prison. Don't mark that off your list or something. You do prison ministry. What's the follow-up when that person gets out? It's like you made them to be saved, but you don't follow up?"*

– Formerly incarcerated woman

Faith-based inside programs with peer support was effective in building an understanding of God's love and forgiveness. This in turn can build hope and confidence in recovery that leads to true reentry.

*"**We had Bible study together** and individual one-on-one sessions every week. When she got out, she was terrified because the wrong people were waiting for her, primarily men that were writing her from prison saying, 'I think about you all the time.' Well, of course in prison a man's going to be thinking about being with this woman when he gets out. And she was so scared that she wouldn't be able to withstand the pressure. There were about four different men, and she really liked all of them, but they had done crimes. They were in crimes together and had been co-defendants and everything, so she kept saying to me, 'I need something that's going to keep me away from these wrong relationships.' She was the first woman [I met before reentry] that was not being optimistic about how it was going to go, and so she and I just became very close.*

We walked through that process together. One by one, she got rid of these wrong men. She changed her phone number, [but] they still found her... The stories of how these men hounded her, because she was so cute, very fun personality, and men liked her. She was able to withstand all of that. A few bumps in the road and a few mistakes, but every time there was a mistake, she would call me and say, 'Okay, I blew it. Here's what happened.' Then we would reaffirm her commitment to walk with God; 'God forgave you, we're putting that behind us, we're going forward, you know?' But then she'd say to me, 'You're not going to drop me, are you?' That fear impressed me so much. 'You didn't hold up your end of the bargain, I'm done with you' ... I just assured her, 'I'm not in it for your success. I want your success. I'm not going to drop you. That's the last thing I would do.'"

– Reentry director

Perspective #3: "I just want to be normal again."

Women reentering after longer prison sentences experience culture shock, where everything has changed. New technology affects their ability to communicate and is necessary for education and most employment. The increased cost of living may be overwhelming as they look at rent and food costs. Rent may have been $500 a month when they were arrested, but now is $800 a month. The demanding fast pace of the free world can be shocking as they have been living in a slow, controlled and reduced stimulus environment.

***"You re-learn all those things.** When I went in the cell phones ... were like bricks... and then you come onto the Nokias, and all that stuff. A lot of people weren't using money anymore; they were using the debit card. You need to re-learn a whole lot of things because you were in your drug addiction. You lose stuff. I think you lose the capacity to process life, so you have to re-learn some things."*

– Formerly incarcerated woman

It takes time to adjust from living in a controlled environment where everything was done for you to living in the free world. One woman expressed how her boyfriend got mad at her for leaving on the lights or not locking the doors. She hadn't turned off a light or locked a door in five years. Everyday activities and tasks are all new and it takes time to get into new habits.

> ***"Watching her agonize over that,*** *removing people that have been in her life, setting healthy boundaries; just watching her work through that has been really awesome... We talked about showing up to work every day... walking through that all the way to how to dress at a workplace..."*
>
> – Case worker

It is important to provide acceptance, support, and patience as women adjust to their new normal, especially those who have chronically dealt with addictions.

> ***"The more they practice [living] this way,*** *the more normal they begin to feel. What we're here to remind them, is that the disease of addiction is incurable... With the looking better, the feeling better, processing gets a little bit better. What they do is associate all of the dark side and negativity and the behavior to the substance use only. Here, what we do is educate them. We engage them and educate them and empower them with information about the illness, the core that's behind the substance use. So that's when sometimes they fall short because they're feeling better than they have in years, and away from the last use, away from incarceration., You know we give them their space because this is their space to have the freedom to move and go and show themselves that they can become trustworthy again. Sometimes they have to work those 12 steps. They have homework to do, and they have a tendency to suffer from the disease of forgetfulness, so I have to step in sometimes to remind them.*
>
> – Reentry director

Many women expressed their desire to be "normal"—to fit in and belong with other women in society; to be part of the family, workplace, and church. For some women, this feeling may manifest itself as they look forward to wearing their own clothes and make-up, since they have lost their uniqueness and identity while incarcerated. The desire to be normal has spiritual ramifications as well.

> ***"Everybody has to come to a point in life*** *where they want to change. I was tired of life; all I wanted was peace. When I did Scripture reading [in]*

Psalms 23, verse two, second part where it says, 'He leads you beside still waters' I thought back to before going to prison. I used to go to the lake all the time swimming. One particular night, a ranger came by about three times. 'Time to go.' I'm still in the water, but it's like the moon was sitting on the water. I would say, 'Peace to you.' I did not want to move… God took me back there to that peace. That's all I ever wanted was peace... It's only because I love water, you know what I'm saying? But if I stopped swimming, I feel like I'm drowning because if it weren't for the word of God, I wouldn't have an anchor. I always remember my grandma used to tell me, 'Hey baby, just pray, pray, pray about it.' When I was younger, I prayed about everything, and now I know that does change things."

– Formerly incarcerated woman

The formerly incarcerated woman may feel emotionally vulnerable and desperate for a relationship with a man. This desire may lead her to unhealthy relationships with those who use drugs or a domestic violence situation. Even with loving rules and surveillance cameras in place after release, reentry program members struggled with the human cost of this emotion.

"Now, I've lost so many girls. *There are girls [in the program] I have right now, when they go to [reentry headquarters] they show them one face. I keep telling [the program directors], they'll show you one face, and have men picking them up. So now I'm over here [in the female residence] and one day something is going to erupt because they're bringing all these different men in. So now they say they put up cameras, but evidently, they aren't watching the cameras. I tell you, I come home from work and I see such and such. You know what I'm saying? It's not really going to work. The girls do get the jobs [but] if they don't want to keep the jobs, what are they going to do? They're going to continue … getting money from men and whatever they're doing. They're not going to do the right things. There's a few of us that do the right things and then we get all the mess. I just stopped talking to them. I shouldn't have to do that."*

– Formerly incarcerated woman

Being "normal" implies a level of social support for acceptance and positive role modeling. Most justice-involved women have strained relationships with family and friends. Family members—tired of empty promises, being manipulated or even harmed by their loved one—may ostracize her. Friends prior to incarceration are long gone.

Yet women returning home need community support, which is identified as an evidence-based practice for reducing recidivism. If social support is not provided by family and prior friends, it is an opportunity for the faith-community to fill the gap through mentors and assimilation into a church.

"I can't really go back to my family *because it was pretty dysfunctional. I couldn't go back to my old playmates, my old playgrounds, so I had to have a support system. And because I became a Christian while I was incarcerated, I didn't know how to be a Christian on the outside. I had to learn. You re-learn all those things. … You have to have a support system."*

– Formerly incarcerated woman

Another woman highlights the critical need for social support for successful reentry.

"When I left prison, I left with nothing. *If I didn't have a support system I would have been out there, probably would have went right back out to the same things, if I was on drugs or whatever the case may be. Thank God that's not my issue, but for other women it is."*

– Formerly incarcerated woman

Faith-based support groups and mentoring for justice-involved women is critically important.

"Because they're in a confined environment, *they have the boundaries set for them. But they need somebody that we can have over to do the reentry part. We can give them everything they need inside, but the reality is will they have a support group once they get out. That is so key, the reentry component of it. I will not refer them to a church that I know is not receptive to men and women getting out of prison, so I try to refer them to places where they will not be rejected. And then*

I encourage them once I get out to make an appointment with their pastor and get them into a Bible study within that church."

– Reentry director

Another complication can be the type of crime committed. For example, there are stringent protections in place for those who have sex offenses.

"These are folks who have other options. *They can go home. They have a home to go to. They don't need to come to our residency program. They have work to do. They can go to a job. They don't need to come to us for employment. Then there are those who've got the goods. They qualify on paper, but don't have any place else to go. So, we're one of the few organizations that accepts sex offenders, that's permitted to house multiple sex offenders in one location. They choose to come to us because they don't have somewhere else to go."*

– Reentry director

Reentry and rehabilitation are long processes that begin before women are released from prison. Much of the research that looks at parole and probation is drawn from studies of male prisoners, which constrains broader applications. This is because the kind of trauma, communication styles, and amount of input each gender uses is different.

Therefore, it is important for practitioners to understand that there are these differences in being able to minister directly to the areas of primary need. However, recognizing the reality of reverse culture shock, effects of realistic and unrealistic expectations, and pathway to "normal" through social support is critical for ministry workers.

"When I start seeing, *I start seeing why people were addicted. I started seeing why people were [not just] their behavior. I started seeing what caused their behavior because I was one of the ones that was molested and didn't know how to deal with the issue. When I realized and finally got help, then I saw that every man wasn't my violator. Then I said, 'Okay, now I could sit down and really have a relationship with the man.'"*

– Formerly incarcerated woman

Questions for Reflection

1. How does knowing the perspectives described in this chapter impact ministry?
2. What should churches and communities be doing to prepare for the return of formerly incarcerated women?

10

Healing the Justice-Involved Woman

***"I think what motivates them is** that they start to feel better. You're meeting a need that they have. They've felt bad for so long, and then they start to experience some healing and they're like, 'Wow this kind of hurts but I'm feeling better.' They start to get more freedom, and they start to look better physically... I think that their pain is definitely a motivator for change. When they're to a point where they ... have to deal with issues and be sober... they have to walk through it. So, they learn that they can walk through it without unhealthy dependencies."*

– Reentry director

Justice-involved women are trauma survivors, marginalized, and broken. They are in need of healing. Healing is the process of becoming whole, including the spiritual, emotional, mental and physical aspects of the person. Healing for justice-involved women involves the integration and implementation of corrections and Christian formation principles. This chapter highlights the impact of abuse and trauma faced by many justice-involved women from the perspective of psychologists involved in clinical work.

The Legacy of Abuse

***"[In elementary school] it was running from the bullies.** You can't catch me if I got away. But sometimes they would catch me. As I got older, it was high school students that picked on me. Not so much me as my age—most of the [students were picked on] because [the high schoolers] would get out before we did. The school even went to let me out the back door; let me go early. I used to have rocks in my pocket, knives. You know the little knife they get in the* *can opener and all that stuff on it, little silver thing? Mama taught me how to sharpen it. Every night I had to sharpen it. She taught me guns. The first ... was a shotgun. This one had the orange bullets and she made me shoot it out the back door. I didn't want to [but] until I can stand up and shoot it, she was going to have me keep shooting out the back door. People just closed the blinds, peeked, and called the police. It never fails. I kept on at shooting people a couple times; peed on myself trying to stop it, though. So that's just something mental she had going on... So like I said: a bullet in the home, bullying outside.*

I still managed. It was rough sometimes [with my mother]; I just had to take it. A few times, even in elementary school, she actually took her foot and kicked me out the door, just because ... I don't even really know what for because I really wasn't a bad kid. I stayed in all the time. I went to school, back in the house, a latch key kid ... If you didn't have a key to get in, you didn't get in. I knew that... The people that are keeping me are also my bullies, so there was a lot of sexual perversion going on there, too. These are teenaged [bullies] -- you got guys and you got girls. I am a kid. So a lot was happening to me and a lot was happening around me. So dangerous; a lot of stuff. It's crazy... I even got raped while [my mother] was next door. She came in and I wanted to tell her. Before I could open my mouth, she smacked me across the room, so I never told her 'You were just next door and I got raped.'

But like I said, kicking me out more than once ... I had nowhere to go... We lived in apartments above the schoolyard, so I'd go to the schoolyard to sleep and try to make it back. She'd been around to working tip service, and I'd come in through my window. I picked the lock. I was getting in because I could watch and go to school, you know what I'm saying? I tried to get in before a few times. The principal almost saw me because he was the first one arrived. But things happen to kids at night in the air because people walk through there. Who was going to tell? So I went through a lot, as far as bad..."

– Formerly incarcerated woman

Abuse is a term broadly used to cover multiple kinds of harm done within a person's lifetime. Some people experience more than one kind of abuse, which is a word that covers emotional, verbal, physical, and sexual harm done to another person. The continuum is from a single experience to a long and chronic history with multiple perpetrators. That is, harm can come from one instance of abuse (e.g., rape) or an ongoing history of harmful behavior. It can involve one relationship in which some kind of abuse took place, or multiple relationships.

Abuse could have taken place as a very young child, as an adolescent, or as an adult. In fact, some women who have been abused as an adult have no experience with childhood or adolescent abuse as others have. Further, abuse may have occurred at the hands of a stranger or be part of a family pattern that has created conditions that enable harm to occur repeatedly (S. Canning, personal communication, September 19, 2018).

Verbal abuse occurs when the justice-involved woman is the object of harmful speech, including insults that in the past have characterized her in ways that are hurtful, negative, and dehumanizing. Verbal abuse may involve threats of harm, intimidation, or manipulation. It can be related to other kinds of abuse, such as when the woman is threatened about things or people she cares about or when hostile words are delivered in a screaming, high emotional state. Manipulation of those kinds of messages is another example of verbal abuse.

Often, verbal abuse is interconnected with other forms, since the words are meant to create **emotional abuse** or harm and can lead to **physical abuse**.

Sexual abuse occurs when an individual is subjected to any kind of sexual behavior that would not be developmentally appropriate or expected, is coercive or against the person's will, or that causes bodily harm. When this kind of abuse involves a partner of some sort as an adult, it is a form of domestic violence referred to as **intimate partner violence**. **Child abuse** is the legal term when this behavior occurs before the age of 18.

It is important that reentry staff and volunteers have the ability to refer the justice-involved woman to professional helpers, as well as be able to move forward themselves when these kinds of conversations come up. This is because the rates of verbal, emotional, physical, and sexual abuse are so high that it is very likely that some people who are listeners in this context may have their own history of abuse. According to psychologist Dr. Sally Canning, helpers must tread carefully when working with abused women:

> ***"The first thing would be to simply focus*** *on their own awareness of that and whether or not there's something that feels like a very open wound emotionally for them. Sometimes people are highly motivated to help others because they've been through things, and they've really grown and had a chance to process."*

In this case, workers may not be aware that they have been through an abusive experience until triggered by a similar story. However, workers may be aware of their own abuse, but not ready to help others with their healing. Canning continues, *"Other times, people are highly motivated to help others [but] … they're much more in the early or beginning stages of processing their experiences."* A related concern is that the justice-involved woman is ready to receive help. Abuse is not easy for people to acknowledge or discuss, and it is highly stigmatized. Dr. Canning points out:

> ***"Sometimes volunteers need to hear stories of hope*** *or need to feel that they are helping. It's understandable and it's a natural motivation. But when we hear tragedy and harm to others, we want often to believe that they can heal and have something better for themselves. To convey an agenda or to try to turn the conversation toward where they can go in positive ways too quickly can really be a disservice."*

The cardinal rule for those working with abused women is that the helpers need help in monitoring their own well-being. It is impossible to listen effectively without proper training, beginning with the helper's ability to reflect on her own history.

Faith-based ministries need to have someone with whom to process these conversations during initial training and provide a person to process these conversations confidentially as they continue in their work. Clinical psychologists and physicians routinely process information that can be more disturbing than they thought with trusted individuals outside the conversation as a preventative for "Do no harm."

Shame, anger, fear, and depression are all common responses from abused women. When abuse is severe, the individual may have a hostile bias toward social interactions. Shame is common as people internalize their emotional and verbal abuse. Anger can lead to aggression or violence, especially if women felt that they were in love with abusers. Fear can result in being hyper-vigilant or overly anxious. Sadness reflects the anxiety or is seen when women panic or relive the experience.

The complexity of emotions that stem from past abuse may include ambivalence and the sense of abandonment as well. The sense of harm strikes at the heart of a person's sense of worth and sense of self. Dr. Canning continues:

> ***"We have to think psychologically*** *and even theologically about all these different emotions. Anger at injustice, anger at being harmed, anger at sometimes even yourself for maybe not avoiding a situation. Anger at another person for not protecting you, or anger at the person who harmed you. These (emotions) are very common and often indicate health. The intensity of the emotion can erupt if someone has not really processed or they've had invalidating experiences where they tried to talk about their abuse... I have many, many, many patients [for whom] the consequences of talking about what happened to them were so severe they were almost more harmful than the abuse itself."*

For these reasons Dr. Canning says, *"I would never force or apply pressure of any kind or make statements about how 'You really need to do that in order to move forward in your life'."* On the other hand, the justice-involved woman may express a concern about how these experiences are affecting her now—even experiences that would seem to have mild impact.

If the woman is concerned about it, then some sort of response is needed beyond soothing the person and keeping her safe. Ministries or correctional facilities need to have a plan for where workers can go with those kinds of needs and include this information in their training. Dr. Canning speaks from her caseload of why directive or specific responses should be the work of a professional clinician:

"Emotions around these things can be very intense. *On the other hand, it can be disconcerting as a listener to [see] … people are smiling and telling you the most horrific things; not a tear in their eye. That's not necessarily healthy. It could indicate that a person is way far down the road in their healing process and they've experienced post traumatic growth. Or it could indicate that they find it very difficult to access the emotions of things that they went through. Or they've had to toughen up so much just to survive…We would expect any of those kinds of presentations to be consistent with how abuse can affect a person on an emotional level and on a cognitive level."*

Good reflective listening is a simple way to keep conversation going. Sometimes things that have happened in the past are still affecting the justice-involved woman's health or well-being. There are several "red flags" to indicate that past abuse is impacting the woman's present and future. She may be experiencing nightmares or avoiding things she needs to engage in to move forward, to find a job, or be consistent with parole.

There may be substance use, or sexual problems. A common concern lies in the quality of relationships, since distrust can isolate the individual more than is healthy. Nonverbally conveying acceptance and learning a few questions to ask can be effective listening when victims of abuse are involved.

Thanking the woman for her openness and validating that the abuse was an important part of her life is more important that coming up with advice. Depending upon the focus of the chaplain, reentry worker or volunteer effort, effective listening might involve asking questions that lead to a future-orientation. *"What connection do you make, if any, between those past experiences and where you want to see yourself going in your future?"* or *"How would you hope that your life could be in that area going forward?"* enables workers to find important ways to gather information, and provide the appropriate referral for professional or spiritual counseling.

Dr. Canning has been doing research looking at literature specifically about women who are incarcerated for prostitution-related offenses (Schultz & Canning, 2018). Past abuse and criminal behavior affects families. However, she advises ministry workers to make no assumptions about the level of meaning the person ascribes to her parenting.

If a woman is separated unwillingly from her children, there is an attachment there and likely to be a lot of mixed feelings about how her incarceration is affecting the children. Common feelings of shame and guilt exist, but these women may also be dealing with depression and hopelessness about being able to repair relationships, get access to or custody of their children, or provide for them. Compounded by the difficulty of finding employment, being unable to keep the kids together is difficult. From a psychologist's point of view, Dr. Canning says:

> ***"Attachment to children can be a really motivating*** *and propelling force. That's one of the functions that we've seen in [research]. It can help people recover and transition and motivate them. It can also overwhelm people's coping resources. The chasm between what they want for the children in their life and their parenting … [is] so large, and they are so overwhelmed and feeling so hopeless about how to get there from where they are… Stigma, lack of opportunity, everything else that can actually erode people's progress and transition [cause] difficulty seeing the path from where they are to where they want to go."*

Professional counselors and physicians understand that if they are listening to stories of abuse, there is a well-recognized cycle. Ministry workers may find it difficult to understand why adult women who experience intimate partner violence return to their abuser. They may find it hard to resist expressions of surprise, blame, shame or condemnation, which can create defensiveness in the woman and kick off the abusive cycle again.

As part of their training, volunteers should receive some information to help their understanding of destructive cycles, as well as be given a few tools so they don't communicate unhelpful or hurtful messages. This training creates a place for acceptance and short-circuits burnout. Dr. Canning provides one final illustration of why counseling dealing with abuse rightly lies with trained chaplains and professional helpers:

"If these volunteers are potentially in a position *where they might be doing some informal counseling, even on a spiritual level, damage can be done when we quickly move over to notions of what's called for in roles... Often women and children have received messages in sermons or from churches, or from pastors and counselors about how they ought to obey or submit, sometimes even to actually physically abusive behavior. Or how they ought to forgive them when those actions are premature, before people really understand the meaning to that person. In these initial conversations or even after talking to someone a few times, we don't know them well enough to really estimate the impact of making these recommendations about forgiveness or possibly trying to frame what God might be doing in their life as a result of it. The potential for damage is high... We wouldn't want volunteers to feel like, 'Oh, I can't say anything spiritual...' but again, just that space for people to talk, validating what they've experienced – you can almost never go wrong there."*

On Stress, Trauma, and Resilience

Everyone has stress and in fact, physiologically, we need stress to keep us alive. Stress is a normal part of daily living that can protect us and help us work through difficult situations. There are several ways to think about stress (J. Aten, personal communication, October 18, 2018).

Acute stress tends to be episodic or event driven. This kind of stress intensifies and spikes but tends to even off over time. For example, many individuals show psychological symptoms of distress in the first weeks and months following a natural disaster. However, a year out only about 10 percent of that same population will have clinically recognizable symptoms of distress.

Chronic stress is the way people talk about issues of burnout or compassion fatigue. For some of the women transitioning from incarceration to society, there is likely to be chronic stress on top of acute stress. Dr. Aten points out:

"They're living in an environment *that at any point in time something could go wrong and wrong quickly and go wrong very badly. Then, on top of* *that is all the mental energy that it takes to navigate being incarcerated, just being within that system."*

For the justice-involved woman, chronic stress isn't new. They may have been living with this their entire life. "Red flags" that signal a bigger problem is when stress starts to interfere with daily life. There may be problems with relationships, or in their jobs. The woman may have problems taking care of herself or have problems in her spiritual life. When the individual starts to exhibit major swings in her life, this is telling. It may be seen in eating too much or too little. The woman may sleep a lot more and then suddenly not sleep at all. These signals may indicate that the normal stress we all experience has become an issue.

New research documents chronic stress within the communities we live in has a direct impact on our health. Stress concerning access to goods or resources has an impact on well-being that is intensified when personal safety is threatened on a daily basis from living in a high-crime area. Essentially even if you are not being mugged or have never been mugged, that possibility is still in the back of your head and has an impact on your well-being.

For some women, there is not just one event; in fact, their lives are not divided into a "before incarceration" and "after incarceration." Rather, **complex trauma** goes beyond the direct impact of an event (acute stress) or lifetime of personal struggle (chronic stress) and can have a cumulative effect. Disaster psychologist, Dr. Aten suggests:

"For some people, there's not a clear stake *in the road of a challenge they've had. It's been one trauma after the next. One of the reasons why they refer to it as 'complex trauma' is that you've got that on-going narrative. It's not post-traumatic stress disorder. The trauma—there's nothing past or post about it. It's still being lived out and within those settings. The other part is that those traumas tend to interact with one another over time as well... We know that if you've gone through a prior trauma, you're more likely to experience a higher level of trauma the next time something really bad happens to you."*

While people commonly think of **resilience** as the ability to bounce back after difficult times, it is best understood as an individual's capacity to withstand stressful events. While some psychologists believe resilience is a personality trait that can be seen in even a young child, resilience can be learned. The thinking is that once you have navigated some problem, you can learn how to get through other tough situations and discover strengths that you can later rely on again.

Dr. Aten gives the example of how in times of physical disaster, sometimes elderly people who are more at risk to be physically hurt have lower levels of psychological distress than their millennial counterparts. Theory suggests that part of this is because they have been there. They know the world's not over just because they have lost belongings. They have a different perspective of life and can learn from the past.

Resilience, which is sometimes called **grit**, can also be cultivated by fostering a sense of self-efficacy. Helping justice-involved women to reflect on their experiences—and just showing up as a survivor of abuse—helps them recognize their own strength. As Dr. Aten told one of his clients who had a horrific background of trauma and difficulty:

> ***"The fact that you're here*** *and that you're able to know what you've been through and are trying to push forward and that you continue despite all this, you really have a strong sense of resilience. You just keep pushing forward."*

Research supports the idea that rethinking weakness as strength can help justice-involved women create a different narrative, and therefore find purpose in their struggles.

On the other hand, some caution is advisable. The way we view resilience is often unrealistic. Most people who go through a significant hardship—a health crisis, loss of a loved one, a natural disaster—need time to rebound, often much more time that we think. Sometimes people can bounce back, but that may be because the stress was not a major event or the individual had the right capacity to deal with it.

For most people, however, it takes a lot longer. Providing social and spiritual support can have a major positive impact on well-being. Dr.

Aten cited statistical scales that measure how people think about God in the aftermath of a calamity. It was found that those who felt positively supported by their spiritual community fared better both emotionally and spiritually. It was not a question of "How much therapy did you get?" or how high the volunteer's empathy rating was. Rather, it was a matter of how much individuals felt people in their faith community cared about them and helped them make sense of what they had experienced. "Were they there for you? Could you count on them?"

A ministry of presence (Aten et al, 2015) emphasizes meeting practical needs. Christians tend to be effective once they perceive a need for help, and work to meet that need. Christians are also good at walking beside someone who is suffering and checking in to see if these women are all right. Both actions are important in creating a "practical presence" with justice-involved women.

However, practical helps are more important than platitudes. Knowing what to do when somebody is really opening up is less important than knowing what to say—and being present will actually speak louder than any words you say. Women who are transitioning out of incarceration need one-on-one help, but also need to consider the broader issues that contributed to their pathway of crime or that pain will keep happening. Focus on the acute reason that the person needs help, without neglecting more chronic or complex issues that have brought that person to you in the first place. In short, intervention occurs on multiple levels. According to Dr. Aten:

> ***"I can help people not feel so overwhelmed...*** *because sometimes it can be like, 'Where do I even start?' Ask the person what they need most help with right now. What is that most basic need that they have? One of the things that a number of our studies have shown is that the physical, the spiritual, the emotional, and the social parts of who we are as humans are all interconnected... If I have lost my home, you can imagine I'm going to feel stressed. We know that somebody who's lost their home is more likely to feel that God is not in control, and maybe have more anger toward God. Then, on top of that, somebody who's lost their home is probably going to be more likely to develop depression and then*

isolate themselves socially.

If somebody comes alongside me, helps me rebuild my home, that's going to reduce my stress. It's going to give me social contact. Oftentimes, we hear people that we've done interviews with talk about that they for the first time saw God in their lives through the helpers that came to their aid. 'Now you've helped me with my spiritual life, too.' Whatever that most basic need is, meet that and trust that God's going to help work through that person's entire life."

Questions for Reflection

1. How does understanding trauma impact your ministry?
2. How can you create a "ministry of presence" within your ministry?

11

Spiritual Formation

"Their incarceration is not just about their crime... *I'll say, 'Your crime is what got you here, but what led up to that is what I'm the most interested in. How did you get to this point?' And that's important to know... What led up to this? What led up to these choices that you made? Then helping them find the pathway to healing, repentance; understanding that God loves you, that this is not the end of your life. God forgives you. You can start again. [Prison] is just a place where you can bring a lot of hope. The other thing that I would say to anybody who wants to be in prison ministry is... It takes a lot of discernment... to know that they're running game and still be able to love them but be able to call them out on it. They know that I am not going to play around, and if you want to play around it's not going to work out with the chaplain. But see, that's what draws them in; that's what they like. They want somebody to care about them like that. A lot of our younger ones raised themselves. Even though they fight it, what they really want is somebody to help them set boundaries."*

– Chaplain

Although some who work with justice-involved women have given up on the possibility of real change after a lifetime of abuse and complex trauma, chaplains and reentry workers see evidence of growth. This is because their work is centered in spiritual formation that leads to healing and hope. Within the Christian tradition, spiritual formation is the process of change at the innermost part of what it means to be human: the heart. It comes from a relationship with Jesus, and the **redemptive process** of forming the inner human world so that it takes on the inner character of Christ himself (Foster, 2008).

This goes far beyond human effort. What is essential to spiritual formation is life with Jesus, an interactive relationship with the great God of the universe that leads to inner transformation into Christ likeness. In sum, the Christian idea of spiritual formation is very simply the **forming, conforming,** and **transforming** of the human personality—body, mind, and spirit—into the likeness of Jesus Christ. This process and the role of the chaplain in spiritual formation is the focus of this chapter.

Spiritual Formation

Spirituality is "a relationship with God, or whatever is held to be the Ultimate (for example, a set of sacred texts for Buddhists) that fosters a sense of meaning, purpose, and mission in life. This relationship produces fruit (such as altruism, love, or forgiveness), which has a discernible effect on an individual's relationship to self, nature, others, and the Ultimate" (Hodge, 2001, p. 204).

> ***"Spiritual formation in the tradition of Jesus** Christ is the process of transformation of the inmost dimension of the human being, the heart, which is the same as the spirit or will. It is being formed (really, transformed) in such a way that its natural expression comes to be the deeds of Christ done in the power of Christ. When we talk about spiritual formation, we are talking about framing a progression of life in which people come to actually do all things that Jesus taught. We biblically and systematically form a people whose character reflects Christ. A person who sees the world and people through the lens of Scripture makes right choices, with love, joy, peace, patience, gentleness, goodness, kindness, faithfulness, and self-control"* (Willard, n.d.).

Christian formation is a divine-human partnership. God initiates the relationship, and we respond by loving him. The Holy Spirit lives in us and changes us as we respond to God in a posture of humility and dependence.

Components of Christian Formation

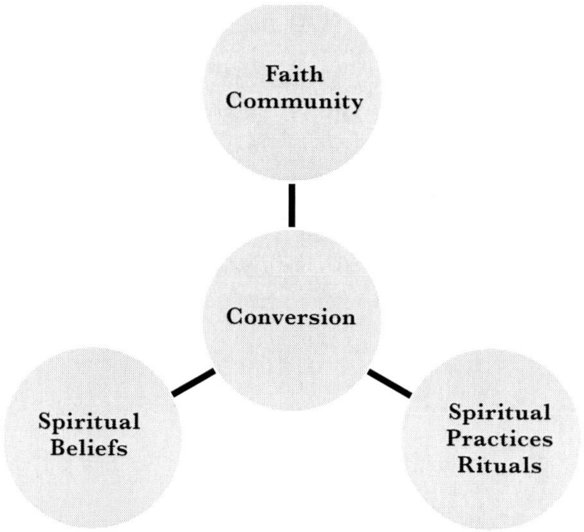

Conversion. Christian formation begins with conversion or initiating a personal relationship with God. "Conversion is the act of believing in Jesus, choosing to follow Jesus and being united with Jesus as Lord and Savior... it is the human response to the saving work of God through Christ" (Smith, 2001, p. 16).

Conversion is more than a "spiritual experience." It is where the person is "born again," becoming a "new creation." There is a radical transformation of one's values, worldview, and life course. Some justice-involved women may have a history of religious grounding and conversion experience, fallen away, and then recommitted their life to Christ. Either conversion or recommitment to conversion is critical for the individual's relationship with God.

Spiritual formation is not optional or only for the "super Christians", but required of all followers of Christ (Willard, 2006). It is not just for personal benefit with God but affects all relationships. Spiritual transformation is "the process by which Christ is formed in us...for the glory of God, for the abundance of our own lives, and for the sake of others" (Barton, 2011).

***"It is a journey into becoming persons** of compassion, persons who forgive, persons who care deeply for others and the world, persons who offer themselves to God to become agents of divine grace in the lives of others and their world—in brief, persons who love and serve as Jesus did"* (Mulholland, 1993, p. 25).

Spiritual formation is not information overload but ongoing renewal of the heart. It is not behavioral modification or self-actualization.

Conversion is foundational for Christian formation, but "the simple claim of being 'born again' has no inherent likelihood of leading the claimant to a crime-free existence" (Johnson, 2011, p. 158). Conversion is initiated and enabled by God and is evidenced through a transformed life of becoming more Christ-like.

This is accomplished through discipleship. A disciple is a student of their teacher. For Christians, converts are students of Jesus. In Jesus' Great Commission, to disciple is explained as "to teach them everything I have commanded you." Discipleship is not a program, but "an intentional relationship in which we walk along-side other disciples in order to encourage, equip, and challenge one another in love to grow toward maturity in Christ" (Ogden, 2003, p. 139).

Discipleship doesn't just happen. The great omission from the great commission is that Christians generally don't have a plan for teaching people to do everything they are commanded to do (Willard, 2006). One model is to assist others to develop *spiritual beliefs*, engage in *spiritual practices* and become part of a *faith community*.

Spiritual beliefs. In the Christian tradition, the Bible is the authority of life. Knowing the main tenants of the faith, especially the character of God, facilitates feeling loved, finding meaning and peace, and coping with life. Knowing that God is holy, loving, compassionate, forgiving, omnipresent, omniscient, sovereign, and wise facilitates feeling loved and not alone; the ability to cope with life.

Unbiblical teaching about the character of God, salvation and sin, and legalism creates **spiritual abuse**. Spiritual abuse can also come from marginalizing women, misusing sacred text (Scripture), speaking falsely for God, manipulation, or spiritual confusion.

One woman in a faith-based program asked if she had to give up her medication to become a Christian. Her chaplain was teaching that Christians should not take medication for emotional issues, because God will meet those needs. Spiritual confusion can come in the form of hearing different denominational beliefs or merging different religious beliefs in forming their own religion. Another example of spiritual abuse is within religions that support marriage over safety, prompting women to stay in an abusive marriage.

Appropriately conveying spiritual beliefs means being intentional about "teaching them all things" by focusing on the tenets of the faith, how they are viewed by God, and how to live the Christian life. Some women struggle with feelings of abandonment by God, being unworthy of Him, or fear he is punishing them. They may have a fatalistic view because there is nothing they can do; God is beyond their reach. Misperceptions and ignorance about God are countered by learning Biblical truth. This knowledge can be relied on to counter lies they face in life.

Spiritual practices. Spiritual practices include prayer, reading and reflecting on Scripture, meditation, worship, and partaking in the sacraments of religious ceremonies. Engaging in spiritual practices or rituals promotes hope, peace, and forgiveness. They help develop relationships with God and others. Studies suggest engaging in spiritual practices may help women adjust to prison life (Levitt & Loper, 2009).

Women rated praying, their relationships with God and Jesus, reading the Bible, and attendance at religious services as more helpful than their family, friends, work, education, and psychiatric programs in facilitating their adjustment to prison. Their belief in a "higher power" or "divine being" helps women cope with their traumatic past, their volatile emotions, and the uncertainty of their future (Clear et al, 2000). Religious activity helps women make meaning and provides intrinsic motivation to desist from criminal activity (Duncan et al, 2018).

In sum, spiritual practices facilitate dealing with the emotional strains of incarceration and dealing with guilt. Religious faith provides relief – the forgiveness of sins and strength to deal with their problems. It enables justice-involved women to take personal responsibility and find a new way of life. Their faith has changed them, creating an active role of God in their lives and giving them a way to deal with the loss of freedom, family, and friends.

Faith community. The faith community provides a sense of positive interaction and group membership otherwise absent in prison life. Christianity, Islam, Judaism, and other faiths command followers to practice religious rituals in a group setting. A spiritual community is vital for a new convert. To immerse herself in the family of faith enables the justice-involved woman to realize spiritual growth and sustainability. The failure of an alleged convert to connect intimately with a congregation is a "recipe for disaster" (Johnson, 2011, p. 157).

The resources of a spiritual community include "increased empowerment, realization of personal strengths, coping ability, self-confidence, lovability, and sense of belonging" (Hodge, 2001, p. 209). The family of faith can come in the form of church, faith-based small groups such as Bible study or support groups, prayer meetings, mentors, discipleship relationships, and spiritual friendships. Faith community can be with peers, volunteers, ministry workers, chaplains, and family.

> ***"Prison chaplains and volunteers** make a valuable contribution to the lives of women in prison and to the correctional system; the prosocial support/modeling and diverse help with meaning-making they offer in prison has a positive influence on the women's journey of desistance in the community after prison"* (Duncan et al, 2018, p.1).

The faith community can be a place of support or a place of spiritual abuse. Spiritual abuse may be the use of the faith community, beliefs, and/or religious practices to coerce, control, or damage another. A faith community that is judgmental, legalistic and creates a culture of shame is abusive.

For example, one group of jail residents identified their experiences within their church community by answering the question, "How does your church feel about you?" Among their responses: *"I will always be judged." "I am always watched and followed." "No one will ever trust me in my church." "I feel more shame when my church does not accept me." "I don't have a lot in common with the congregation." "I felt like I was in a pit." "There's a 'sour' face when you tell someone you were in jail."* One woman whose crime was sex with an underage male recalled returning to her home church and being made to sit in the balcony with an escort. Churches do need to be diligent about protection of their congregants but may use restrictive ways to provide accountability and restore the person back into the family of faith.

The Role of the Chaplain in Spiritual Formation and Healing

There are few data-driven studies focused on chaplains working with women in jails and prison ministries, and these are limited in terms of both number of people studied and geographic location. Therefore, the Institute of Prison Ministries (IPM) initiated interviews with 12 chaplains working with justice-involved women. One male and 11 females clarified perceptions of prison culture and ministry issues. From their responses, a survey representing chaplains' training and experiences was developed, and to which 44 chaplains responded.

In addition, a survey of prison ministry organizations yielded another 50 responses highlighting priorities in their work. These responses referenced practices in 32 states that capture some of the challenges and rewards of working with justice-involved women. Outsiders' perceptions of prison culture and ministry issues showed broad engagement in the healing process.

> ***"Once they hit their unit,*** *our goal is to prepare them for release, because they've already done their time. Our goal is to key in on them, help them deal with those issues, and to help them to get free from those issues and those bondages, and have them to begin to look at their past life. In that sense, also help them to adjust to transitioning from being incarcerated to being free. To help them to change their mindset, and basically to give them hope; that is the goal."*
>
> – Chaplain

Another way this goal was illustrated was in holistic patterns of behavior.

***"It's all about showing them compassion...** Some of these women have never been shown compassion and love, and they don't know what a healthy relationship is. They don't know what it's like to be loved and for people to look at them for who God made them to be and not for what they've done. When you show that compassion, and you take time with them, and you sit down and you look them in the eyes… Not just 'I'm talking to you and you're just a number'. No. 'You mean something to me, and I'm concerned about your soul'. Even when I've talked to the women that are not of my faith, I really take time with them. That really, really blows them away.*

So that is what is very key to me, that they get foundationally rooted and grounded. And as I tell them, 'If you don't remember anything else, remember that God loves you… There's nothing that can separate you from the love of God. So when you get out there and you falter and you fall (and that is going to happen from time to time), you just repent and you get up, and you continue in your walk. Don't go backwards.'"

– Chaplain

One of the challenges of working in a faith-based program is facing skepticism from justice-involved women who do not recognize spiritual formation as a valid goal.

***"This makes a difference in the women's lives.** When women come into the program, they realize how difficult it is to follow the rules, think differently and change their lives so they quit before the miracle happens. The women that quit end up in a relationship with another woman or a fight and end up in lock down."*

– Chaplain

However, spiritual goals can work in tandem with institutional goals to create real change.

***"It's all in a way to say,** 'Hey, let's start looking at life differently. There are different coping mechanisms than just going out and getting stoned or running away.*

There are different ways that you can handle life's problems. There are different ways that you can cope with your anger'—those types of things... We actually have very similar goals to what probation has, except on our side God is going to be the one that's going to come in. He's going to bring the equipping and he's going to bring the training, and he's going to be bringing the change of thinking that is required. We always want to impress that upon the Probation Department."

– Chaplain

In interviews, chaplains spoke realistically of their workday within the jail or prison.

***"The challenge that I have [is] the courts** and the administrative work, and all those things. What I've learned is that I have to do my administrative work in the morning and do my counseling and crisis counseling in the evening or the afternoon. Now there's days that I come in with intentions on doing one thing, and then if a man or a woman has a crisis in their family—they have a death, their family's calling or they're just going through some things—all my administrative work has to go to the side. And sometimes I spend 45 minutes to an hour with one person, because I don't want them to leave my office, leave the chapel, without being able to release all their frustrations, or at least get them on the path. There is my main frustration."*

– Chaplain

When chaplains are at odds with prison administrators or the courts, they walk a fine line between faith issues, meeting the needs of the women, and more apathetic community members.

***"To be honest with you,** as a chaplain what I get all the time is grievances filed. I have my rights to practice my faith. When they go into the courtroom and they have a public defender that is just trying to get the next case done, not really fighting for them, and they want that faith-based rehab, they never pull that card. That's my right to my faith. Really, that could change the world.*

An area that needs to be focused on to help these people... It's just recidivism, the recycling. I work really hard with women. I can sense they're in the life. I bridge them to sex trafficking organizations. We try to get them into those programs. We have more success with that because they're working with the police department too, so they have another advocate on their side helping them. As far as programming and things like that, I really try to meet them where they're at. We run probably 140 classes a month. We offer the full church services weekly, but midweek I do [alternative programming] because it's meeting them where they're at."

– Chaplain

With differing goals and roles, chaplains talked about both positive and negative experiences with other workers inside and outside of the correctional institution.

"We have a lot of freedom *and a lot of favor, but still many times you have to work with line staff and sometimes you can get a frustrating relationship … or you get line staff that really doesn't value the ministry as part of a positive program... Overall, sometimes just being seen—especially since we've been there for over 30 years—having our specific team being seen as part of the treatment team and being seen that what we do actually does change hearts, and minds, and lives… 'Change the way that you think and then that will change the way that you behave' and that's what the Lord's all about: transforming our minds… It's just [difficult] working within the confines of the probation system."*

– Chaplain

Chaplains play an important role with others within the facility, sometimes with unexpected methods and sensitivity. Often overlooked and underpaid, correctional officers have more face time with incarcerated women than chaplains do.

"I'm doing presentations on compassion fatigue *and moral distress because you can feel it. When you go from the medical field back into corrections, because I was flip-flopping every other day, I felt like I was on vacation in the hospital because… Corrections is so heavy. It's like depression. It's there all the time, so you don't realize how long-term it's weighing on them* *as staff or inmates. I debrief the inmates when we have suicides and … they just hang on him and weep. That's all part of healing, that they need that, and the officers need it, too. That's another area that dog therapy has been relevant because we debrief staff too. An officer won't open up, but I'll see them trying to get [the dog] to come by them. When they start petting him, then they start talking and they get it out. It's just different tools to use in your tool kit."*

– Chaplain

Even with success, the fact that women are coming in and out of jail and prison can be confusing and demoralizing. Not all chaplains find their calling within this work.

"I felt like on the inside *that I was beating the walls, teaching and praying and helping and supporting and some of those ladies who had the greatest responses were cycling back in. When I would talk to them, they would often drop their head and say, 'Well you know, I really had nowhere to go. I went back into the same environment, among the same people.' I began to think, it just seems to make so much sense that we would have somewhere for them to go. There's got to be more thought into this process, that if we're working on this side, that the outside has to collaborate, and there has to be this partnership. That was sort of the beginning.*

Now I work in victim services. I made this incredible journey from being on the yard, serving every day, working with women every day, helping them work through just the transition in and the process of being there. Then the transition out and what that looks like, to actually working with the people whom they have caused harm and pain to. What has happened in my career in that regard is something called "balance", this crazy balance that you would never expect to have, and most of the time, most prison workers don't have because they strictly work with offenders… They're not really engaged with the victim aspect, whereas through a course of events, I end up serving the victims of our state that are tied to the offenders that are in prisons in our state. It's amazing work, very much like chaplaincy work. Very, very fulfilling, but always working with broken individuals who have been impacted by crime."

– Victim services staff

The survey collected responses from a separate group of 44 chaplains, including 39 who worked in state institutions, two in federal correctional sites, and three employed in for-profit institutions. Nineteen surveys came from male chaplains; 25 surveys were completed by female chaplains.

At least 17 of the chaplains worked in a facility that had a faith-based pod or dorm unit. More than two-thirds of the chaplains were white; the next largest group was comprised of five black or African American women. In our survey, we found a well-educated population: 22 percent of the respondents had college degrees. Another 16 percent completed some post-graduate coursework along with their four-year degree, 31 percent had a post-graduate or professional degree, and three chaplains held doctorates.

From interviews and survey responses, there were two strong, positive patterns mentioned by chaplains that contributed to their high level of satisfaction. First, female inmates came across as open, genuine, motivated, and willing to talk. They were perceived overall as nurturers, and more engaged with others. (*"They'll talk about deep issues without the reticence I'm used to with people outside the prison. They will seek reconciliation with one another, and they learn some things about how to do that while they're in prison."*)

The second positive attribute is the number who were seeking reconciliation, which lead to reconnections with a professed faith in Christ, successful returns to families, and impact as leaders in their units. (*"Some of the positive experiences that I have had is hearing about the very traumatizing life these women have had and God using me to motivate them to change or to see something different about their life. To watch God heal them from their trauma is absolutely remarkable"*). The connection between positive attitudes and a healthier future is strongly connected, as one chaplain noted: *"Those who react to the gospel get better; those who do not generally remain the same or get worse."*

Negative aspects of the chaplain's role were first seen in the (*"daunting"*) difficulty justice-involved women have in making big life changes. *"The biggest frustration has been those who have struggled not finding the aftercare they needed and as a result… died in their addiction. Such a loss of potential talent and mission for Christ."*

Chaplains saw this failure impacted by personal traits and characteristics, including a lack of personal responsibility, and "faking faith" for gain.

Several chaplains were concerned about younger inmates who seemed out of control, harder to reach, disrespectful, or exhibiting a "want it now" demeanor. (*"The women that are coming in are much younger than ever before… There are so many more fights, and attempts with suicide. Because they are young, it's very difficult for them to realize or recognize that they need to change their life. They get caught up very easily in the drama that is going on in the prison, so not as many women are interested anymore in coming to faith programs."*)

Among negative institutional concerns is the lack of recognition of religious programming as important (*"They fail to look at us with the same 'evidence-based' lens that drives everything else"*), the inability to talk openly about religious differences, and correctional officers who fail to see female inmates as worthy of grace. In assessing their clients and resources, 93 percent of the chaplains taking the survey agreed that the services and programs offered were relevant to the needs of the women.

There was less agreement, however, that the financial and physical resources to do the job well were available. The need for more resources—space (*"A chapel or holy place, meeting rooms… due to the demographic location of the facility, targeted women-based programs are difficult to organize."*) and donations (*"Due to the drug issues, we are now greatly limited in our outside resources that can come in as donations. We were always very well stocked but are now struggling"*) were issues.

The interviews and surveys raised some issues to be addressed. Noteworthy was the need for society—and especially churches—to welcome back formerly incarcerated women to their communities. Most programming is focused on preparing the women to reenter society, but little to nothing is done to prepare the church or community to welcome these women home. According to one chaplain, *"Society must welcome back and support those returning, and the Church has the first responsibility to model forgiveness, the dignity of the human person in the felon, and to do more than say, 'Be warm'."*

A second concern raised was addressing the needs of women in a system built for men. One warden explains that women's correctional facilities are shifting to more of a human service type of field from a punitive incarceration mindset. The focus is on evidence-based practices and having what is deemed to be the right program that provides the needed outcomes. According to one prison administrator, *"We'll select programs and assessments like that as opposed to homegrown programming or gut feeling."*

Addressing the needs of women in prison might include more addiction beds, decriminalizing addictions, interventions for abuse, and greater support for the women's children. While overall positive, surveyed chaplains felt that prison culture among staff and inmates changed as the female population has increased.

A third concern is the need for more Christian volunteers with greater confidence and appropriate training. According to one person, *"Our volunteers need to manage their class with confidence—and respect authority themselves."* Finally, the need for on-going training and education in corrections care and spiritual formation is essential.

> ***"I really think the standard of chaplains*** *has to be raised. I'll tell you why. Because correctional facilities are hiring pastors that are just taking it as a second job; social workers, maintenance workers too. There's no respect for a trained chaplain. If you understand a professional chaplain and the years it takes to become one, it can change a whole program because you come in equipped, because this is your church. That's your church that the Lord has given you to minister to. Then it needs to bridge to the outside body. What has been the most frustrating for me is to see the inmates shortchanged, and the staff. There's this misconception out there that you can't minister to inmates and staff. Yes, you can, if you're trained. You absolutely can."*
>
> – Chaplain

The individuals who took the survey completed a series of questions about themselves and their perceptions of strengths and weaknesses in "typical" ministry encounters. One third of the chaplains did not feel well trained for their position, and more than half wanted the opportunity for more training.

***"I have a desperate need to understand** trauma now because I know that's where they've come from, because they've shared stuff with me that infuriates, sickens, and frightens me all at the same time about things that are in their past. Every time I have an opportunity to learn about trauma, trauma healing and those areas of focus, I'm now trying to gain knowledge in order to assist them specifically."*

– Chaplain

All interview and survey participants felt their role as chaplain made a difference in others' lives. More than 80 percent felt their position within the correction facility was used well, and they had opportunity to interact with others (82 percent). The majority of chaplains responding to the survey said stress and burnout, keeping healthy boundaries with inmates, getting women to attend programs and classes, having volunteer and staff resources to do the job well, and having enough communication with correctional staff and supervisor were not problematic.

***"I think that going into jail is probably** one of the most wonderful experiences I've ever had in my life. I'm never exhausted… to get to be able to go in and give women hope, give them the ability to know that they are special in spite of what's happened to them; that they are not what they did. That they've made mistakes, but we can… try and restore the dignity to some of these women."*

– Chaplain

Perhaps the most telling fact coming out of the chaplain survey results is that a full 84 percent would recommend this career to others.

***"Every day I go there it's a new experience.** I have been gifted with the ability not to internalize the depravity of some of the women's lives that I hear and that I see. God has just been gracious to me and when I leave, I'm able to go home and not think about what I've heard or what I've seen… Those that work in this industry know some of the horrible things that have happened to the inmates prior to them becoming incarcerated. It's more awful for the women because of the sexual violence a lot of them experienced…*

I don't have the words to explain how wonderful it is to get to do this, to get to be able to go in and give women hope, give them the ability to know that they are special in spite of what's happened to them. That they are not what they did. That they've made mistakes, but we can fix that and try and restore the dignity to some of these women."

– Chaplain

Questions for Reflection

1. What are the spiritual goals of your ministry, and how intentional are you about pursuing them?
2. How can we develop a healthy faith community inside the jail or prison and in the community where they can be welcomed and loved?

12

A Primer on Volunteers

***"The volunteers that come into the prison** with the programs … gave me some comfort, and some encouragement, and that was what kept me going. There were people that did care, despite how bad the situation looked, or how bad it really was in the building, or with some of the staff and things: there were people that did care… People were praying for me... so I turned to God, and I believe God placed these people in my path for a reason."*

– Formerly incarcerated woman

In the summer of 2018, the Institute of Prison Ministries (IPM) initiated interviews with over 30 volunteers and collected 471 surveys from ministry workers across the country. This chapter demonstrates the exceptional dedication of volunteers represented in our survey and personal interviews, as well as the challenges they face.

Volunteer Motivations

Nonprofit organizations in America rely on volunteers to accomplish their mission. When people give time or money to aid others, they act on their values and human need to belong and contribute to others in community. This gives them a sense of connection with the future as well as immediate help for the individual or ministry goals.

"Serve the Mission, Save the Life"

Although there are few studies available on volunteers working in female prison ministries, the best predictor of service is the volunteer's religious values. For volunteers who self-identify as Christians, serving others is a way of living out a personal faith consistent with their calling.

Visiting the incarcerated as well as caring for their needs after release is an extension of Christian purpose. Says one volunteer, *"Being a witness for Christ means to show up and let God do His amazing work and all are rewarded—the volunteers and the participants."*

Echoed in the words of another volunteer, *"My goal is to train the ladies to trust Jesus for everything by helping them know Him personally. Joy is when one accepts Him as Lord … and then works through her hurts, habits and hang-ups, inside [prison] and outside, too."*

> ***"I am an advocate for God*** *and the life change He can make in the most downtrodden, guilt ridden individuals. I believe strongly in second and third chances. I believe some of us were born into a failed life from birth. I believe society let a lot of women down and did not protect them as they should have been protected. I believe in rehabilitation and the love of Christ shown through a volunteer."*
>
> –Jail Volunteer

Volunteering activities reinforce the individual's values in other ways. As one prison volunteer observed, *"Even though I have not been incarcerated, I feel at a point in my past that my mind was imprisoned. Receiving Christ and allowing my mind to be transformed has empowered me to help others overcome."*

Another volunteer pointed out, *"It is a challenging ministry in a sense that I have so much compassion for each woman. I wish that I could take each one of their places. I receive such a tremendous reward in serving them anyway I can."* Team members project other values as well, for example: *"Forgiveness is extremely important for volunteers as well as prisoners."*

Similarly, one long-term volunteer remarked: *"Meeting the women right where they are and sharing the love and forgiveness of Jesus Christ is as rewarding to us as a volunteer as it is to each of the inmates."* However, a number of volunteers were once incarcerated, and in this sense, correctional ministry remains part of their identity.

> ***"I was inmate [number]*** *and [this ministry] saved my life. I have had a lot of health issues [that have prevented me from volunteering] since I have been*

> *home. But I so hope and pray that I will be back inside the gate soon. These women and men are people just like all of us. They deserve to be treated and respected and know that God's love will help them during this time of their life. Being in prison is the hardest thing I ever had to go through, but it's saved my life and made me a better person. It takes each one to reach one to teach one. If we don't give back what we were given the healing process will not work."*
>
> – Prison Volunteer

Volunteers see lives changed, and this is highly motivational. According to one, *"The chance to bring hope and light to despair and darkness is such a wonderful gift from the Lord. We have seen lives changed for eternity – what an amazing thing!"* Another volunteer asserts, *"The women are hungry for what God offers … hope, forgiveness, and love … and it is a joy to offer it and observe how the Holy Spirit meets their needs."*

Another stated, *"It is rewarding serving in this volunteer program. All these ladies who are incarcerated have souls and that is what this is all about; winning them to Jesus. I feel my time is not wasted by having the opportunity to share God's love."* Many volunteers had stories like this one to illustrate:

> ***"I mentored a woman addicted*** *who had lived on streets since she was 13 years old. Her parents were addicts. She is now in her 30s. This inmate received Jesus as her Savior. She came to value herself, passed her GED, achieved the highest grade and is now knowing all things are possible through God for her. She is presently pursuing a degree while she serves time at a state facility. [Before ministry] this beautiful broken woman had no hope, no value, no worth… Presently she is a priceless Bride of Jesus Christ who knows her future is glorious."*

However, correctional ministry volunteers are often confronted by the needs and injustices they see. Chief among the observed needs are a lack of staff and resources. *"It is hard not to have a chaplain at our jail at this time. I pass the book cart and every time there are less and less books available from the chaplain's office. It is discouraging not to see the books back on the shelf."*

Another perceived unfairness lies in a lack of programs. *"The longer you work in prison ministry or jail ministry [the more] you see the lack of programs that are going to produce any success for these people. That makes it hard when you yourself are facilitating a program where you see change happen in people's lives, but you know that we can only allow 25 women in our group."*

As one volunteer testified, *"I work with women in the prison. Thus far, I've encountered women who have asked for and WAITED numerous months for religious mentors. There clearly are not enough women who are able to volunteer for this ministry."* Within the prison structure there are other roadblocks.

> ***"Just the loopholes,*** *and then the over-crowdedness of our systems ...the disarray or disorganization that sometimes happens when we're reaching out for certain services. It's like, okay, it's there but we can't get it, because we need this, and we need that... The trickiness... can be incredibly frustrating when you're serving such a high or at-risk population."*

It is easy to forget that the priority for staff is security and safety, rather than individual programs. Other volunteers put blame on the church and ask for more investment in the volunteers and their ministry to overcome the perceived needs and injustices.

> ***"I think the church today doesn't quite understand*** *what it means to pick up your cross. These people are broken, and when they come to find Christ, the church inside, there is nothing like it. The church outside falls very short... [The women] admit how sinful they are. They don't deserve mercy. But I've never seen such love, not only for each other by these people, but the love for me. They don't have any masks on, whereas one will go to church and say, 'I'm fine'. [Volunteers shouldering these crosses] need to be encouraged and embraced..."*

"Strengthen Self Identity and Grow as a Person"

While a sense of calling was the number one motivator, survey respondents often cited the effect the experience of volunteering has on individuals. Volunteering produces direct and tangible rewards for the person who helps, as well as those receiving help. These rewards can be highly personal for each worker. One volunteer expressed the reward she received from helping: *"The feedback from incarcerated women at the prison is always positive. I am continually amazed at the outpouring of thanks and gratitude."*

Another claims a tangible reward in that "working in this ministry has changed my life and given me a greater sense of purpose." A long-time volunteer admits, *"I feel at times that I have learned more from them than they may have learned from me."*

Volunteer experiences can impact identity in other ways. Some studies indicate that volunteers tend to have more diversity in friendships, a higher level of education, greater intensity of religious belief, increased involvement within informal social networking, and more formal group engagement among volunteers (Ertas, 2014). This testimony bears witness to the extended impact volunteering can have on identity and engagement.

> ***"I have been volunteering in the adult detention center.*** *A year ago, I received my Certificate of Correctional Ministries from the Institute of Prison Ministries. Now I'm serving as a commissioned lay chaplain teaching bible study to women on a weekly basis. I am currently on track for certification from the Trauma Healing Institute [and] co-facilitating an eight-week class at a church. [I recently] attended two closing services sponsored by another local prison ministry and am in my 10th year of involvement with a children's home [overseas]. And I just confirmed the leader of a jail and prison ministry with a vision to connect local volunteers to [other ministries] where there is a need."*
>
> —Chaplain

Volunteering gives individuals an opportunity to reflect more intentionally and over extended periods on their own experiences.

> ***"I think those who sin much love much,*** *and their relationship with God is deep. So many times I will say to myself, 'My church is the church inside'. I do talk to my pastor about that, because we as the church get so caught up in materialism and things, we don't think we're that bad. We don't understand God's love and respond to that with a gratefulness and total commitment."*

Another volunteer, concerned about her own nervousness and lack of confidence in correctional ministry, was unsure as to whether she would be able to handle the emotional work. As she reflected on her experience:

> ***"I feel very strongly that programs to support women*** *in prison are tremendously important for their personal growth and well-being. Most of them have such low self-esteem and are struggling with issues of addiction, abuse, self-harming, mental health challenges, loss of children… they need programs at every level that will build up their sense of self. Some of them have amazing gifts that they are not even aware of. I have met some of the most inspiring women behind bars, each with a unique voice and story. Meeting and more importantly getting to know many of the women with whom I have interacted over the past three years has been life changing for me.*

Another volunteer tells of a woman in her ministry who is imprisoned for life, but whose powerful voice and work to inspire other women in prison to be better has been a personal encouragement.

> ***"She has helped many of them*** *with their own appeals and is participating in a mentor program for younger women. She writes and speaks eloquently about what prison ministry has meant in her life, and you cannot be around her without feeling the depth of her faith… She remains a person whose courage and strength behind bars is uplifting to those of us with whom she interacts monthly as to her sisters in prison."*

Notably, long-term volunteers often have family and friends whose life and volunteer experience influenced their level of involvement.

> ***"My 80-year old mentor*** *has been going into prison for 50 years now, writing and leading her own Bible Studies, and often being the only female volunteer there on a Wednesday night, going to all three units. She's my hero and is truly a faithful servant to God. The inmates love her."*

A similar pattern of family or teacher/mentor influence is seen in young adults who are positively engaged as volunteers. However, millennial engagement tends to be more self-serving. For them, volunteering is not only as a way of helping others but a means to develop practical or professional experience. Given prison population demographics, it was sobering to see that in our survey of 471 people, only three individuals were under 30 years of age and nine respondents were in their thirties.

Volunteers in our study noted that programs outside of Bible study, prayer, and discipleship were not connected to the underlying problems the women still face in their ability to establish and maintain healthy relationships. They do not use skills that are needed to contribute to their community, family, and church.

> ***"Finding employment for women with a felony*** *background isn't easy, so getting them those certifications, which Corrections is trying to bring in more, is important. But regardless of how able and ready they are to work, if they don't work on their addiction, codependency, toxic relationships, the sex industry—they don't learn how to teach people how to treat them."*

When dedicated and satisfied volunteers are able to make a connection, it is especially satisfying.

> ***"It's a rare privilege to see the Holy Spirit transform*** *women's lives, right in front of me. I see them going from despair to hope, making vulnerable, open connections with the volunteers and each other. When they 'get it' that they are loved and worthy, their attitude really changes. One Trans woman shared how she had been beaten by her family after going to church each week. When she saw a bunch of older white women Friday night, she wasn't sure what our reaction would be. However, she said she felt complete love and acceptance from us. I glow with God's love after each team training meeting and prison weekend. While we can't stay on the mountain top all the time, it is rejuvenating to visit once a year or so."*

"Create Social Impact and Social Justice"

A third motivation for involvement in correctional ministries lies in the volunteer's desire for change. Specific insight into the communication between volunteers and the women they serve needs more study but for those women whose histories involve abuse, volunteers can be allies in the struggle for justice and social change (Tewksbury & Dabney, 2004).

Washington Post columnist Mike Gerson (2018) wrote about the need for social justice as essential to Christian faith, and not just a by-product of good works.

> ***"It is neither realistic nor fair*** *to ignore the current damage of mass incarceration and failed educational institutions on minority groups. Prejudice and institutional evil are ongoing—deeply ingrained in social practice and ratified by indifference. Repentance is in order—along with a passion for social justice that is inseparable from the Christian gospel."*

For politically minded volunteers, advocacy is possible. There is proposed legislation currently on the Senate floor that would benefit from social support. See Appendix C to read about this bill [S. 1524: The Dignity for Incarcerated Women Act]. Appendix D highlights the possibility of real criminal justice reform that recently took place (Oklahoma Department of Corrections, 2019).

For volunteers working in reentry, the realities of social impact are clear. These problems start the moment women exit the jail or prison doors. Despite the desire for rehabilitation, justice-involved women often live in places that make it difficult to create real change.

> ***"We're all the product of our environment.*** *With addicts, geographical change can help but if you want to use, you're going to use. Not having stability sets you back… Anyone that's coming out of the prison system, whether they're an addict or not, they're in recovery from something... They're going to find a way to get by. I think that's why my heart is here at [ministry]… It's a place for somebody to go when they get out and say, 'I don't know what to do. I don't know how to live. I know what I was doing wasn't living, but I don't know how [to change]'… they say the only thing that has to change when you're trying to change is everything … Housing's probably the biggest one because… everybody wants us to rehabilitate, but in poverty-stricken areas. Drug use is more common, but we're condemned to being in these poverty-stricken areas. Even if we worked so far to get a career and make money and do what we're supposed to, we've got these felonies*

in our background. So we're condemned to stay in these areas."

– Formerly incarcerated woman and volunteer

Volunteers motivated by the need for social impact and change sometimes have unrealistic expectations that do not fully acknowledge negative realities, or the role played by other partnerships with family, church, and friends who are needed for support. One award-winning volunteer notes:

> ***"I was trying to do such big things*** *in there and that probably wouldn't be a normal experience for people who are … not really making waves and just leading a devotional or whatever every week… If I could change anything about the churches' involvement in the prison system, it would be… to also care for their physical needs and fight for real justice… So on one hand, I'm encouraged by how many people in the church are in there, but on the other it's like, 'Can you do a little more?'… Can you seriously approach this [ministry] without the lens of recognizing how inherently racist the system is and not work to combat that?"*

Volunteering is a commodity: the individual picks where she wants to work as well as the work she wants to do. The volunteer imagines the experience she expects to have and anticipates a certain level of satisfaction in the effort (Glasrud, 2007).

However, this expectation is quickly challenged. One volunteer noted: *"Most prison ministries are ministries of hope and healing and yet people feel a 'stigma' of working with the incarcerated. I was one of them."* While understanding the need for change and desiring to participate in that change, the volunteer may not find supportive behavior. Resistance can come from corrections staff.

> ***"There was a challenge last week*** *by an officer that was giving me a hard time in the past… he says, 'Why are you here?' He's trying to figure out why I keep coming... I have no ulterior motive. I don't get paid, but I know that Christ loves them, and it's his love that compels me to go. And I care. I care about these people, especially knowing what they've been though."*

Another volunteer wrote of enthusiasm tempered by her pastor's resistance:

> ***"God called me to serve as Clergy****... I could offer one-on-one Biblical counsel and prayer to the inmates, with legal clergy protection of privileged/ protected communication for the inmate... My husband and I prayed and moved forward in faith to obey God, writing a long letter to our pastor, asking if I might stand before the elders of our church and ... "be ordained to minister to incarcerated women as Clergy. He said no. He would not ask the elders... After three months of praying [we contacted another pastor] and explained the situation. The pastor expressed his awareness of the spiritual gifts God has given me, and he agreed with this calling to prison. He ordained me... When I arrived with the team, I learned one of the inmates had JUST written a letter to the church that ordained me, asking them to please send someone."*

Volunteers who have worked with both incarcerated men and women have seen a bias that views ministry with justice-involved women as less important or no different from ministry work with incarcerated men. Social justice and change are difficult.

> ***"We're all broken obviously,*** *but due to the pathways that women in our program came to us through... they're pretty beat up by the time they get to us. Their challenges go... really deeply into relational issues. Where you have [males] being on the assaultive abusive end of the spectrum, you have the [female] battered abuse end of the spectrum ... That's a huge gulf. So, working with them has been really challenging. Some of the women that I've seen who have returned, they had serious trust issues. They have been told stories about 'we're going to do this and do that' and people haven't followed through."*
>
> – Formerly incarcerated woman and volunteer

Correctional ministry encourages stewardship and responsibility centered on the incarcerated ("We need to help change lives—not only save them but make them better"), which also affects the individual volunteer attitudes. (*"My team members are strong Christian leaders who help me to grow in my servant ministry for Christ."*) However, sometimes justice and compassion can be sorely tested and raise other theological issues.

> ***"I had been meeting with a woman for five years;*** *she murdered her son. She never really talked about the extent of her crime, but the regret and how the other inmates and officers treated her was hard for her. But I saw her find a relationship in Christ and continue to deepen that and grow. When it became time for her trial, I decided that I would attend. And it was... absolutely horrific... It was so gruesome I just couldn't believe it. The courtroom was so dark... I think that was the hardest thing for me over the five years, to understand the forgiveness of God in such a horrific situation... If I believed that he had forgiven her, as I had been telling her all that time, I knew I would have to go back to the courtroom and stay throughout the trial, which I did."*

Barriers Faced by Correctional Ministry Volunteers

Many volunteers experience a push-pull of emotions that inevitably produce tension. They must balance a desire to help without giving handouts that will build further dependency. They must learn to set limits that will allow them to listen compassionately but detach emotionally from their clients. They must engage competent supervision and substantive training to deal with the inevitable changes.

Multiple and conflicting values

Volunteers are often confronted by multiple and sometimes conflicting values that can make it more difficult to effectively work within their assignments (MacNamee & Peterson, 2014). For example, one volunteer noted her discomfort with alternative lifestyles. *"Coming down to the prison, you soon find out that many of them have lesbian relationships in the prison setting. Trying to orchestrate around that as a Christian and give counsel has been very challenging."*

Volunteers often experience multiple and conflicting values when they fail to see the social impact from their efforts (Ronel 2006). Training promotes a warm but professional attitude, with the aim of building independence for reentry. However, volunteers sometimes need affirmation on the process as well as outcomes of their work.

One volunteer simply said she *"would like feedback from inmates or the chaplain as to how the visits impact the inmate."* Another said, *"I'd like to be allowed to do more follow up with those incarcerated after they are released."* Volunteers may not understand that most jails and prisons enforce a no-fraternization policy where inside volunteers are not allowed to have contact with those who are released. Volunteers may need to make sense of what is happening as well as learn mechanisms for handling these tensions since:

> ***"I don't have people I can really process with****... Last year, I had a really tough case. One of the women down at [prison] just opened up to me... and it was so horrible, I didn't think that I would be able to handle it... I know no sin is greater than another... I needed to talk to someone, but at the same time, I wouldn't even want anyone else to know what she had told me... When I was getting my chaplaincy, one of my professors said to me, 'Never underestimate the depth of evil that a person is capable of.' That was a wake-up call, but it also prepared me for not being totally shocked by some of the things that people have done because if you look too much at that, you can't assure them of God's forgiveness."*

As volunteers learn, multiple and conflicting values create unique training opportunities if not meaningful change.

> ***"You know, I think anybody that works in this very long*** *knows that the numbers are very small ... You maybe meet hundreds to thousands of inmates a year, and there is a handful a year that really make a dramatic life change and come to Christ. I think that's probably one of the difficult parts about this ministry..."*

In spite of these tensions, only eight percent of those who had also worked in men's prison ministries thought working within women's ministry was more difficult. Competent supervision and substantive training can help volunteers resolve conflicting values. Even if volunteers struggle to "feel good" about their work, their work can be effective.

Enduring Challenges to Change

A second barrier is the realization that there are long-lasting challenges to full recovery and change. *"Sometimes I feel I can only plant seed, offer emotional support. I think many of the women will revert to the drugs or other life choices when they leave the jail. But while they are here, I can help meet their needs for today."* While acknowledging the work of the Holy Spirit in individual lives, volunteers must strike the balance between creativity and constraint that ultimately will determine in their own minds whether their efforts will be worth it. One volunteer explains the challenge of ministry with justice-involved women:

> *"**Trauma distorts people's view of who God is.** They almost always think that God gave them that trauma, that it was visited on them because there's something intrinsically wrong with them and that they deserve this. Maybe they've had so many bad things [happen] or whatever. So when they begin to see through our program what Scripture has to say about God, and begin to unravel these untruths that they believed about God, themselves, and others—that's when the path is cleared and then they're really ready to receive the gospel..."*

It is disheartening if those "helped" respond with resentment, humiliation, or resistance toward the volunteer. But as noted by a long-term volunteer, *"We are not called to judge. We are called to love unconditionally."*

> *"**One young lady, seven times incarcerated,** didn't want to see me the last time she was in the jail because she was so embarrassed. In conversations and meeting one-on-one, she would say 'I left my family because these guys deserve better.' And I said, 'Let's look at this. You can be that better they deserve, and let's make that our goal. Things don't have to stay the way they are.' But you know, in her case, she was deeply wounded as a child...and many of them don't want to have anything to do with God because it's like, 'Where was he? Where was he when all of this was going on?' I particularly think of one case where this woman told me that as a child, she would come home from Sunday school and be sexually molested. And so working with these people to even mention that God loves them, it can be dangerous because in their minds, they see what God could have done and he didn't, and that's not love."*

Volunteers may be best served by a "bounded love" rather than an all-embracing commitment to the women they serve. This allows individuals to find balance as they separate themselves from the roles they play (Wuthnow, 1992). Volunteers must be attentive and flexible to what is happening in the moment, but with a clear sense of where these women have been and what is possible in the future.

> ***"Making Christ the priority*** *and staying hidden behind the cross helps a great deal with any boundary struggles. I am not there to have my needs met or have my voice heard or get my way. I am there to introduce them to my friend Jesus and pray and hope for them to become friends with Him too. I just listen and love and point to Him. He alone can rescue and save – that's not for me to do."*

Structural, Organizational and Cultural Constraints

Volunteers face barriers when their ability to bring expertise and skills needed for effective change is challenged.

> ***"In the 1990s, we were welcomed as volunteers.*** *Now so many rules are in place that it is difficult to show the love we would like to show. So much of this is due to the rules the prison warden has put in place and the way the chaplains interact with the prisoners. At the prison I usually go to the chaplains do not act as friendly to the prisoners as the previous chaplain did and this is reflected in the attitude of the prisoners."*

Time constraints and safety needs are common examples. One volunteer noted: *"We need more help from the prison staff in getting the ladies to us at the proper time for all our meetings there."* Another said, *"Our biggest problem is prison understaffed for security to go in."* Correctional staff can be the point of resistance for female volunteers. A volunteer said:

> ***"I have been yelled at.*** *I have been frisked inappropriately. [Officers] are lazy. Sometimes they tell me that the women don't want to come to class, when the women really do… Some of the administration actually would like to see us*

fail. The officers... don't want to see us in there helping the inmates. They don't feel they deserve that."

Other ministry workers said, "Prison chaplains can be an asset but in past situations chaplains have been aggressive and challenging while volunteers stay obedient to rules and regulations." One volunteer explained how lines of authority can be blurred:

> ***"[Women] have to apply,*** *but down at [prison] they do not have many programs, and the waiting list is horrific. We offer a presentation of the class and women come, and then we interview them. But the chaplain down there, and particularly this year the warden, just gave input to who they thought would be good to be in the class because it is a good program to take before re-entering life again."*

Another volunteer lamented that, *"I watch many women get saved and then monthly begin to fall away... because there is a lack, within the prison, concerning the setting up of bible studies for these women. If the chaplains could set up a few weekly bible studies, these women could not only become 'saved' but anchored in their faith, which in turn would help lead others within the system to Christ."*

However, not all chaplains are Christians, so they may delegate Bible studies to volunteers to determine what is taught. In addition, some ministries have no coordinated discipleship effort but only random studies. Volunteers often disagree as to the best way to foster common ground that helps others see mutual advantages in helping.

> ***"Our corrections staff are great,*** *and we serve at their pleasure. I strongly feel we are guests in their facility, and it is a privilege to enter their facility, disrupting their work. Any volunteer who pushes for more from them is poorly representing Christ. Part of our calling is to represent Jesus to staff as well, many who don't know the Lord yet. As servants, we are called to be humble and compliant to their rules in this role."*

When the ability to bring expertise and skills needed for effective change is hindered by structural constraints that prevent implementation, brainstorming and feedback is key. Fostering relationships while respecting others' time and boundaries can be challenging. One volunteer found her own way to confront this attitude:

> *"**I believe that anyone who volunteers** in a prison has to understand that the prison has other priorities than what you are there to do. Security will always take priority over education or religion. We always have to understand that we are not in control and have to trust God through lockdowns, emergency counts, and other inconveniences. This is not a ministry for everyone... I have to have a very open and flexible attitude so that I can adapt to whatever the needs are each day that I am there."*

"Successful" Volunteers

Successful volunteer efforts are often comprised of people "doing with" others rather than "doing for" them. Organizations that provide "plug-in" volunteer opportunities (e.g., Angel Tree parties) often engage people in situations where volunteers are more concerned about doing the job well, being useful, and making the justice-involved women happy rather than seeing themselves as part of a bigger picture.

These volunteers know little about the organizational context beyond the activity they are part of and may learn little or nothing from their experience. The result is temporary relationships in which volunteers do things without consistency, sustained contact, or lasting results for the women or ministry.

For long-term volunteers, it is a different story. Nonprofit organizations often depend on volunteers to survive, so retention of key personnel is an important priority. Established organizations have procedures in place that easily allow volunteers to contribute their time and effort. However, ministries must also offer assurance that volunteer time and effort will eventually be beneficial to others. In this case, hearing the volunteers' voice, ensuring they feel supported, and having opportunities to connect with other people in their volunteer work are important. Listening is critical, especially early in the process.

> ***"It's looking for a sense of connection,*** *just being seen, being validated, whether it's pain, or joy, or just as a person. So for me going in, that's always the perspective that I take: 'How can I connect with this person in front of me?' No matter what the background, what the history or experience is. And so we laugh all the time. The women that I serve currently are just really such a joy to be around. They have incredible gifts, incredible talents. Their pasts and their histories and their struggles are just a part of who they are in the grand scheme of things... seeing that tenacity for life and that drive to keep going after you've been through so much trauma, so much personal failure, so much failure of others to you. I mean, it's phenomenal… Something that we say a lot is that 'We're better for knowing you' and I truly believe that…"*

Effective volunteers in strong ministries see that only a very flexible, willingly self-critical kind of person is likely to build bridges across social divides. Organizations may struggle to find a realistic standard for performance—or poorly communicate those expectations. Volunteers need to know the organization will allow areas of deficiency as well as excellence, but the ministry's "success" requires continuous vigilance, adjustment, and improvisation on the part of both volunteer and manager.

Questions for Reflection

1. How can ministries recruit younger and diverse volunteers?
2. What kind of training is required or provided for your volunteers?

13

Correctional Care

*"**The number of people who come,** and the amount of care and guidance and leadership that they provide... I've never had as many volunteers as I ever have here... Faith-based organizations are so revered inside of institutions, more than anyone. I mean, there's a reason that you can have a Kairos event and have 500 offenders for a three-day weekend, and never have a fight. A lot of it's the fellowship and the expectation. You know that someone took time out of their day and away from whatever's going on to spend time with you because they care about you. That is transformative in and of itself..."*

– Chaplain

Working with justice-involved women is a specialty area. For effective ministry, it requires integrating both correctional and spiritual formation principles. Justice-involved women need holistic healing, yet because of their multiple needs, one agency or ministry cannot meet all the demands.

The application of corrections care principles is an opportunity for government, community and faith providers to learn from one another and partner together for the sake of justice-involved women and their children. In chapter four, we identified five approaches to correctional care: criminogenic risks and needs, strengths-based, trauma-informed care, evidence-based practices, and gender-responsive practices. This chapter aligns principles and components of each to implement effective prison and aftercare ministries.

Significance of Correctional Care

According to a study by PEW (2014), women have a higher degree of spiritual depth than men in terms of spiritual beliefs and practices. Religious programming provides an opportunity to facilitate prosocial behavior and cope with institutional life. Spirituality contributes to institutional adjustment in several ways. It reduces infractions, provides hope, deals with guilt, provides a sense of meaning, offers a new way of life, copes with loss, extends social support, and connects with outsiders.

> ***"That's where I really began seeing*** *quite encouraging success is with women getting out and having someone to walk with them as they began to try and piece their lives together. I have not been an addict, I have not been incarcerated, anything like that. I always say to the women, 'My whole thing is I've not been there, but I care. I care.'"*
>
> – Reentry worker

Ministry Implications of Criminogenic Risks and Needs

Criminogenic factors identify major risk factors and needs associated with criminal conduct that predicts recidivism. For effective healing, several program components are seen to be effective. In terms of *criminal history*, programs that help women identify risky situations, ways to avoid risky situations, and discover alternative prosocial responses can be effective in developing a moral compass and problem-solving skills.

Antisocial attitudes are addressed in programs that enable responsible thinking and taking responsibility for past actions. For women raised in *dysfunctional or abusive families*, effective programs help women parent from behind bars and connect them with their families to develop and maintain healthy relationships. Programs that work to help women obtain job skills and education will help increase their successful reentry.

Women are relational, but because of their high rates of abuse and trauma need to develop relational skills for safe, healthy relationships This will enable them to replace *antisocial connections* with prosocial ones.

Finally, treatment agencies such as Alcohol Anonymous (AA), Narcotics Anonymous (NA) or Celebrate Recovery provide specialized care to deal with *substance use*. Ministries can partner with these agencies, but if there are differing views on medication need to remember they are not professionals. They should not interfere with medication, and always refer women to contact her doctor for what she needs.

Ministry Implications of Strengths-Based Approach

A strengths-based approach recognizes all women have strengths that can be utilized to increase positive behavior changes and reentry success. Programs that work to build *family support* (unless her family is engaged in criminal activity) can help women develop a faith family that encourages and supports her efforts for a prosocial life. Ministries that build hard skills (e.g., GED classes, vocational training) and soft skills (e.g., conflict resolution, relational communication) are *educational assets* which not only increase confidence, but also enable these women to succeed in their future employment.

Self-efficacy programs strengthen the belief that the justice-involved woman's life is under her own power and control, and that she can take positive steps to improve it. These ministries provide positive reinforcements as the woman progresses toward reentry or in her life plan. A final strength is increasing parental involvement, since this is a strong motivator for women. Programs that increase the connection with her children enable her to make prosocial changes.

Ministry Implications of Trauma-Informed Care

Trauma-informed ministries acknowledge that traumatic experiences often play an important role in a number of disorders, such as PTSD, depression, anxiety, and psychosis. Ministry workers should be aware of behavioral "red flags" that trigger the need for established programs and alert mental health professionals. Some symptoms of PTSD include re-experiencing a traumatic event through flashbacks, nightmares, intense or prolonged distress, and viewing the world as unsafe. There may be emotional numbness, memory loss, a mistrust of others, and avoiding people, places and situations.

Negative emotions and thoughts such as blaming, fear, anger, shame, diminished interests, feelings of isolation, and loss of faith and hope may be observed. Arousal symptoms include angry outbursts, reckless and dangerous behavior, hypervigilance, and difficulty sleeping. Symptoms of depression and/or anxiety include excessive crying, irritability, restlessness, or social isolation. There may be anxiety, fear, apathy, hopelessness, loss of interest, changes in sleep and eating habits, lack of concentration, and suicidal thoughts.

Some psychotic symptoms are aggression, self-harm, social isolation, thoughts of suicide, difficulty thinking and understanding, anger, anxiety, and loneliness. Justice-involved women may exhibit fear, depression, manic episodes, deficiency of speech or rapid speaking, and hallucinations.

The six core values of trauma-informed care programs emphasize physical, psychological and emotional *safety* for both providers and survivors that create opportunities for survivors to rebuild a sense of control and empowerment. Physical and emotional safety is a high priority. Women should not be subject to spiritual abuse or judgment. Verbal and nonverbal expressions should be warm and empathetic.

Trust and transparency are built through structured programs that start on time, are consistent with expectations and discipline, and that maintain healthy boundaries. Participants are not there to meet the needs of ministry workers.

Peer support and mutual self-help contribute to these core values when participants share their stories and peers promote recovery and healing. *Collaboration and mutuality* ensure shared power and decision-making. Everyone has a role to play and creates a sense of belonging as healing happens through relationships.

Empowerment builds the justice-involved woman's voice and choice. Sensitivity to *cultural, historical, and gender issues* means there is no stereotyping or biases. These programs offer gender responsive services, leverage cultural connections, and address historic trauma. Ministry workers must be educated in cross-cultural ministry in order to bring love, compassion, and hope. Scripture used wisely can speak to issues of suffering, forgiveness, and healing.

Ministry workers should assume that trauma exists. It is safe to presume that all justice-involved females have a history of traumatic stress and that universal precautions should be exercised. The question ministry workers are to ask is not 'What is wrong with her?' but 'What has happened to her?' and listen with empathy.

Ministry workers should recognize their limitations when working with those in their trauma. If a woman is triggered or re-traumatized and not able to stabilize, alert those working in mental health so she can receive proper care. This is effective if there is already a relationship with those in mental health prior to referring women to them.

Applying trauma-informed care principles can be challenging when working in a corrections facility. The space, setting, interruptions, culture of distrust, limited materials, lack of privacy and sometimes lack of a supportive staff can hinder implementing a trauma-informed program. Recognize potential trauma situation and triggers.

Ministry workers who are aware of potential trauma situations and triggers (such as those who are restrained with chains or in solitary confinement) can be ready to provide ministry through presence and empathetic listening. Resist re-traumatizing women. There are times that ministry workers create stressful or toxic environments that interfere with recovery (e.g., using shame or guilt as a motivator, not keeping confidentiality, or being judgmental rather than providing empathetic listening).

Ministry workers may experience secondary (indirect) traumatic stress (STS) which occurs when the listener begins to experience trauma symptoms as a result of hearing firsthand the pain and suffering of others. The vivid recounting of trauma by the survivor and the ministry worker's mental or emotional representation of that event may result in a set of symptoms and reactions that parallel PTSD.

Constant exposure to graphic accounts of victimization can challenge basic spiritual beliefs, create a pervasive distrust about the motives of others, and contribute to a pessimistic attitude about human behaviors. Ministry workers need be aware of STS and have coping strategies such as prayer, scripture engagement, meditation, journaling, or talking with others to keep them healthy and balanced.

Ministry Implications of Evidence-Based Principles

Evidence-based practices (EBP) apply eight principles derived from empirical research and expertise on risk reduction. Programs first *assess the risk and needs* of their participants using gender-specific, credible assessment instruments to inform programming and case management.

A recommended tool is the Women's Risk/Need Assessment (WRNA).

Program directors then *enhance intrinsic motivation* by using interviewing techniques to coach, engage substance use treatment, and case management to initiate and maintain positive behavioral changes. *Target intervention* implements risk principles to prioritize supervision and treatment resources for higher risk women, as well as match women by temperament, learning style, motivation, culture and gender. *Training staff skill with directed practice* builds strong communication skills along with an understanding of social learning theory, cognitive behavioral strategies, and trauma-informed care.

Skill is promoted by modeling, reinforcement, role-playing, graduated practice, and extinction. *Positive reinforcement* promotes behavior changes. Ministry workers need to look for opportunities and a variety of ways to provide verbal encouragement and material rewards. Research also indicates that *engaging ongoing support in natural communities* can increase positive outcomes. Involving significant others in case plans and having meaningful connections to the prosocial community fosters the development of healthy relationships. Implementing EBP practices include *measuring ongoing processes and practices* of the program and workers' effectiveness.

Formal evaluation rather than anecdotal evidence is needed in ministry programs, and this is often missing. Finally, the program must *provide measurement feedback* to the women they work with, as they move through reentry or their life plan.

Implementing these principles matters. Otherwise, the ministry may focus on the wrong type of individual, and over or under program her, resulting in higher institutional infractions and recidivism rates among program participants. In addition, it may be poor stewardship of resources to continue to fund an ineffective program or ministry.

Gender-Responsive Correctional Care

Gender-responsive means creating an environment through site selection, staff selection, and program development, content, and material that reflects an understanding of the realities of women's lives and addresses their issues. Corrections administrators point out that policies, programs and procedures are male oriented, since males comprise most of the prison population.

Incarcerated women are expected to fit into policies, procedures and programming designed for their male counterparts, yet some of these policies, procedures and programs do not make sense for women. While there is movement toward implementing gender-responsive strategies, the dominant (male) corrections environment still heavily influences state and federal corrections policies and programs.

In a recent interview with prison administrators, we learned of efforts in a state correctional institution to create a gender-responsive prison.

> ***"Over the last two and a half years*** *our leadership team put a focus on it because this prison was built as a gender-responsive prison. When I drove up and came in, I'm thinking this place is no different than when I left, other than a new building. The culture is still the same. The vibe is still the same. So it was [the warden and deputy warden's] task—and then the executive team, the leadership team, the supervisors and some line staff—that we were going to change the culture to fit what we built because it felt like we weren't 'walking our talk'. I think that giving women choices when I walk in a man's prison is about compliancy and probably respect that we don't deserve... I don't want a woman just to respect me because of my title. I think that we also have to earn it and how we treat them in providing a safe place and how we listen to them and how we ebb and flow with them. That is focused on in here. And I think that part of holistic approaches is not just asking somebody to say 'Yes, ma'am.'"*
>
> – Warden

These prison administrators observed that *"Women in general like [the warden] as a female leader. The women that are living here want this. I think staff want this. I think they expect accessibility. That's not necessarily expected of a male leader. There are expectations around what that accessibility looks like."*

Gender-responsive principles were used to expand our understanding of correctional facilities designed for women. For instance, men as well as women experience trauma. Trauma-informed practices try to understand the different kinds of trauma and that what is experienced by men and by women is gendered. To apply the same things to both sexes is limited. One warden said, *"I think that it's difficult sometimes ... because we are the world in here... But then you throw in the dynamic that when somebody becomes incarcerated... she becomes asexual...We want her to ... fit into policy, to fit into [asexual] clothing, to [be] compliant."* Another difference noted:

> ***"The majority of our women will get out.*** *And whether they have children or not, [they'll need] salaries that enable a livable wage [to] support themselves without the assistance of another person... That then plays into some things that we've been trying to do differently here. I am not saying education is not important. [I have my master's degree], but some populations in here... need a trade. You know, they come in here at 40 years old... Education is a focus and it needs to be a focus, but also identifying individual needs as well and what actually that one woman needs as opposed to the lump of people...*
>
> *More women come in already having a high school diploma than compared to a male prison... So where do we focus our energy at for the women...? What kind of jobs were they holding with that? We have apprenticeship programs here. I think that's something, so that's the other piece that I think we try to be vocal about. Male prisons have a cadre of apprenticeships and so then people try to mirror it over with us and it's like, 'Wait a minute, our average length of stay is 10 months and just because you offer it in a men's prison doesn't mean that we need to offer all of it here.' [We're] getting people to narrow down and offer the right kind of apprenticeships, not the kind just because it worked somewhere at a men's facility... It doesn't need to happen that way. Then it feels like we're spread too thin and we aren't doing anything well... so I think it's really pulling out [hundreds of women] from that population of [thousands of men] and focusing on mental health, trauma, and holistic care.*
>
> *In the last two and a half years [we worked] to have a safe environment. We want safe reporting... We want women to speak up about things that aren't right with them. And I've said this before: I don't want a compliant woman*

in here... We don't want people that just go along with the flow because that's what they think they need to do in order to be supported...They're relational... [At this facility] I walk in, I get stopped. I think that women want to explain more, talk more. They call me [by first name]. At the men's prison they called me a warden... I think that in their hierarchy, [first name] didn't work. In this [female] environment [my first name] works... There's one prison. They're not housed according to their classification. They're housed according to their behavior."

– Warden

A gender-responsive approach affected their prison in several ways, including creating a fluid environment that sometimes can appear a little uneven. Core correctional practices start with training.

***"There's some staff that have been around** for a long, long time and never worked anywhere else. Staff might view gender-responsive as softer; that we're not holding people accountable, that there's an allowance for women to be disrespectful to staff.*

– Deputy warden

Leaders may ask, "Is disrespect worthy of segregation or is it worthy of a conversation? Is this a pattern or a one-time deal for her?" Long-term staff may struggle with this approach, believing it does not hold women accountable for acting out. Several prison administrators reported spending a lot of time discussing issues staff are concerned about that relate to being women not discussed in a men's prison. One example is the "shorts" issue. Can the incarcerated women wear shorts? How short, and when and where can they wear them?

***"It seemed like there was an ordinary amount** of focus on women's behavior that was not connected to any sort of criminogenic need. I think since we've been here, we've had this conversation a lot... From staff to us in administration talking about policies, we were giving an inordinate amount of time to things about women that are not connected to criminogenic needs. For instance, whether or not a white tee shirt is going to be allowed, whether or not a*

> *family can send a bra, the color of jeans, how snug their clothing can be, whether the shirt sleeves if you're outside can be pushed up to be like a tank top... They're nothing to do with criminogenic needs. It's simply 'You're a woman and we want to control how you come across as a woman'. The female piece of it is not criminal, just femaleness.*
>
> – Warden

For those providing leadership and working in a women's facility, building a gender responsive culture involves several steps.

> ***"Get a good leadership team around you*** *that are skilled and smart and educated. I couldn't do it without [my deputy]. I've said that multiple times. [Then there's] our treatment director or a security director. We have a new business manager. So having a skilled team and a team approach is important. My old boss used to say, 'You got to remember you're a warden' ... [but] I'm thinking, 'Oh no, I'm really part of a team.' I try not to make decisions without the team's input. There're some decisions that just need to be made. Get a good team and lay out your strategies. It's not going to happen overnight."*
>
> – Warden

Hiring the right people, training them in safety matters and core correctional practices is important. The warden noted that having decentralized training on site for everyone regardless of where they are going to work helped.

Workers learn "these are the things you need to understand about women" as central to their employment. Once you have a team on board, you also need central office support in order to move anything forward. The final step is holding the counselors accountable with contact standards.

Ministry Implications of Gender-Responsive Principles

The principles of gender-responsive correctional care are:

- **Relational,** working with women in a way that promotes mutual respect and empathy;

- **Strengths-based,** recognizing all women have spiritual, educational and experience strengths that can be mobilized;
- **Trauma-informed,** recognizing the history and context of abuse plays an important role in how women respond to programs, services, people, and God;
- **Holistic,** providing a comprehensive case management model that addresses the complex and multiple needs of justice-involved women, including the spiritual component;
- **Culturally competent,** services that value and acknowledge the diverse cultural backgrounds of women (Modely & Giguere, 2010).

Wardens and chaplains receive many requests for groups or individuals to come into the facility and offer an event or program. These requests often further the mission of the requester, but not the mission of the facility. All requests require staff time and attention, so it is a challenge to respond to the requests and stay focused on the mission of the facility. There is pressure to accommodate requests from taxpayers who fund the prisons.

A common mistake is for ministries to take a successful program created for incarcerated males and implement it with incarcerated females. Yet, often the program does not meet the needs of women or is not implemented in ways that take gender into account.

When working with justice-involved women, corrections experts recommend rehabilitative rather than punishment focused efforts and implementing gender-responsive practices. Gender-responsive means creating an environment through site selection, staff selection, program development, content, and material that reflects an understanding of the realities of women's lives and addresses the issues of the participants (Bloom, Owen, & Covington, 2005). This reality takes into account her unique pathway to criminal conduct, relational and social/cultural factors.

Understanding, supporting, and applying the following corrections principles will strengthen your relationship with corrections administrators and increase ministry effectiveness. Implementation strategies or suggestions are provided along with ministry questions, but additional training is highly recommended. The number of corrections principles can seem overwhelming, so you may want to start with one area at a time.

Be intentional and purposeful. Establish the goals for participants in your program. What does a mature spiritual believer look like? What do you want participants to be able to know, do and be committed to by the end of their participation? For example, participants should be able to 1) explain the foundational truths of the faith, 2) describe their new spiritual identity, 3) feed themselves spiritually through prayer and scripture engagement, 4) identify ways their faith transforms their behaviors and thinking, and 5) connect with other faith followers through worship and small groups.

Use a framework to guide your spiritual formation program. One framework is to help participants develop their spiritual beliefs (tenets of the faith), practices/rituals (prayer, reading and reflecting on Scripture, worship), and community (spiritual friends, small groups, congregation). Other frameworks are the Reveal study that identifies catalysts of spiritual growth (Hawkins, Parkinson, & Arnson, 2007), and for evangelism, Thresholds for Unbelievers (Everts & Schaupp, 2008).

Align programs and curriculum with program goals. Every class, program, and activity should align with the program goals. Select curriculum that is culturally relevant, taking into account gender, ethnicity, and social economic status. What works in church in the free world may not connect with justice-involved women. Give the women a voice by including them in program development and curriculum creation or selection.

Integrate corrections principles. For example, provide classes on parenting, anger management, decision-making, thinking biblically, moral compass, and healthy relationships. These need to be presented through the lens of Scripture.

Train volunteers. Volunteers can be beneficial or detrimental to a program. Select and train volunteers in corrections principles and spiritual formation. This will help prevent spiritual abuse by volunteers who, while well-meaning, may bring in their denominational differences or speak about issues relevant to justice-involved women in a judgmental way.

Assess the program and the participants. Correctional facilities measure success by lowered recidivism rates. To gain credibility, use the same standard state or federal systems use to measure recidivism rates. Ministries recognize that desistance is a byproduct of spirituality. The program goal is not just lowered recidivism, but that participants are committed, growing followers of Christ.

One assessment tool is the Lifeway Spiritual Growth Assessment Process (2006). Another way to track participant progress is to provide a pre- and post-test. Self-studies can also be helpful to determine if program goals are being met. The bottom line is the need for program, participant and processes evaluation.

"What do you think are the motivations *behind why some of the residents either will join the programs, or why they'll stick with it? I want to see my kids on the weekend. I don't want to stay in the pod. I hate my roommate. She stinks. She hates me. I hate her. I don't want to be in the room with her. I need something to do. I'm full of anxiety and stress. I don't have anything to do. I'm nervous. I've already written everybody. They're not writing me back fast enough. I'm angry that I'm in here.*

The motivation is usually very self-serving. It's not because I really want change. I accidentally run into change. I just need to do something. Then if the facilitator is good, before long they're under the skin and into the heart. You know what I mean? The women say, 'I really need a change' and they have a false expectation of that change or how it's going to be. Most of the time, I just need a change of environment, a change of pace. I need to do something… I just want out of the scope of this room. You know, cells aren't even half this size [of the office where the interview took place]. This is almost three cells, this office space. Almost three."

– Formerly incarcerated woman

Questions for Reflection

1. What changes need to be made in ministry to be more effective in reducing recidivism among justice-involved women?
2. How can ministry workers be trained and cared for in coping with secondary trauma stress and ministry fatigue?

14

Programs of Hope

"Sometimes it's important to realize *that prison has a stigma as being the bad place and the horrible place. But it's the place called Change and the place of redemption to the man or woman that hears and listens. It can be the greatest turning point in a person's life that has no hope and no self-esteem. Where they fall into the hands of what we call 'jailhouse religion'. Jailhouse religion is that experience of desperate crying out to God. Clergy come in and bring a real life-changing experience... It's the beginning of hope and the beginning of new life. Those are my thoughts."*

– Formerly incarcerated woman

Effective institutional and reentry faith-based programs integrate both corrections and faith development principles. While the ultimate goal and measure for program success for corrections is reduced institutional infractions and recidivism rates, for faith-based programs the goal is spiritual transformation with reduced institutional misconduct and lower recidivism rates as products.

Spiritual transformation means a heart change, not just a behavioral change. Anyone can modify their behavior to fit in or conform to the culture. But once the person is out of the culture, does the changed behavior continue? If it does, it demonstrates a deeper heart change, not just modified behavior. Measuring changed lives through faith-based programs is the ultimate challenge and focus of our attention in this last chapter.

Faith-Based Correctional Programs

Faith-based programs lie on a continuum from "religious" to "irreligious". There are seven key organizational areas to determine the extent of an organization's religiousness. These include: 1) *self-identity*; 2) *participants* (the number of stakeholders sharing the same religious convictions); 3) *resources*; 4) *goals, products, and services;* 5) *decision-making* procedures; 6) *power and authority* (religious values); and 7) inter-organizational relationships (Jeavons, 1998).

A typology then places faith-based programs on a continuum including "faith-saturated", "faith-centered", "faith-related", "faith background", and "secular" (Sider & Unruh, 2004). Most of the highlighted faith-based programs described later in this chapter are "faith-centered." Religious faith is explicit throughout the organization and shared by virtually all staff. Religious content is explicit in some or all programs, but not mandatory; secular content is also available. Most funding comes from private, religious sources, and there is often an explicit policy of refusing secular funds.

All correctional institutions' faith-based programs must be available for women of any faith or no faith. They must provide an alternative curriculum for those who do not want the specific faith's curriculum.

Christian faith-based programs offer teachings that focus on promoting a relationship with Christ, rely upon biblical values and morals, impart accountability and responsibility, and provide positive social support networks and skills that can affect behavioral and social change. Components of unconditional love, forgiveness, dignity, hope and supportive community contributes to creating prosocial cultural values and behaviors.

The premise is that spiritual transformation acts as a turning point in an individual's life, leading to desistance from crime (Goebel, 2012). Evidence to support this premise suggests "intermediaries" (i.e., organizations that mediate between two different parties) can provide the structure and tools leading to change, as Johnson (2011, pp. 208, 216-217) states:

> ***"Not only are faith-based approaches beginning*** *to show promise when it comes to the issue of effectiveness, but they are cost-efficient since so much of the work is completed by faith-motivated volunteers. In fact, a number of faith-based organizations are adopting programs that are completely or almost completely*

staffed by volunteers. Congregations, more than any other institution in America, are volunteer-rich organizations able to leverage millions of talented people to feed these faith-based efforts… approaches [which are] already making a difference in confronting difficult-to-solve social problems from delinquency, crime, offender reform, and prisoner reentry. If we only consider the costs and benefits from a purely economic perspective, then we can no longer afford to discount faith-based approaches to crime reduction. Imagine what might be possible if we can overcome the last acceptable prejudice that continues to deter the building of partnerships and networks of support where sacred and secular efforts come together in addressing and solving many of our current crime-related problems."

The number of faith-based institutional and reentry programs for women and girls is unknown because faith-based efforts are broad and shift according to need. For example, they may involve the children of incarcerated women and individually motivated members of the community who see a need. (*"We did a program to… provide school supplies for the children that came to visit their moms. I reached out to several area churches and told them who I was and what we were doing, and would they be interested in getting some school supplies? For the most part I was able to get a lot of donations…"*)

On the other hand, faith-based initiatives may include sanctioned residential programs inside the prison, regular group efforts to provide religious training while incarcerated, or a combination of aftercare ministries for justice-involved women.

To illustrate the challenges behind identifying common features of "faith-based" correctional programs for justice-involved women, the Institute for Prison Ministries initiated a 2018 survey of member organizations located in 20 different states. Forty-three of the first 50 respondents described themselves as being faith-based or faith-related organizations, mostly nondenominational. Seven respondents claimed no religious affiliation but admitted (along with the other 43 agencies) that their strongest held belief was "Demonstrating God's love to participants."

Within this sample of 50 organizations, 14 distinct program areas are named. Most work was accomplished with one or two full-time employees, and sometimes one or two part-time employees. A third of the respondents were working with budgets of $10,000 or less, and all 50 organizations in this study admitted that only a small percentage of faith-based budgets were designated solely for women's ministries.

Common Components of Faith-Based Programs in Correctional Facilities

Prosocial changes within a correctional institution may include specific programs that affect cognitive awareness and self-esteem. They may involve behavior modification as women live in a faith-based dorm or associate with the Christian community inside the facility. While the programs may look different, there are common components of faith-based programs inside correctional facilities.

Voluntary Participation

All jail and prison faith-based programs must be voluntary and open to all women who apply and meet the selection criteria (typically related to institutional conduct and release date). Motivation for participating varies from sincere (e.g., wanting to grow closer to God and make positive life changes) to insincere (e.g., wanting to be with their girlfriend).

In the case of dormitory-type living arrangements, a few participants request to go back into the general population if the faith-based program does not meet their expectations or they feel uncomfortable. Program directors encourage participants to give it more time rather than responding to a decision often based on emotion. While most participants decide to stay with the program, a few choose to leave. Some graduates return as volunteers.

Targeted Gender-Specific Criminogenic Factors and Preparation for Reentry

Faith-based classes target various criminogenic factors by addressing topics such as thinking errors, addictions, relationships, anger management, forgiveness, and parenting issues. These classes also help prepare women for reentry or in some cases the women attend an institutional reentry program. Some of the curriculum is from a faith perspective or faith is integrated into the learning.

Case management and connections for reentry are provided in most faith-based programs. Some justice-involved women start their own nonprofits, and even return to their former home with programs to help others.

> ***"The truth is that when they come,*** *we treat them just like any other volunteer. The prior incarceration, it's really irrelevant to us. That's not who they are. We don't have an obligation. They're a parolee, or not, and we just go down the road. Such is life… to see growth and the ability to thrive and be comfortable with oneself, and to rekindle relationships."*
>
> –Warden

An interview with Warden Ryan Long provided insight into how a correctional facility approaches faith-based programming. Warden Long has worked his way through the ranks of both men and women's facilities, starting as a correctional officer. He now oversees several prison populations, including the Denver Women's Correctional Facility, where he spoke about gender responsiveness (R. Long, personal communication, January 14, 2020):

> ***"Statistically, [where you came from*** *and who you are] does lend to your chances of incarceration, but once you get there and you become accountable… it's you and you alone. We provide opportunities for offenders. College courses and empowerment, community involvement that you would be hard pressed to get in any Homeowners Association… We do trauma-informed yoga and things like that where we provide multiple levels and opportunities for offenders to open up to someone, to change perspective, paradigm and narrative in reference to where they're going and what they're doing... This winter the Women of Influence ran a drive where they got money for socks for homeless people, and they challenged the staff to raise as much as they did. I won't even give you a number, but they embarrassed us… Those things help them be part of the community and… be much more equipped to become part of it as opposed to become isolated from it."*

Spiritual Development

Hodge (2011) defines spiritual interventions as "therapeutic strategies that incorporate a spiritual or religious dimension as a central component of the intervention" (p. 150). Faith-based programs offer opportunities to strengthen participants' relationship with God, learn more about him through study of the Bible, and engage in spiritual practices such as prayer and study of sacred text.

Warden Long has been an enthusiastic supporter of the work of faith-based ministries:

> ***"A lot of offenders will say they're doing great.*** *They're involved in church services, and they're like, 'Well, it's really easy to find God when there's nothing else to do!' For us, regardless of the factual basis of that, it matters not to us because you're being exposed to something that provides you with a higher morality compass, and that's what we want."*

Alternative religious options are available for those who are not of the Christian faith tradition. In addition, many faith-based programs work closely with the Chaplain or encourage participants to attend religious programming. Warden Long noted:

> ***"I would want [people working in prison ministries]*** *to know that regardless of how they believe they're perceived, how staff see them, and how offenders see them in the institution, they are the single most important component of everything that we do, because they provide something that we can't necessarily always [provide]. Their sacrifice, willingness, and really, unfaltering love is something that in a lot of these people's lives has never, ever existed in any way, shape or form."*

Caring and Moral Community

The prison culture of survival, distrust, and self-preservation does not facilitate rehabilitation. Separating women from the general population into faith-based living units allows the women to be with others who share their desire to grow spiritually and make positive life changes.

The separate unit provides both social support and an opportunity to learn or hone social skills through interaction with peers, volunteers, and faith program workers. Volunteers and workers also bring a sense of care from society that the women, who have little contact with the "outside," may feel has abandoned, marginalized or rejected them. These relationships are especially important for incarcerated women who receive fewer visits than incarcerated men. Warden Long said:

> ***"I think that the greatest need is just programs****—delivery of programs and presentation of programs or concepts that teach them to value relationships and value themselves first in their relationship and what they can do, because there are relationships all around. Most of them have children that family are taking care of. They have relationships inside, relationships with those that are on the outside. When they came in, a lot of time they burn those. Then they come in, and they're forced to sit in a cell at night all alone and ponder. For the female population anyway, a lot of negative self-talk occurs."*

Positive Role Models

Faith-based program participants are exposed to positive role models through volunteers, ministry workers, and peers. These role models demonstrate living out their faith and moral behavior. Warden Long told us in consideration of faith-based programs:

> ***"The majority of females for sure are going back****... in some way, shape or form, [these women] are going to be returning to the community. So that's been a component of our partnering with outside entities, community partners, nonprofits, nondenominational groups, denominational groups. Building confidence through cognitive awareness and self-awareness is a huge, huge, huge piece for me."*

One-on-One Mentoring

Faith-based programs offer one-on-one mentoring with a volunteer or ministry worker. Most programs also offer peer mentoring through program graduates or a type of "Big Sister/Little Sister" relationship between those who are further along in the program. Training is required to prevent controlling or judgmental relationships such as 'this worked for me so it should work for you'. However, prisons are seeing value in these opportunities. Warden Long noted:

> ***"We're transitioning into where*** *some of those church-based, religious-based mentors [can come in]. We may allow them, based on risk and proximity to release, to come and grab [inmates] for half a day and take them to church in the community and engage them with community partners... We haven't done that yet, but we're close... because those people sometimes have the ability and the network to get 20 more things than we have in the first place. It doesn't mean that you have to be a believer, and it doesn't mean that you have to profess all of these things. They really just want to help, and them being part of that community helps us with that relationship piece."*

Accountability

The faith-based program provides accountability and structure. Accountability is different than support in that it basically measures if one is doing what they are supposed to be doing. The faith-based program has a specific schedule of required classes and rules for living in the unit, and violations can be cause for dismissal. Warden Long pointed out:

> ***"None of us love everyone we work with*** *or love our bosses or love our job every day, and that's part of, for us, what we really believe to be the rehabilitative part of it: having real life consequences... Our goal is to make inside of prisons look as close to outside of prisons as we can so that when you walk out the door... it's about your comfort level. You know what society expects of you, and then you move forward into the world as such."*

Faith-Based Inside Community Culture

There is a wider contrast between the culture in the faith-based unit and the culture in the general population for males in custody than for females. Male culture does not allow any kind of weakness, vulnerability, or care to be shown. This culture values toughness and is more violent than their female counterparts. Yet participants in a male jail faith-based program report it as a "caring community" where there was love, freedom to cry and share feelings, encouragement and accountability (Swanson, 2007).

For women, the difference between the faith-based unit culture and the general culture is not as drastic but still important. The differences between the general population and faith-based culture involve calm and less drama. There are fewer fights and less theft, facilitated by accountability to the rules of the program since rule violation could result in program dismissal. In addition, faith-based units have a higher level of trust, unity, friendship and accountability among participants.

These relationships may be facilitated in smaller dorms that show more stability than the general population, since women in the faith-based program stay through the program. However, faith-based living units also come with some unique challenges, with issues of gossip, jealousy, judgment, and spiritual pride. One alumna shared her expectation of the faith-based unit culture being full of grace and mercy. Instead, she found the women talked about grace and mercy without understanding and praxis.

Faith-based programs hold participants to a higher standard, but alumni expressed a "feeling of being watched by their peers to see if they are a Christian." One former resident sees this as competition about who can be the best Christian. Residents watch one another to "prove you are a Christian" with the expectation that you perfectly live out the Christian life, or at least according to their list of how a Christian should live.

Failing this standard was met with judgment, condemnation, and verbal accusations (e.g., *"You call yourself a Christian and you do X?"*). Legalism, a list of do's and don'ts (spoken or unspoken) of how a Christian conducts herself, jealousy from peers meant to put others down so they feel better about themselves, or faith judgments (e.g., calling a woman a "Bible thumper" or "Holier than Thou" or saying *"You think you're better than we are"*) came from a few staff as well.

In evaluating faith-based programming, there are two questions: *"Do program participants exhibit faith that is externally motivated or internally motivated (i.e., when women are released from incarceration and free from the controls of the system and Christian culture)? Do they seek out the Christian faith community or return to a non-faith centered life?"*

Creating a beloved community requires continuous work and intentionality. Legalism, condemnation and jealousy demonstrate the need for intentional discipleship that teaches love, mercy, grace, humility, forgiveness, restoration and the "one anothers" in the Bible.

Benefits of Connectedness Through Faith-Based Programs

Humans are created with the basic need for relationships. First, a relationship with God provides a sense of love and purpose, answers or guidance to make sense of puzzling and difficult life events, strength to persevere in trying circumstances, peace and comfort, and empowerment. Second, relationships with others provide love, care, and belonging. "People connected to other people thrive and grow, and those not connected wither and die. It is a medical fact, for example, that from infancy to old age, health depends on the amount of social connection people have" (Cloud, 2001, p. 122).

Spiritual director Anne Fletcher Grizzle states, *"I now believe the greatest tragedies lie not in suffering, but in suffering alone; not in pain, but pain born on one's own without community and communion."* Through faith communities, God provides healing, support, and an abundant life. Faith-based programs provide a sense of belonging and connection. One faith-based program identifies themselves as the "women in white" since their prison garb was white scrubs. Opportunities to establish or restore a personal relationship with God and with others are encouraged and those relationships nurtured. In the Christian tradition, all the commandments can be summed up in two actions: loving God and loving others.

Personal Growth

Connection with God and a loving, supportive community provides healing for emotional problems such as trauma and depression. Feelings of alienation and isolation are often at the core of depression and addiction. It is rare for an individual to experience complete recovery from an addiction without connection to a support system such as Alcoholics Anonymous,

Narcotics Anonymous, or Celebrate Recovery. People behave like those they associate with, so surrounding one's self with those who support the desired changes increases success.

Moral Behavior

Connection with a prosocial community such as found in faith-based programs promotes moral behavior. As one study notes, "An individual's religiousness alone seems unable to constrain delinquent behavior. Only within a significantly religious social climate—a moral community—does the individual's faith generate this power" (Stark et. al, 1982, p. 20-21).

Faith Development

Connection within a faith-based community is required for faith sustainability and spiritual growth. Engaging in community spiritual practices and connecting with others on the same faith journey allows deeper connection with God through deeper connection with others in the family of faith. Similarly, when individuals disconnect from their faith community, they often feel disconnected from God. A consistent element in spiritual growth is to establish community with others who share their spiritual beliefs, which is built into the inside of faith-based programs.

The Practice of Presence

To practice the presence of people is "To see people as Jesus does—as the most important things in the world… lets people know that they matter and have our undivided attention" (Calhoun, 2011, p. 56). It is to love others as Jesus would love them, never marginalizing them or making people feel invisible. He interacted and healed those despised by society. People matter to Jesus and when we listen to others, we give them the gift of mattering.

What Works? The Missing Piece in Reentry

Ever since Martinson's (1976) landmark study concluded "nothing works" for rehabilitation, researchers have refuted his overgeneralization and challenged his findings through other recidivism studies and established evidence-based practices. The missing piece for successful reentry from incarceration to society, even for those who participate in education and religious programs is a supportive community that addresses the need for prosocial peers.

When faith-based program participants go back into society, they take with them knowledge and skills gained through the classes and gains in their faith and moral development, but they leave behind the supportive faith community. One woman expressed her concern of feeling spiritually supported by chaplain and volunteers in jail, but not as confident of societal support after release.

The supportive faith community is often the missing piece for transitioning from a correctional faith-based program to free society. "Successful ex-offenders overwhelmingly identify poor social support as a major barrier that oftentimes remains neglected in government and non-profit organizational programming" (Denney et al, 2014, p. 39). "Those involved in the work of providing religious support to ex-offenders in the community, reaffirming that supporting the work of faith community reintegration and the provision of social support should not go overlooked (Mowen et al, 2018, p. 1098).

Many governments and some faith-based programs implement evidence-based practices, trauma informed care, and gender responsive strategies. They address basic reentry needs such as safe housing, employment, education, and substance use treatment. However, findings suggest social support persists as an issue even for women provided with other basic needs when returning to society. Faith-based ministries are in a position to connect participants with both survival resources and a social support system.

A strong social support system may come from family or friends, yet some women return home to family or significant other who is engaged in illegal activities or substance use, or a violent domestic partner. She may live in an unsafe situation because she has nowhere else to go. Some women may feel ostracized from family or friends especially if they have a sex offense.

Positive social support provides moral, faith and often financial support.

"Among the most frequently expressed desired forms of social support were a mentor to guide them to make everyday decisions, peers with whom to share struggles, and a support system to hold them accountable for their lifestyle and behavior" (Denney et al, p. 47).

In reentry, women in transition connecting with support groups containing successful alumni are especially beneficial. These alumni offer relevant, hopeful and practical guidance. Potential connections with a 12-step program, a faith community, reentry coach or even Facebook can help. The Institute for Prison Ministries can also be a resource for working alongside the church to seek social support and social justice.

Faith-based programs that primarily provided a supportive community, including peers who had successfully reentered, were more successful than programs that either handed off participants to an unfamiliar outside staff person or ministry. The continuity of relationships inside and out along with peer support was seminal.

Measuring Success

> ***"I think that a lot of [prison administrators]*** *share in the vision that although prisons were effective for a long while -- they existed for a long time and they did what people thought them to believe -- we can all agree that we know two things are certain. Number one, that mass incarceration doesn't work, and [two] that programming does… Recidivism rate is the end all, be all. Regardless of how you account for it, how long you go out, the truth is that the needle hasn't moved. Whether we put $100,000 or $100 million into reentry, if the recidivism rate doesn't change, then it's not the program in which we're delivering. It's the way in which we deliver it, and the content and value in which we have in it… I know that our executive director, our director of prisons, our deputy directors all believe that we need innovative and new concepts to move ourselves forward and fix what has been broken for a very long time."*
>
> – Warden Long

Among Christian ministry workers, moral rehabilitation is a by-product of spiritual transformation. Rehabilitation is clarified significantly by linking it to the concept of conversion, suggesting that conversion is primarily a moral transformation. That moral transformation is, arguably, a vital component in the life of one who has been rehabilitated (Skotnicki, 2014, p. 120).

As women experience spiritual conversion or recommitment to Christ, and grow in their faith, moral behaviors and prosocial attitudes develop. However, these behaviors also must be taught. Success is not measured by recidivism rates, since this may not necessarily indicate law abiding behavior but only that the person has not been caught. Success is measured through spiritual transformation of the heart, evidenced through justice-involved women who engage in a growing faith, increased Christ-like behavior, and connection with a faith community.

There is a lack of research studies on faith-based corrections and reentry program effectiveness (Johnson, 2011). The few existing studies are based on justice-involved males. There are a few studies of religion and female inmates, but little published research studies on faith-based female programs. See Snodgrass (2019) for a noteworthy exception.

In the Institute for Prison Ministries' survey of 50 faith-based organizations, participants were asked about how they measured the success of their ministry. Three-quarters of the respondents said there was a documented process for training volunteers. Over 70 percent of the programs claimed to set up measurable objectives before a program begins, and 62 percent of ministries had performance indicators for each program objective, and regularly report on each program. Half the respondents said they routinely monitor their programs through external evaluation.

Both faith-based and corrections programs seek rehabilitation, yet they have different approaches. In faith-based programs, rehabilitation is a by-product of spiritual transformation. As women grow in their Christian faith, the Holy Spirit begins to change them into becoming more Christ-like in their thinking and behavior. In contrast, corrections programs utilize cognitive behavior therapy and social theories to guide its programming. The two most common measurements for success in correctional programs are in-prison misconduct and recidivism.

In-prison Conduct

The misconduct of females in prison is less violent than among male prisoners. Incarcerated females tend to engage in fewer violent assaults, stabbings, and drug-related incidents than incarcerated males and pose less threat of escape. Women are most often cited for minor incidents such as interfering with a count, disobeying orders from correctional officers and asking for justifications of those orders, being in unauthorized areas, or interfering with security measures (Handyman & VanVoorhis, 2004).

Women's unmet and untreated needs actually function as risk factors for their misconduct while in prison (Wright, VanVoorhis, Salisbury, & Bauman, 2012). In general, victimized (abused) women, those who reported substance use and mental health problems (depression, anxiety, anger, psychosis), and those with problematic intimate relationships adapted poorly to the prison environment. These women were more likely to incur serious misconduct violations in their first year behind bars than women who did not display such characteristics.

Recidivism and Desistance

Recidivism, a return to crime, is the gold standard for measuring program effectiveness. Yet criminologists do not agree upon the criteria and method used to measure whether a crime has occurred. Not all crimes committed are detected—only the ones recorded in the criminal justice system. The National Institute of Justice (NIJ) says, "Another way of assessing criminal activity is to interview study participants and ask them to recall the crimes they have committed. Because of memory decay and other methodological issues, this, too, is an imperfect measurement." As a compromise, recidivism is measured in different ways to see whether the different assessments correspond (National Institute for Justice, 2008).

The NIJ recommends the following key considerations be involved with measuring recidivism. First, how does the study determine that a re-offense has occurred? Is it measured by arrest, conviction, supervision violation or commitments to jail and prison? Second, when does the offender recidivate? In other words, what are the starting and stopping points for tracking recidivism? Is it at release or the start of a faith-based community program? Third, how is risk factored into the research design? Women with a high level of risk factors who are released into an "at-risk environment" will be more likely to recidivate. Clearly, the range of these considerations makes it difficult to compare recidivism rates between states and programs.

Christian programming supposes living in the free world with the pressures of life, lack of structure, added temptations, and ability to find a supportive faith community. Rather than focusing on those who recidivate, some studies examine those who are able to desist and identifying what is helpful for women achieving successful reentry. One study (Cominna, 2009) reported women saying the following was helpful in their successful transition to the community:

- relationships with family, friends, and other women who were positive role models;
- positive support from social networks, particularly once in the community (e.g., housing, job connections, transportation);
- positive support from relationships with corrections (especially female) staff;
- safe environments in which to live (e.g., efforts to reduce trauma in their lives such as avoiding the use of restraints);
- programming such as substance abuse, mental health, parenting, and education or vocational training within the institution and in the community; and
- an ability to secure employment/financial support.

Evaluative Measurement Tools

Evaluation is a key component to effective faith-based programs and involves a determination of whether goals are being reached. Measuring the impact of ministry is challenging, however, because it is not easy to assess the supernatural work of the Holy Spirit in the lives of participants.

Yet, the ministry must establish an evaluation system to accomplish this. Directors need to gather a team of staff, volunteer leaders and board members to define what success looks like in the ministry. This is accomplished by reviewing the ministry's mission and program goals. For example, "to become more like Christ" can be broken down into identifiable and specific objectives that also translate into prosocial behavior changes similar to rehabilitation.

A second step to measuring ministry success is to determine what needs to be measured. This allows the team to know they are making progress toward meeting their goals. Again, goals need to be specific and related to institutional objectives. Beyond spiritual goals, there might be graduation rates, recidivism, misconduct, spiritual practices (bible study engagement), faith decisions, and prosocial behavior to consider.

The third step is to identify current measurement tools that your ministry is using and analyze if these are effective. Two standardized assessments created specifically for correctional programs are The Correctional Program Assessment Inventory (CPAI) and the Evidence-Based Program Checklist (Duwe, 2017).

Remember that "effectiveness" is measured by whether or not the ministry is meeting their goals. With this information in hand, each ministry can determine what new assessment(s) to use in order to measure the areas identified in step two. This process of measuring success may also lead ministry workers to a clearer focus on their mission and encourage them in the process.

Once the goals and measurement tool are in place, the ministry may find evaluating success is as simple as counting the program completion rate. That is, how many women enter a faith-based program, and how many complete the program? If attrition rate is a problem, this is cause for reevaluating the program itself.

Anecdotal Evidence

Even with well-designed measurement tools, hard data will not tell the full story. Most faith-based correctional ministry programs highlight individual participants' success and share stories of how participants have benefited or been transformed through their participation in the program. However, the stories told should not be just about the one person who was considered the "star" of the program and who may be an anomaly.

Just as we have included first-person narratives throughout this text, the stories you use must represent multiple participants providing evidence of the "norm" rather than the "exception" for graduates. The following narrative reflects a theme mentioned by several of the women approaching reentry when asked why they were interested in participating in faith-based institutional programming.

> ***"Some of these volunteers will help you*** *where they're signing [for] transitional housing. Or if you don't have anywhere to go, they'll try to help you find somewhere safe that you can go. There were few things they asked you, and in general you had to have a recommendation such as the Chaplain or somebody that would say, 'Hey, we've watched this person. They've been in prison this amount of time. They do seem to have made some changes in their life... I'm not saying they wouldn't try to help somebody if maybe they didn't take classes, but generally they're going to be way more willing to help somebody that does seem to want help."*
>
> – Formerly incarcerated woman

Common Core Components

There are many effective ministries. Common core components for measuring ministry success are these criteria for evaluation:

- **Faith-saturated.** The program is able to integrate their Christian faith, which is a key motivator for providing their program and for the volunteers.
- **Relationship with the Department of Corrections.** The faith-based ministry has strong support from correction administrators. This relationship often allows for quick approval of volunteers and dedicated space. Volunteers and ministry staff are able to have contact with women in the program on the inside and when they are released. Most states do NOT allow this contact.
- **Partnerships.** The ministry has partnerships with churches, corrections, other non-profits and community agencies.
- **Relational.** The ministry is highly relational, connecting the women

with God, their children, faith-friendly peers, volunteers, and ministry staff.

- **Community.** The faith-community living within a designated unit within the prison and relationships on the outside provide a therapeutic environment important for women to be able to express their feelings and receive support from others (Covington & Bloom, 2006).
- **Inside/outside program.** There is a continuum of care inside and outside ministry often including the same staff and volunteers, or in providing a hand-off to outside staff.
- **Holistic.** While faith and faith development is the driving force for ministry, the ministry provided for or partnered with other agencies to provide holistic care addressing criminogenic needs/risks.
- **Dedicated volunteers.** The ministry has a solid volunteer base with most volunteers coming from churches.
- **Humble leadership.** Leaders care about the women in the program more than themselves. Most are willing to accept substandard salaries so more funds can be used for ministry.

Recommendations

We know that successful ministries have a clear mission and purpose, with a strategic plan that extends several years into the future. The process of getting there involves all stakeholders and a solid foundation based on the core values of the organization. The process begins with the efforts of the organization's Board and the Director, who work in tandem to clarify the ministry's purpose, analyze relevant issues and resources, and develop a fiscally sound budget.

The Director and board leadership should model core organizational values as they steer all work towards meaningful, measurable, and financially sustainable results.

However, a good plan is not enough. Leaders must recruit, train, and retain the right staff and volunteers to enable them to do their jobs well and achieve the organization's mission. Providing the necessary tools for workers to do their jobs to the best of their ability enables them to support the values of the ministry and meet the needs of justice-involved women.

Staff and volunteers know their purpose, measure what they are trying to accomplish and assess where changes are needed.

Providing opportunities for board members to contribute strategic capital through their time, financial resources, networks, and skills complements the professional staff and volunteers' daily commitment and focus on the mission. With this foundation, the ministry builds a sustainable model for operation understood by key stakeholders and potential collaborators alike. Additionally, a solid mission statement, measurable objectives, and plan of evaluation enhances funding efforts to increase the ministry effectiveness, stability and sustainability.

The necessity for all ministry workers and their partners to work together strategically underscores the benefit of being part of networks, coalitions, or collective impact teams to achieve goals. In working with justice-involved women, it truly "takes a village".

Whatever your mission, there may be other organizations that are also working with the same population. Regular, multi-directional communication with other public, private, and nonprofit players sympathetic to the mission and activities is beneficial. Giving and receiving thoughtful feedback from peers amplifies your impact and improves community response. Regardless of ministry focus, you can ensure that you build your work on an effective framework that incorporates each of these players in order to be more successful.

The following recommendations reflect standards of practice among nonprofit organizations as applied to the work of individuals involved in the healing of justice-involved women. They underscore the importance of leaders managing and marshalling organizational resources to adapt and improve the consistency and quality of this important work. These recommendations also allow for strategic collaborations that can leverage others in the church and community for greater impact.

1. Enhance funding efforts for program effectiveness.

The **Executive Director** is the fundraiser. She may not be trained in this area, receive little help from her board members, or be unable to give it the attention it needs. Most programs operate with a minimal budget, so ministries have limited data on program effectiveness, which is an incentive to give or receive grants. Increased fundraising training and board participation provides support for the Executive Director, relieves some of her responsibility load, and provides increased funding for ministry growth.

2. Train volunteers, increasing the ethnic diversity and age of staff and volunteers to reflect the population of women served.

All ministries utilize **volunteers** and rely on their efforts to be successful. Volunteers are valued members of the organizational team, but often receive minimal training, on-going training, or feedback on their efforts. Ministries may provide minimal procedures for safety and security inside the correctional facility but neglect ongoing training. Volunteer experiences are not usually included in assessments of the program goals and challenges. These issues need to be addressed by organizational leaders in order to enhance effectiveness. Finally, ministries are strongly encouraged to increase ethnicities that reflect the justice-involved women they serve.

3. Implement program assessment and evaluation.

The majority of faith-based programs do not implement program assessment and evaluation, much less research. To increase program quality, **staff** must add program assessments and evaluations that focus on the implementation of evidence-based practices, trauma-informed care, gender-responsive strategies and faith development principles. Finding grants or donors to fund research can be challenging, but regardless of your mission, the data collected can be a clear and compelling guide toward reaching the intended impact. Assessment and evaluation allow you to make smarter use of your resources to achieve your mission and direct future efforts.

4. Plan for succession.

One of the goals in writing this text was to encourage ministries to use data to continually improve engagement with justice-involved women and recognize when you are on the right track. However, data can also help identify problems or failures as opportunities to improve and innovate. For example, **Board Members** need to have succession plans in place, A succession plan is a strategic document that lays out what to do in the event that a member of your leadership team leaves your organization, as well as how to prepare for the departure before this event occurs.

It is the responsibility of the Board to manage transition intentionally. They must identify current challenges and those that lie ahead, along with the leadership qualities needed to navigate these challenges. A succession plan should have an emergency plan for transition, consider whether an interim leader is appropriate for the ministry, have a timeline for leadership successions that are planned, and identify development opportunities for staff so that the organization will have a "deeper bench" of future leaders. Finally, determining what your organization will say before, during, and after a transition of leadership is important.

Questions for Reflection

1. What does your ministry's evaluation process look like?
2. What does the strategic plan and succession plan for your ministry look like?

Epilogue

Jails and prisons are hotbeds for the spread of COVID-19 due to the numbers of people in tight quarters, inaccessible cleaning and grooming supplies, lack of adequate medical care, visits from the outside population, and a staff that enters and exits the facilities each day. These factors all share the potential for rapid spread of the disease.

As we finish this book, the pandemic has led to a complete disruption of prison operations and the chaplaincy. Extended daily lockdowns and isolations in cells or pods is the norm to prevent the spread of disease. Food is delivered to the cells, and the flow of resources (e.g., books, counseling, services) has stopped.

"Hand to hand, face to face, group to group has ended" says one chaplain. The lack of interaction for women as well as an inability to connect, touch, and be with others is like doing jail time again. *"The women are weary. Prison is difficult, and this is adding to it."*

There is little that justice-involved women can do to prevent contagion from the virus. Once infected, the women may be hesitant to report symptoms since doing so means more isolation. Solitary confinement limits their contact at all levels and heightens anxiety.

In addition, incarcerated women often have preexisting health conditions—diabetes, heart disease, high blood pressure, tuberculosis, asthma—that make them particularly vulnerable to this virus. In jails and prisons, you can't social distance and you can't breathe different air.

Quarantine in prison is not like staying home. Many live in a dorm-like setting with hundreds of other women. You are in the dorm 23 hours a day with limited access to phone, emails, or healthcare. There is guilt over an inability to see family members or grieve those lost to the virus. Most women are not working, so boredom sets in. Anxiety is heightened by an unknown timeframe for seclusion and the threat of a second surge. With limited capacity for success, a familiar feeling of failure is present.

Andrea Circle Bear was a member of the Cheyenne Sioux River Tribe. Prosecuted for a low-level drug crime on her reservation, she was not allowed to get drug treatment in South Dakota. Leaving behind five children and eight-months pregnant with a sixth, Circle Bear was transferred to a federal prison in Texas. She soon was diagnosed with pneumonia-like symptoms that turned out to be COVID. A limited phone call informed the family that the baby had been delivered by caesarian and Circle Bear was on a ventilator. After her death, Circle Bear's 70-year old grandmother drove the thousand miles to a Fort Worth hospital to bring her baby home (Aspinwall, Blakinger, & Neff, 2020).

Limited infrastructure and policy options pose other difficulties. Nonessential workers have been restricted from entering correctional facilities during the crisis, and in some jails and prisons chaplains are viewed as nonessential workers. Volunteers so critical to programming likewise are not permitted to enter. This has severely limited the number and quality of services and available programs.

While state and federal chaplains have kept their jobs, contract chaplains are kept out of the jails, prisons, and youth facilities. Without volunteers to help with ministry, chaplains who are working are overwhelmed. They risk exposure to the virus, bringing it home to their families, and if infected, enduring long periods of quarantine before reentry. Although justice-involved women have been able to act as peer ministers and volunteer ministers have sometimes been granted access, these stopgap practices may threaten future programming and sponsorship.

The longest-serving female inmate in Louisiana is Gloria Williams. Charged as an accomplice in a 1971 robbery that resulted in the death of the grocery store owner, Williams' family has worked tirelessly for years to secure her release. In July 2019, the Board of Pardons unanimously approved her clemency application. However, it still sits on the Governor's desk awaiting his signature. Williams contracted the virus nine months later and spent weeks in the hospital without family contact before being returned to prison on oxygen. An estimated 180 of the 213 incarcerated women at her correctional facility tested positive for the virus (Law, 2020).

On the other extreme, the COVID-19 crisis has led to more communication with upper management. Supervisors have been learning what the chaplain does and the value of ministry to justice-involved women. The increased use of social media has enhanced some jail and prison ministry programs. Through Facebook and online Bible studies, chaplains have been able to reconnect with women they had lost contact with. Recovery-centered studies online, the delivery of free Life Recovery Bibles to women in reentry programs, phone calls, and Zoom meetings have created alternative outlets for contact.

Early intervention from jail and prison administrators is credited with limiting the number of COVID cases. Sensitive to other limitations during this time of crisis, strong leadership has enabled justice-involved women at some prisons to have extra phone calls, and more appealing options on the menu. In addition, making masks for nursing homes and hospitals has given some justice-involved women a sense of purpose and ability to fight the virus.

Awareness of the growing number of positive cases as well as health risks to justice-involved women and correctional staff have led several states to consider decarceration. This involves release of women who have little time remaining in their sentences. Additionally, federal, state, and local officials have released pregnant, aged, sick, and nonviolent offenders in order to reduce the prison population.

However, this action puts additional strain on reentry ministries that may be ill-equipped to deal with early releases or who may be reluctant to put others at risk for exposure. The justice-involved woman's family may have limited resources, harbor mixed feelings toward her, or carry their own baggage of addiction or abuse. With the threat of little food and poor job opportunities, early release actions can set back gains achieved during incarceration.

Reigniting stress and complex traumas limit the ability to focus, stay in the moment, and maintain a sense of control and strong identity as a deeply loved child of God. However, those involved in ministry to justice-involved women bring hope and encouragement. They have creatively shown their love through messages of support, cash donations added to accounts, donated videos, prayer journals and pens, Mother's Day cards, and (for staff and security) hot meals, protein drinks, and protein bars. In response, many of these recipients have been led to look out for one another.

God works in mysterious ways, and in the end the COVID-19 crisis may prove effective in changing attitudes and collaborative solutions that impact justice-involved women. A study meant to reduce juvenile crime in New York considered essential mindset shifts regarding who is engaged, how they work together, and how progress happens (see Kania, Hanleybrown, & Splansky Juster, 2014). The findings underscore the belief that change occurs at "the speed of trust" (p. 3) and "success comes from the combination of many interventions" (p. 5).

As we move beyond the horizon to a new "normal", fundamental mindset shifts will have significant implications on the design and implementation of our ministries. And as the work of faith practitioners comes alongside compassionate judges, probation and parole officers (Hardy, 2020), policymakers, and funders to bring solutions, we all rise.

Appendix A

Glossary

Abusive sexual contacts only—unwanted contacts with another resident or any contacts with staff that involved touching of the resident's buttocks, thigh, penis, breasts, or vagina in a sexual way.

Administrative Segregation—housing inmates separate from the general population who pose a serious threat to institution's safety. Sometimes known as protective custody.

Acquittal—judgment that a criminal defendant has not been proven guilty beyond a reasonable doubt and is free.

ADP—average daily population of an institution or program during a certain period of time and taking into account daily fluctuations.

Adjudication—the legal process where the judge reviews the evidence and argumentation to pronounce judgement in the case.

Ankle monitor (tether or ankle bracelet)—a homing device that individuals under house arrest or parole are required to wear. At all times, the ankle monitor sends a radio frequency signal containing location and other information to a receiver.

Arraignment—the accused is brought into court, told of the charges, and asked to enter a plea of guilty, not guilty or no contest.

Asexual—a person who is not romantically or sexually attracted to any gender.

Baby programs—prison nursery programs for women who give birth while incarcerated. In 2012, eight states had in-prison nursery programs.

Bail—cash amount paid to the court to guarantee that the defendant will appear before the court for their case.

Bail bond—the monetary amount the defendant has to hand over to the court as security to guarantee that the defendant will appear before the court for their case. The amount is 10% of the set bond. For example, if bond is set at $5000, the defendant, their family, friends, or a bail bond agent must pay $500 for the defendant to be released from custody.

Beds—a way of measuring space available to house offenders in a correctional facility. A bed is equal to one offender.

Bible Thumper or Church Rat—a derogatory name given by other inmates to the incarcerated who participate in Christian religious services.

Bisexual—a person who is romantically or sexually attracted to more than one gender or sexual category.

Bondsman—an individual who collects cash, securities and property deeds to pay the bail bond for the defendant. Bondsmen keep a non-refundable fee from the defendant.

Bunkie (or cellie)—the other person who shares the same cell.

Butch—women who have masculine characteristics and play the dominant, or male, role in a homosexual relationship in prison.

Canteen—a store within a correctional facility from which inmates can purchase personal items, such as personal hygiene supplies, snacks, electronics and writing materials.

Chaplain—may or may not be a religious person but coordinates volunteers and religious services for the incarcerated. Often is the person who delivers death notices to inmates.

Cell block—a group of cells within a common day room or a group of cells considered a block because of their location or classification.

Classification—the process of scoring an offender's risks and needs in order to determine his or her appropriate custody level and placement in a prison.

Conviction—a judgment of guilt against a criminal defendant and sent to jail until his or her sentencing trial.

Close custody—the second most secure custody level, between medium-high and maximum security.

Code of Silence—an informal institutional norm (rule) that says members of the group will not inform on or give evidence of testimony against other members of the group, even though actions of the other members may involve breaches of policy or even the criminal law. Also referred to as the "Code of Blue."

Cognitive Behavioral Treatment—therapeutic techniques designed to help individuals address problematic thinking patterns and actions.

Coming Out—the process through which people acknowledge, express, and share with others information about their sexual orientation and gender identity. This experience can be affirming and healthy, resulting in a sense of belonging. It can also create stress in the lives of youth and put them at risk for negative outcomes caused by LGBT-related stigma and the responses and behavior of others. This process may include coming out to oneself, to friends and other peers, at school, to family, at work, and in one's community over time.

Commissary Ho—a name incarcerated women give to other women willing to trade sexual favors for commissary items.

Community Corrections —personnel and programs that oversee those who are justice-involved outside of jail or prison and are administered by agencies or courts with the legal authority to enforce sanctions such as probation and parole.

Continuance—the postponement of a date of a trial, hearing or other court appearance granted in response to a motion made by one of the parties. The judge determines to grant or deny the continuance.

"Cop"—slang term used by the incarcerated for corrections staff.

Contraband—any substance, material or object that is illegal for an incarcerated person to possess.

Correctional officer (CO)—frontline staff with the responsibility of safety and security of everyone in custody, volunteers, and other staff. [Slang—"Cop"]

Count—several times each day all movement stops, and staff count those in custody to make sure no one has escaped.

Crime—conduct in violation of the criminal laws at the federal, state or local level. The type of punishment for a crime depends on whether it is a felony or misdemeanor.

Criminogenic factors—risks and needs that research has shown to be highly correlated with future criminal behavior and that can be changed.

Death penalty (capital punishment)—used by the federal government and 33 states.

Defendant—the person accused of the crime.

Defense attorneys—lawyers who defend the accused against the government's case. They are ether hired by the defendant or assigned by the court (public defender) and represent the defendant.

Detention—imprisonment or confinement for an offense, detention by a police officer.

Diversion—placement of an offender by a court or the department in a facility or program as an alternative to prison such as drug treatment or boot camp. The offender must volunteer for the program or be sentenced.

Dope sick—an individual who is going through withdrawal from drugs (heroin, methamphetamine, crack or cocaine). Symptoms include vomiting, diarrhea, profuse sweating, intense cramping, and paralyzing anxiety.

Electronic monitoring (EM)—the use of electronic equipment to verify that an offender is at home or in a community correctional center during specified hours.

Evidence-based practices—using the best available research and clinical experience within the context of the inmate's characteristics, culture, values and preferences to make decisions about the care of those who are justice-involved.

Felony—a crime carrying a penalty of more than a year in prison. Felony has two categories: violent crime and non-violent crime. Violent crime uses force or threat of force and includes: murder, non-negligent manslaughter, rape, robbery (theft through the use of force or fear), and aggravated assault. Non-violent crimes are those crimes that do not involve the use of any force or injury to another person. The seriousness of a non-violent crime is usually measured in terms of economic damage or loss to the victim. Non-violent crimes include property, drug, prostitution, and tax fraud.

Femme—the female "girly girl" role in a homosexual relationship within prison society.

Fine—monetary charges imposed on an individual convicted of a crime. If the fine is not paid, the individual is imprisoned.

Fraternization—to associate on friendly terms with a justice-involved person or their family.

Gate money—$50.00 and a bus ticket provided to the released offender on parole or mandatory supervision by correctional institutions.

Gay—commonly refers to men typically attracted to other men.

Gay for the stay, straight at the gate—heterosexual women who engage in homosexual behavior while incarcerated but return to heterosexual once released.

Gender—a socially constructed concept classifying behavior as either "masculine" or "feminine," unrelated to one's external genitalia.

Gender expression—how a person expresses their gender identity, including appearance, dress, mannerisms, speech, and social interactions.

Gender identity—distinct from sexual orientation, this refers to a person's internal, deeply felt sense of being male or female.

Gender non-conforming—gender characteristics and/or behaviors that do not conform to those typically associated with a person's biological sex.

Gender "norms"—the expectations associated with "masculine" or "feminine" conduct, based on how society commonly believes males and females should behave.

Gender variant behavior —conduct that is not normatively associated with an individual's biological sex.

Gender-responsive, gender-specific, gender-sensitive—creating an environment, programs and materials that reflect an understanding of the realities of women's lives and addresses the issues of the women.

Good time—an early release procedure under determinate sentencing regimes. Prison inmates get an automatic reduction in sentence for every day they spend without being written up for a violation of prison rules, and participation in educational programs, community service projects, or medical experiments.

Grand jury—a group usually composed of 12 members that determine whether a person should be charged with an offense. A grand jury indictment is required in some states only for serious offenses.

Habitual offender—an offender with two or more separate prior convictions.

Heterosexual—sexual or romantic attraction to a sex differing from one's own.

"Hooch"—an alcoholic beverage made by prisoners using fruit, candy and bread.

Hug-a-thug—programs such as drug court or mental health court which use programs to rehabilitate individuals rather than punish. Viewed by some as being "soft on crime."

ID number—the unique number assigned to each offender under department supervision.

Imprisonment—sentenced to a length of time. If more than a year (in most states) sent to a prison, less than a year in the jail. Most often time served is counted toward the sentence.

Indeterminate sentence—the prison term ranging a number of years (e.g., five to ten years) rather than a specific period of time.

Inmate account—funds deposited by family or friends and income generated from working while incarcerated. These funds can only be used for purchases from the canteen.

Inmate handbook—information given to each incarcerated person at intake which includes information such as programs, policies, and procedures that pertain to all of life within the facility.

Inmate welfare fund—an account holding money from involuntary contributions by inmates and used to assist inmates in need.

Intake—new inmates go through a diagnostic process which includes medical, mental health and academic examinations. Court papers are reviewed, counselors gather information and a general orientation takes place. The individual is photographed and classified and given personal hygiene items and clothes.

Intersex—a condition in which a person is born with external genitalia, internal reproductive organs, chromosome patterns, and/or an endocrine system that does not fit typical definitions of male or female.

Jails—correctional facilities that primarily hold pretrial individuals who are pending arraignment (charges are read, and the individual enters her plea) and those awaiting trial, conviction, or sentencing. Individuals sentenced to a one year or less (two years or less in PA) are held in the jail.

Justice-involved—individuals under the criminal justice system, their family members, and victims.

Kinship networks—a type of prison socialization in which women deal with incarceration by becoming part of make-believe families.

Kite—a form the incarcerated use to submit written requests to corrections staff.

LGBTI an acronym for a group of sexual minorities including lesbian, gay, bisexual, transgender, questioning and intersex individuals.

Lesbian—commonly refers to women typically attracted to other women.

Lockdown—securing a cell, unit or entire jail by locking residents in their cells as part of a daily routine or to control an incident or disturbance.

Medical—the location and personnel of the correctional facility which provides physical and mental health care.

Med Line—inmates waiting in line to receive their medications.

Misdemeanor—usually a petty offense, a less serious crime than a felony, punishable by less than a year of confinement. Misdemeanors are sub-classified as Classes A through C, with Class A warranting the maximum penalty for misdemeanors. Every state has a system for classifying criminal offenses. Common misdemeanors include petty theft (item stolen below a particular monetary value), simple assault (an attempt to cause serious physical harm to an individual, or causing minor harm), drunk driving without causing injury, and disturbing the peace.

Nonconsensual sexual acts—unwanted contacts with another resident or any contacts with staff that involved oral, anal, vaginal penetration, hand jobs, and other sexual acts.

Off-paper—no longer on probation or parole.

Pat-down—the act of searching a person for concealed items such as contraband or unapproved items made by passing the hands over their clothing.

Parole—the supervised release into a community of an inmate prior to the completion of a sentence, as a result of a decision by the state Board of Pardons and Parole, and subject to conditions imposed by the board.

Parole Officer (PO)—monitors the post-release activities of parolees and provides information about various resources to help parolees fulfill their parole requirements.

Plea—the accused's response in court to the indictment or information that is read at their court hearing. Plea options are guilty, not guilty or no contest.

PREA—acronym for the Prison Rape Elimination Act, which was passed by Congress in 2003. It imposes requirements on state and local governments under threat of losing federal funds. It mandates development of standards for detection, prevention, reduction and punishment in custody assault, and collection of data on the incidence of correctional facility sexual assault.

Preliminary hearing—appearance before the judge to determine whether there is probable cause to support the charges against the defendant.

Prison—facility that house adults serving typically one year or more. Prisons have state, federal or private funding.

Prison time—everything takes longer to do and moves at a slow pace. No one is in a hurry.

Probable cause—the facts and circumstances are sufficient for the police officer to believe that a crime has been committed.

Probation officer (PO)—person who manages a caseload, supervises those on probation, and makes presentence investigation and other reports to the courts.

Probation—a sentencing alternative to imprisonment in which the court releases convicted defendants under supervision as long as certain conditions are observed. Conditions may include community service, drug testing, substance abuse treatment, and fees.

Programs—activities inside correctional facilities including education, vocational training, substance abuse treatment, and religious services.

Prosecutors—lawyers who represent the state or federal government (not the victim) throughout the court process from the first appearance of the accused in court until the accused is acquitted or sentenced.

Proselytizing—unwanted or forceful attempts to persuade another individual to convert from one religious belief to another religious belief.

Protective custody—a term describing the status of being housed in a secure location away from other prisoners in an effort to provide safety from other prisoners.

Public defenders—lawyers assigned by the court to represent defendants who can't afford an attorney in criminal matters.

Questioning—an active process in which a person explores her own sexual orientation and/or gender identity and the cultural assumptions that they are heterosexual and/or gender conforming.

Reception—part of a jail where individuals are initially housed pending intake and transfer to an assigned cell.

Recidivism—the rearrest, reconviction, and reincarceration of an individual. Reincarceration can occur through violation of post-release requirements or committing a new crime.

Reentry—the term given to pre- and post-release programs serving justice-involved adults and youth as they transition back to communities.

Restitution—money paid to the victim, either a person or society as a whole.

Restorative justice—a criminal justice philosophy that focuses on healing the harm and restoring the losses to individuals and communities affected by crime. This philosophy is based on offender-accountability, habilitation and restitution.

Retaliation—when an inmate or staff injures, harms or intimidates a person who has reported sexual abuse and assault—or attempts to do so—in response to the report.

Retributive justice—a philosophy that a crime is committed against the state and the offender is held personally liable through punishment.

Search—when items in your possession are searched by staff to make sure there is no contraband and that all items are preapproved.

Sentencing—the formal pronouncement of a judge imposing the punishment inflicted on a defendant found guilty.

Security threat group—sometimes called STG's, these most often refer to prison gangs.

Segregation—housing inmates in units separate from the general population for administrative or disciplinary reasons.

Sex—one's anatomical make-up, including external genitalia, chromosomes, and reproductive system.

Sexual Abuse—any of the following acts of which the victim does not consent, is coerced into by overt or implied threats of violence, or is unable to consent or refuse:

- sexual contact;
- penetration of the anal or genital opening of another person, however slight, by a hand, finger, object or other instrument;
- any other intentional touching;
- any attempt, threat, or request to engage in sexual activities;
- any display by a staff member, contractor, or volunteer of his or her uncovered genitalia, buttocks, or breast in the presence of an inmate, detainee, or resident; and
- voyeurism by a staff member, contractor, or volunteer.

Sexual Harassment—repeated and unwelcome sexual advances, requests for sexual favors, or verbal comments, gestures, or actions of a derogatory or offensive sexual nature by one inmate director toward another. This also includes repeated verbal comments or gestures of a sexual nature to an inmate, detainee, or resident by a staff member, contractor, or volunteer, including demeaning references to gender, sexually suggestive or derogatory comments about body or clothing, or obscene language or gestures.

Sexual identity—the sex that a person sees themselves as. This can include refusing to label oneself with a sex.

Sexual orientation —romantic and/or physical attraction to members of the same or different sex.

Sexual victimization—all types of nonconsensual sexual activity with others inmates (that involves contact with the penis and the vagina or anus; contact between the mouth and the penis, vagina, or anus; penetration of the anal or vaginal opening of another person by a hand, finger, or other object; and rubbing of another person's penis or vagina by a hand), abusive sexual contacts with other inmates, and both willing and unwilling sexual activity with staff.

Shake down—corrections staff searching the inmate's personal property and living quarters for contraband.

Solitary confinement—locking up an individual in a cell for 23 hours a day with little or no human contact because of a major infraction.

Staff sexual misconduct—includes all incidents of willing and unwilling sexual contact with facility staff and all incidents of sexual activity that involved oral, anal, vaginal penetration, hand jobs, blow jobs, and other sexual acts with facility staff.

Status offense—conduct illegal for minors but legal for adults such as possession of alcohol or tobacco, skipping school, or violating curfew.

Strip search—used with the incarcerated. The individual must strip naked and is searched by the same gender staff to make sure there is no contraband on or inside the individual.

Suicide watch—an intensive monitoring process used to ensure that a person cannot attempt suicide. Suicides rates are higher in jails than prisons.

Technical violation—the person who is on probation or parole that fails to abide by rules and conditions of probation or parole (specified by a judge or parole board) resulting in revocation of probation or parole.

Ticket—a written disciplinary report, made by corrections staff, for an inmate's rule violation.

The "mix"—women's involvement in problematic prison behaviors and activities.

Transgender—a person whose gender identity differs from their birth sex.

Transgender girl—a person whose birth sex was male but who understands herself to be, and desires to live her life as, a female.

Transgender boy—a person whose birth sex was female but who understands himself to be, and desires to live his life as, a male.

Transsexual—a person who engages in gender non-conforming behavior, such as adopting the gender expression of the opposite sex for purposes of sexual or emotional gratification, but does not necessarily consider their gender identity to be different from their biological sex

Trauma—the experience of violence and victimization including sexual abuse, physical abuse, severe neglect, loss, domestic violence and/or the witnessing of violence, terrorism or disasters.

Two spirit— term used by many Native Americans to identify LGBTI and gender variant persons within their community. Historically, in some Native American traditions, two spirit people were viewed as privileged and sacred.

Unwilling activity—incidents of unwanted sexual contacts with another inmate or staff.

Urinalysis—a technique where the individual must urinate in a cup, which is tested to determine if they are using drugs.

Victim-impact statement—a report presented by a victim to the court before sentencing, or to the Board of Pardons and Parole before a parole hearing that summarizes the trauma caused by the crime. The victim often offers his or her opinion about an appropriate sentence or whether parole should be granted.

Visit—an incarcerated person receiving personal contact from an individual in the free world.

Voyeurism—an invasion of privacy of an inmate, detainee, or resident by staff for reasons unrelated to official duties, such as peering at an inmate who is using a toilet in her cell to perform bodily functions; requiring an inmate to expose his or her buttocks, genitals, or breasts; or taking images of all or part of an inmate's naked body or of an inmate performing bodily functions.

Willing activity—incidents of consensual sexual contacts with staff. These contacts are characterized by the reporting inmates as willing; however, all sexual contacts between inmates and staff are legally nonconsensual.

Work-release center—a correctional facility which allows the residents to work in the community during the day while residing in the center during nonworking hours.

Zero Tolerance—policy of correctional facilities stating sexual abuse, sexual harassment, and sexual misconduct will not be tolerated. There is no such thing as consensual sex between residents and volunteers and residents and staff. All sexual contact between residents and staff or volunteers is considered sexual abuse. It is against the law for volunteers or staff to have sexual contact with residents, even if the resident agrees or seems willing.

Additional sources: National PREA Resource Center, Sexual Victimization in Prisons and Jails, and https://www.justice.gov/usao/justice-101/glossary

Appendix B

Position Statement

National Commission on Correctional Health Care (NCCHC, 2014) recognizes that the number of female inmates is large and growing annually, presenting unique and increasing issues for health services in correctional facilities. Therefore, NCCHC recommends the following:

1. Correctional institutions need to be required to meet recognized community standards for women's services as promoted by standards set by NCCHC.
2. Correctional health services and women's advocacy groups need to collaborate to provide leadership for the development of policies and procedures that address women's special health care needs in corrections.
3. Correctional institutions need to implement intake procedures that include histories on menstrual cycle, pregnancies, gynecologic problems, contraception, current breastfeeding, sexual and physical abuse, and a nutritional assessment (ACOG, 2012a).
4. Correctional institutions provide comprehensive services for women's unique health issues:
   A. Considering women's special reproductive health needs, the frequency of repeating certain tests, exams, and procedures (e.g., Pap smears, mammograms) needs to be based on guidelines established by professional groups such as the American Cancer Society, the U.S. Preventive Services Task Force, and ACOG, and should take into account age and risk factors of the female correctional population.
   B. Correctional institutions need to provide intake examinations that include a breast exam and, depending on the female's age, sexual history, as well as past medical history, pelvic exam, Pap smear,

and baseline mammogram (ACOG 2012b; Anno, 2001).

C. All women at risk for pregnancy should be offered a pregnancy test within 48 hours of admission. Sexually active women remain at risk for pregnancy until they go through menopause.

D. Considering the high levels of victimization (sexual and physical) among the female inmate population, and considering the circumstances of incarceration of violent female offenders (i.e., many have committed interpersonal altercation violence against a family member or intimate), counseling to resolve issues of victimization and perpetration of violence against intimates (such as conflict resolution skills or parenting skills) needs to be available.

E. Considering the large number of incarcerated women who have dependent children, counseling on parenting and child custody issues needs to be available.

F. Considering the unique needs of pregnant women, women need to have access to options counseling and pregnancy termination when desired, to routine prenatal care from a qualified health professional, and to specialty and emergency obstetrical care when indicated (ACOG, 2011).

G. Because of their high risk of postpartum depression and psychosis, women who deliver while in custody and who enter a facility within one year of childbirth should be screened for and educated about these conditions.

H. Considering the known benefits of early mother-infant attachment, correctional facilities need to facilitate contact visits for mothers with their infants.

I. Given the benefits of breastfeeding and breast milk, correctional facilities should make arrangements for postpartum women to either breastfeed their infants or to pump, freeze, and transport breast milk for their infants (ACOG, 2011).

J. Considering the high rates of mental health issues women report upon incarceration, counseling needs to be available.

K. Considering the high rates of alcohol and/or drug problems women report upon incarceration, counseling and treatment need to be available to address this issue.

L. Considering the high risk of unintended pregnancy upon release, correctional facilities need to offer contraception services in a noncoercive manner while women are in custody, and allow women to continue methods they are already on, especially if their incarceration is short term or if the method is for medical reasons. Emergency contraception also needs to be made available to women, especially at intake (ACOG, 2012a).

M. Correctional institutions should conduct laboratory testing for chlamydia and gonorrhea on all women up to age 25, and when possible age 35, and among pregnant women regardless of age, unless the inmate is transferred from a facility where testing was done. Because many STDs are asymptomatic, all females should be screened for risk factors for chlamydia and gonorrhea according to CDC guidelines (e.g., new sexual partner, multiple partners, previous STD) and tested if risk factors are present regardless of age. Syphilis screening protocols should be determined based on local prevalence and in consultation with local public health departments, in addition to screening all pregnant women. The CDC recommends routine opt-out testing for HIV in correctional settings, and such testing should be performed on all pregnant women.

N. Considering the aging of the prison population, correctional institutions need to address the unique health care needs of older women including symptom management and treatment of menopausal hot flashes.

5. Correctional institutions need to provide pre- and post-release services for women reentering the community. Strong partnerships are encouraged between public health, community, public assistance, and correctional agencies. Programming such as employment and vocational training, health education, and parenting education also should be available.

Appendix C

The Dignity for Incarcerated Women Act (S.1524 Dignity Act)

U.S. Senators Cory Booker (D-NJ), Elizabeth Warren (D-MA), Richard Durbin (D-IL), and Kamala Harris (D-CA) have introduced a bill to reform the way women are treated behind bars. **The Dignity for Incarcerated Women Act** would make a series of common-sense reforms to how the federal prison system treats incarcerated women in order to reduce the negative impact incarceration has on the family members of women behind bars, especially their children, and better prepare incarcerated women to return to their communities. It proposes the following:

Visitation

- Require the Bureau of Prisons (BOP) to consider location of kids when placing incarcerated persons in prison facilities.
- Require BOP to create better visitation policies for primary caretaker parents.

Treatment

- Prohibit the solitary confinement of pregnant women.
- Ban the shackling of pregnant women.

Programming

- Require BOP to provide parenting classes to primary caretaker parents.
- Mandate BOP provide trauma informed care to individuals who are

primary caretaker parents and train correctional officers on how to handle victims of trauma.

- Allow returning citizens to mentor current incarcerated people and assist with reentry.

Oversight

Create an ombudsman at the Justice Department to monitor certain violations in prisons.

Telecommunications

- Prohibit BOP from charging incarcerated persons for phone calls.
- Require BOP to make video-conferencing available at every facility free of charge.

Health

- Require BOP to provide certain health products, such as tampons and pads, free of charge to incarcerated people.
- Restrict BOP employees from entering restrooms of incarcerated individuals of the opposite sex except in exigent circumstances.
- Allow all pregnant women and primary caretaker parents to enroll in the Residential Drug Abuse Program.

Overnight Visit Pilot Program

Require BOP to create an overnight visit pilot program for children and parents.

Appendix D

Case Study: Criminal Justice Reform in Oklahoma

November 1st, 2019 was a historical day for criminal justice reform in Oklahoma, the state that has the highest incarceration rate in the nation.[1] The Oklahoma Pardon and Parole Board (OPPB) voted unanimously to commute the sentences of 527 inmates, the largest single-day commutation of prison sentences in U.S. history.

In 2016, Oklahomans passed criminal justice reforms that made simple drug possession a misdemeanor and increased the felony dollar threshold from $500 to $1000 for felony property crimes. The first day HB 1269 took effect, that act enabled the Board to review the sentences of hundreds of inmates in prison for crimes that would no longer be considered felonies if charged today. This decision gives hundreds of non-violent, low-level offenders an opportunity at a second chance.

Oklahoma has the highest rate of incarceration for women.[2] Susan Sharp, a national expert on female incarceration and professor *emerita* at the University of Oklahoma, says women are collateral damage in the war on drugs. Her research shows that poor women in rural areas receive longer sentences, while those who can afford private attorneys get less time for the same crimes.

Sharp also explains that Oklahoma "… is an extremely conservative state and an extremely religious state and very evangelical and a lot of biblical literalism. So, the belief that women have a certain role in

1. Retrieved November 22, 2019 from: https://www.governor.ok.gov/articles/pressreleases/oklahoma-pardon-and-parole-board-recommends and https://www.nbcnews.com/news/us-news/hundreds-oklahoma-inmates-will-be-released-monday-largest-commutation-u-n1076056
2. Herrera (2017). Retrieved 29 November 2019 from: https://www.pri.org/stories/2017-10-03/why-oklahomas-female-incarceration-rate-so-high

society — that role is to give up themselves and put themselves and their own wants, goals, desires secondary to taking care of their husband and children."

When Governor Kevin Stitt approved inmates for release, 25% were female. The average age of all commuted was 39.7 years old. Most had been incarcerated for the past three years, and the recommendation commuted 1.34 years from their sentences. Early release saved the State of Oklahoma approximately $11.9 million.

Whatever the motivation, the State of Oklahoma put much thought into preparing for this day. The first ever transition fairs for inmates were held at 28 facilities across the state. More than 200 people from 45 community partners, nonprofits, and state agencies attended. These fairs connected 781 inmates with the services they may need once released. The Oklahoma Department of Corrections (ODOC) collaborated with the governor's office to be ready to release the commuted inmates on Monday, November 4. ODOC received the signed commutation certificates from the governor's office Friday afternoon, and their facilities worked over the weekend to process discharge paperwork, transfer inmates' trust account money to debit cards, and prepare necessary inmate discharge medications. Another hurdle was removed by allowing recommended inmates to have a valid state-issued driver's license or state-issued ID prior to discharge.

Change is difficult. The people of Oklahoma needed to care about issues of justice and mercy. The vote on the single-stage commutation docket needed the support of numerous state entities: the Pardon and Parole Board, the Oklahoma Department of Corrections, Office of the Governor, Oklahoma Department of Mental Health and Substance Abuse Services, Oklahoma Employment Security Commission, Oklahoma Department of Human Services, Oklahoma District Attorneys Council and Oklahoma Department of Public Safety. Final collaborations with special grant funding from several family foundations were also involved in this important reform.

In reviewing this long effort Governor Stitt included thanks to "the many non-profits who are stepping up and working hard to connect our inmates with the resources they need for a successful transition." Steven

Bickley, Executive Director of the OPPB, noted that from the beginning:

> *...the goal of this project has been more than just the release of low level, non-violent offenders, but the successful reentry of these individuals back into society. It has been a moving experience to see our state and community partners help connect our inmates with the resources they need for a successful reentry and I thank... the many local nonprofits, churches, and job creators that stepped up to ensure these inmates have every opportunity for success.*

As the governor stood outside an all-women's prison in shaking hands with an estimated 70 women who filed out of the Dr. Eddie Warrior Correctional Center, it was an emotional scene. Former inmates embraced family and friends, many crying as they saw their children, their joy palpable. *"We really want you to have a successful future,"* Stitt told the crowd. *"This is the first day of the rest of your life. Let's make it so you guys do not come back here again."* Republican State Representative John Echols noted, *"These are real lives—real people with real families and with real friends—and they get to go home."*

REFERENCES

Alpher, M., Durose, M. R., & Markman, J. (2018, May). *2018 Update on prisoner recidivism: A 9-year follow-up period* (2005-2014) (NCJ 250975). U.S. Department of Justice Bureau of Justice Statistics.

American College of Obstetricians and Gynecologists. (2012a). Health care for pregnant and postpartum incarcerated women and adolescent females (Committee Opinion 535). *Obstetrics and Gynecology* 120, 425-429. Retrieved February 14, 2020 from https://www.acog.org/Clinical-Guidance-and-Publications/Committee-Opinions/Committee-on-Health-Care-for-Underserved-Women/Health-Care-for-Pregnant-and-Postpartum-Incarcerated-Women-and-Adolescent-Females.

American College of Obstetricians and Gynecologists (2012b). Osteoporosis (Practice Bulletin 129). *Obstetrics and Gynecology* 120, 718-734.

American Correctional Association (2019). *Performance-based standards, expected practices, adult correctional institutions*, (5th ed.). Annapolis Junction, MD: American Correctional Association.

American Psychiatric Association. (2018). *Diagnostic and Statistical Manual of Mental Disorders* (DSM-5). https://www.psychiatry.org/psychiatrists/practice/dsm.

Andrews, D. A., & Bonta, J. (2010). *The psychology of criminal conduct* (5th ed). New Providence, NJ: Matthew Bender.

Anno, B. J. (2001). *Correctional health care: Guidelines for the management of an adequate delivery system.* Chicago: National Commission on Correctional Health Care.

Aspinwall, C., Blakinger, K., & Neff, J. (2020). *What women dying in prison from Covid-19 tell us about female incarceration.* The Marshall Project. Retrieved 28 May 2020 from https://www.themarshallproject.org/2020/05/14/what-women-dying-in-prison-from-covid-19-tell-us-about-female-incarceration

Aten, J. D., O'Grady, K. A., Milstein, G., Boan, D., Smigelsky, M. A., Schruba, A., & Weaver, I. (2015). Providing spiritual and emotional care in response to disaster. In D. F. Walker, C. A. Courtois, & J. D. Aten (Eds.), *Spiritually oriented psychotherapy for trauma* (pp. 189-210). Washington, DC: American Psychological Association.

Bandele, M. (2017, October 23). *Here's how prisons and jail systems brutalize women.* Retrieved October 12, 2019 from https://www.aclu.org/blog/womens-rights/women-and-criminal-justice/heres-how-prison-and-jail-systems-brutalize-women.

Beitsch, R. (2017, September 13). *Breaking the cycle of incarceration by keeping mothers and children together.* Retrieved October 12, 2019 from https://www.pewtrusts.org/en/research-and-analysis/blog/stateline/2017/09/13/breaking-the-cycle-of-incarceration-by-keeping-mothers-and-children-together.

Bloom, B., & Covington, S. (2008). Addressing the mental health needs of women offenders. In R. Gido & L. Dalley (Eds.). *Women's mental health issues across the criminal justice system.* Columbus, OH: Prentice Hall.

Bloom, B., Owen, B., & Covington, S. (2003). *Gender-responsive strategies: Research, practice, and guiding principles for women offenders.* Washington, DC: National Institute of Corrections. https://s3.amazonaws.com/static.nicic.gov/Library/018017.pdf

Bogue, B., Campbell, N., Carey, M., Clawson, E., Faust, D., Florio, K., Joplin, L., Keiser, G., Wasson, B., & Woodward, W. (2004). *Implementing evidence-based practice in community corrections: The principles of effective intervention.* Washington, DC: U.S. Department of Justice, National Institute of Corrections.

Bronson, J., Stroop, J., Zimmer, S., & Berzofsky, M. (2017, June). *Drug use, dependence and abuse among state prisoners and jail inmates, 2007-2009* (NCJ 250546). U.S. Department of Justice, Office of Justice Programs, Bureau of Justice Statistics. https://www.bjs.gov/content/pub/pdf/dudaspji0709.pdf.

Bussell, H. & Forbes, D. (2002). Understanding the volunteer market: the what, where, who and why of volunteering. *International Journal of*

Nonprofit and Voluntary Sector Market 7(3), 244-257.

Carlen, P., & Tombs, J. (2006). Reconfigurations of penalty: The ongoing case of the women's imprisonment and reintegration industries. *Theoretical Criminology*, 10(3), 337-360.

Childress, S. (2013). *Michelle Alexander: 'A system of racial and social control'.* Retrieved October 12, 2019 from https://www.pbs.org/wgbh/frontline/article/michelle-alexander-a-system-of-racial-and-social-control.

Clear, T.R., Hardyman, P.L., Stout, B., Lucken, K., & Dammer, H.R. (2000). The value of religion in prison. *Journal of Contemporary Criminal Justice* 16, 53-74.

Cobbina, J. E. (2009). *From prison to home: Women's pathways in and out of crime.* Dissertation submitted to the Department of Criminology and Criminal Justice, University of Missouri–St. Louis. https://www.ncjrs.gov/pdffiles1/nij/grants/226812.pdf.

Couloute, L. (August, 2018). *Nowhere to go: Homelessness among formerly incarcerated people.* Prison Policy Initiative. https://www.prisonpolicy.org/reports/housing.html

Covington, S. & Bloom, B. (2006). Gender-responsive treatment and services in correctional settings. In E. Leeder (Ed.), *Inside and out: Women, prison, and therapy.* Binghamton, NY: Haworth Press.

Davidson, J. (2018, March 9). *Federal prisons fail to provide adequate services for female inmates.* Retrieved October 12, 2019 from https://www.washingtonpost.com/politics/2018/09/19/report-federal-prisons-fail-provide-adequate-services-female-inmates.

Decker, S. H., Spohn, C., & Ortiz, N. R. (2010). *Criminal stigma, race, gender, and employment: An expanded assessment of the consequences of imprisonment for employment.* Phoenix, AZ: Arizona State University.

Dignity for Incarcerated Women Act (S. 1524 Dignity Act). Retrieved February 14, 2020 from https://www.congress.gov/bill/115th-congress/senate-bill/1524/text.

Driskell, G. W., Meyer, J., & Mirivel, J. C. (2012). Managing dialectics to make a difference: Tension management in a community-building organization. *Communication Studies* 63(2), 243-261.

Duncan, J., Stansfield, R., Hall, S., & O'Connor, T. (2018, May 25).

Women's engagement with humanist, spiritual and religious meaning-making in prison: A longitudinal study of its impact on recidivism. *Religions 9*(6), 1-16. https://doi.org/10.3390/rel9060171.

Ertas, N. (2014). Public service motivation theory and voluntary organizations: Do government employees volunteer more? *Nonprofit and Voluntary Sector Quarterly* 43, 254-271.

Everts, D., & Schaupp, D. (2008). *I once was lost.* Downers Grove, IL: InterVarsity Press.

First Step Act of 2018. H.R.5682 Retrieved February 13, 2020 from https://www.congress.gov/bill/115th-congress/house-bill/5682/text.

Forbes, K.F., & Zampelli, E. M. (2014). Volunteerism: The influences of social, religious, and human capital. *Nonprofit and Voluntary Sector Quarterly* 43, 227-253.

Foster, R. (2008). *Ten counsels: Richard Foster on spiritual formation.* Retrieved November 3, 2019 from https://www.reformedworship.org/article/march-2008/ten-counsels-richard-foster-spiritual-formation.

Foster, H. & Hagen, J. (2009). The mass incarceration of parents in America: Issues of race/ethnicity, collateral damage to children, and prisoner reentry. *Annals of the American Academy of Political and Social Science* 623, 179-194.

Frost, N.A., Greene, J., & Pranis, K. (2006, May). *Hard hit: The growth in the imprisonment of women 1977-2004.* Institute on Women and Criminal Justice. Retrieved January 8, 2019 from http://csdp.org/research/HardHitReport4.pdf.

Garner, J.T., & Garner, L.T. (2011). Volunteering an opinion: Organizational voice and volunteer retention in nonprofit organizations. *Nonprofit and Voluntary Sector Quarterly* 40, 813-828.

Gelb, A., & Velazquez, T. (2018, August). *The changing state of recidivism: Fewer people going back to prison.* Pew Research Center. Retrieved January 9, 2019 from https://www.pewtrusts.org/en/research-and-analysis/articles/2018/08/01/the-changing-state-of-recidivism-fewer-people-going-back-to-prison.

Gerson, M. (September 11, 2018). Statement on social justice misinterprets gospel truth. *Daily Herald* syndicated from Washington Post Writers Group.

Glasrud, B. (2007). Volunteerism vectors. *Nonprofit World* 25, 3-4.

Glaze, L., & Maruschak, L. (2008, August). *Parents in prisons and their minor children.* (Special Report, NCJ 222984). Washington, DC: U.S. Department of Justice, Office of Justice Programs.

Hager, E., & Flagg, A. (2018, December). *How incarcerated parents are losing their children forever.* New York: The Marshall Project. Retrieved January 9, 2019 from https://www.themarshallproject.org/2018/12/03/how-incarcerated-parents-are-losing-their-children-forever.

Haney, C. (2001, December 1). *The psychological impact of incarceration: Implications for post-prison adjustment.* Washington, DC: Office of the Assistant Secretary for Planning and Evaluation.

Hardy, J. (2020). *The second chance club: Hardship and hope after prison.* NY: Simon & Schuster.

Harlow, C. W. (January 2003). *Education and correctional populations.* (NCJ 195670). U.S. Department of Justice, Bureau of Justice Statistics.

Hawkins, G. L., Parkinson, C., & Arnson, E. (2007). *Reveal: Where are you?* Barrington, IL: Willow Creek Association.

Hodge, D.R. (2001). Spiritual assessment: A review of major qualitative methods and a new framework for assessing spirituality. *Social Work*, 46(3), 203-214.

Huang, Y., Strawderman, L., Babski-Reeves, K, Ahmed, S., & Salehi, S (2014). Training effectiveness and trainee performance in a voluntary training program: Are trainees really motivated? *Nonprofit and Voluntary Sector Quarterly* 43,1095-1110.

Hughes, T., & Wilson, D. J. (2002). *Reentry Trends in the United States.* Washington, DC: U.S. Department of Justice, Bureau of Justice Statistics. Retrieved February 14, 2020 from https://www.bjs.gov/content/reentry/reentry.cfm#highlights.

Hyle, K. (2018, April 30). Annual determination of average cost of incarceration (Document 2018-09062). Washington, DC: Bureau of Prisons. Retrieved January 9, 2019 from https://www.federalregister.gov/documents/2018/04/30/2018-09062/annual-determination-of-average-cost-of-incarceration

Johnson, B.R. (2011). *More God less crime: Why faith matters and how it could matter more.* West Conshohocken, PA: Templeton Press.

Joy, T. (2018, February 2). *The problem with private prisons.* Retrieved October 12, 2019 from http://www.justicepolicy.org/news/12006.

Kaebel, D., & Cowhig, M. (2018, April) *Correctional populations in the United States, 2016.* NCJ251211. Retrieved January 9, 2019 from https://www.bjs.gov/content/pub/pdf/cpus16.pdf.

Kajstura, A. (2018, November 13). *Women's mass incarceration: The whole pie 2018.* https://www.prisonpolicy.org/reports/pie2018women.html.

Kania, J., Hanleybrown, F., & Splansky Juster, J. (2014). *Essential mindset shifts for collective impact.* California: The Stanford Social Innovation Review.

Kopak, A., & Smith-Ruiz, D. (2016). Criminal justice involvement, drug use, and depression among African American children of incarcerated parents. *Race and Justice* 6(2), 89-116.

Law, V. (2020, May 14). *Louisiana's longest serving incarcerated woman returned to prison after being hospitalized for Covid-19.* Retrieved 28 May 2020 from https://theappeal.org/louisianas-longest-serving-incarcerated-woman-returned-to-prison-after-being-hospitalized-for-covid-19/

LeBel, T. P. (2012). Invisible stripes? Formerly incarcerated persons' perceptions of stigma. *Deviant Behavior* 33, 89-107.

Malcolm, M. & Seibler, J.M. (2017, March 7). *Collateral consequences: Protecting public safety or encouraging recidivism?* The Heritage Foundation. Retrieved February 14, 2020 from https://www.heritage.org/crime-and-justice/report/collateral-consequences-protecting-public-safety-or-encouraging-recidivism.

Martin, E. (2017, March). *Hidden consequences: The impact of incarceration on dependent children.* (NCJ 250349). Washington, DC: National Institute of Justice, NCJ250349.

Maruschak, L. M. (2006, November). *Medical problems of jail inmates.* (NCJ 210696). Office of Justice Programs, Bureau of Justice Statistics.

Maruschak, L. M. (2008, April 1). *Medical problems of prisoners* (NCJ 221740). Office of Justice Programs, Bureau of Justice Statistics.

Maruschak, L. M., & Berzofsky, M. (2016, October). *Medical problems of state and federal prisoners and jail inmates*, 2011-2012 (NCJ 248491). U.S.

Department of Justice.
McNamee, L. G., & Peterson, B. L. (2014). Reconciling "third space/place": Toward a complementary dialectical understanding of volunteer management. *Management Communication Quarterly* 28(2), 215-243.
Meyer, J. P., Wickersham, J. A., Fu, J. J., Brown, S. E., Sullivan, T. P., Springer, S. A., & Altice, F. L. (2013, December 26). Partner violence and health among HIV-infected jail detainees. *International Journal of Prison Health*, 9(3), 124-141. https://www.ncbi.nlm.nih.gov/pmc/articles/PMC3873166.
Miller, K. (2006). The impact of parental incarceration on children: An emerging need for effective interventions. *Child and Adolescent Social Work* 23(4), 472-486.
Modely, P. H., & Giguere, R. (2010). *Reentry Considerations for women Offenders.* U.S. Department of Justice, Office of Justice Programs National Center on Addiction and Substance Abuse at Columbia University.
Mulholland, M. R. (1997). *Invitation to a journey: A road map for spiritual formation.* Downers Grove, IL: InterVarsity Press.
National Commission on Correctional Health Care (Reaffirmed with revision on October 19, 2014). *Women's Health Care in Correctional Settings.* Retrieved October 12, 2019 from https://www.ncchc.org/womens-health-care.
Neuwirth, K., Frederick, E., & Mayo, C. (2007). The spiral of silence and fear of isolation. *Journal of Communication* 57, 450-468.
Ney, B. (January 2018). *Don't forget About women justice reform.* Retrieved from the National Resource Center on Justice Involved Women October 11, 2019 https://cjinvolvedwomen.org.
Ogden, G. (2003). *Transforming discipleship.* Downers Grove, IL: InterVarsity Press.
Owen, B. (1998). *"In the Mix": Struggle and survival in a women's prison.* Albany: State University of New York.
Pew Research Center Religious Landscape Study (2014). *Religious and Public Life.* Retrieved November 19, 2019 from https://www.washingtonpost.com/politics/2018/09/19/report-federal-prisons-fail-provide-adequate-services-female-inmates.

Reichert, J. & Bostwick, L. (November 2010). *Post-traumatic stress disorder and victimization among female offenders in Illinois.* Illinois Criminal Justice Information Authority.

Ronel, N. (2006). When good overcomes bad: The impact of volunteers on those they help. *Human Relations* 59, 1133-1153.

Roos, J. (2017). *What life is like after prison.* United Way of Central Iowa. Retrieved January 25, 2020 from https://www.unitedwaydm.org/blog/summit-shows-what-its-like-to-re-enter-society-from-prison.

Sawyer, W. (2017, April 10). *How much do incarcerated people earn in each state?* Prison Policy Initiative. Retrieved November 3, 2019 from: https://www.prisonpolicy.org/blog/2017/04/10/wages.

Sawyer, W. (2018, January 9). *The gender divide: Tracking women's state prison growth.* Prison Policy Initiative. Retrieved February 13, 2020 from https://www.prisonpolicy.org/reports/women_overtime.html.

Schultz, S. & Canning, S.S. (2018, December 3). What we long for the church to know about sexual violence. https://www.christianitytoday.com/edstetzer/2018/december/what-we-long-church-know-about-sexual-violence-gc2-summit.html.

Sentencing Project. (2007. May 1). *Women in the criminal justice system briefing sheets.* Retrieved February 14, 2020 from https://www.sentencingproject.org/publications/women-in-the-criminal-justice-system-briefing-sheets.

Sentencing Project. (2019, June 6). *Incarcerated women and girls.* Retrieved February 13, 2020 from https://www.sentencingproject.org/publications/incarcerated-women-and-girls.

Serin R. C., & Lloyd, C.D. (2009). Examining the process of offender change: The transition to crime desistance. *Psychology, Crime & Law* 15(4), 347-364.

Shapiro, R. (2018, October 16-18). *Iowa, a commitment to make prison work better for women.* National Public Radio. Retrieved October 12, 2019 fromhttps://www.keranews.org/post/iowa-commitment-make-prison-work-better-women.

Snodgrass, J. L. (2019). *Women leaving prison: Justice-seeking spiritual support for female returning citizens.* Lanham, MY: Lexington Books.

Sufrin, C. (2019). Jailcare: *Finding the safety net for women behind bars.*

Retrieved October 7, 2019 from https://www.hopkinsmedicine.org/news/newsroom/news-releases/first-of-its-kind-statistics-on-pregnant-women-in-us-prisons.

Tewksbury, R., & Dabney, D. (2004). Prison volunteers: Profiles, motivations, satisfaction. *Journal of Offender Rehabilitation* 40(1/2), 173-183.

VanWormer, K. (2010). *Working with female offenders: A gender-sensitive approach.* Hoboken, NJ: John Wiley & Sons.

Wagner, P., & Sawyer, W. (2018). *Mass incarceration: The whole pie 2018.* https://www.prisonpolicy.org/reports/pie2018.html.

Willard, D. (n.d.). *Spiritual formation: What it is and how it is done.* Retrieved February 14, 2020 from Sentencing Project. (2019, June 6). Incarcerated women and girls. Retrieved February 13, 2020 from https://www.sentencingproject.org/publications/incarcerated-women-and-girls

Willard, D. (2006). *The great omission: Reclaiming Jesus's essential teachings on discipleship.* New York, NY: Harper One.

Wolff, N., Blitz, C. L., Shi, J., Bachman, R., & Siegel, J. A. (2006). Sexual violence inside prisons: Rates of victimization. *Journal of Urban Health,* 83(5), 835-848.

Woods-Giscombe, C. L. (2010). Superwoman schema: African American women's view on stress, strength, and health. *Qualitative Health Research* 20(5), 668-683.

Wuthnow, R. (1992). *Acts of compassion: Caring for others and helping ourselves.* Princeton, NJ: University Press.

Yochelson, S., & Samenow, S. E. (1976). *The criminal personality, volume I: A profile for change.* Northvale, NJ: Jason Aronson.

Zeng, Z (2018, February). *Bureau of Justice Statistics Bulletin: Jail inmates in 2016* (NCJ 251210). U.S. Department of Justice Office of Justice Programs. https://www.bjs.gov/content/pub/pdf/ji16.pdf

Made in United States
North Haven, CT
10 November 2026

22088277R00152